Performance of Financial Institutions in India

Performance of Financial Institutions in India

Editors

Abhijit Sinha
Tagar Lal Khan
Brajaballav Pal
Tarak Nath Sahu

ALLIED PUBLISHERS PVT. LTD.

Noida • Mumbai • Kolkata • Chennai • Bangalore

ALLIED PUBLISHERS PRIVATE LIMITED

D-5, Sector-2, **Noida**–201 301
Ph. Nos.: 0120-4320295/2542557/4352866
E-mail: delhi.books@alliedpublishers.com

17 Chittaranjan Avenue, **Kolkata**–700072
Ph.: 033-22129618 • E-mail: cal.books@alliedpublishers.com

15 J.N. Heredia Marg, Ballard Estate, **Mumbai**–400001
Ph.: 022-42126969 • E-mail: mumbai.books@alliedpublishers.com

No. 25/10, Commander-in-Chief Road, Ethiraj Lane (Next to Post Office)
Egmore, **Chennai**–600008
Ph.: 044-28223938 • E-mail: chennai.books@alliedpublishers.com

P.B. No. 9932, No. 15, 3rd Floor (Next to Vijaya Bank), 5th Cross, Gandhinagar, Karnataka, **Bangalore**–560009. Ph.: 080-41530285/22386239
E-mail: bngl.books@alliedpublishers.com

Website: www.alliedpublishers.com

ISBN: 978-93-89934-71-7

Professor Susanta Kumar Chakraborty
Vice-Chancellor
Vidyasagar University
Midnapore - 721102
West Bengal, India

VIDYASAGAR UNIVERSITY
MIDNAPORE - 721102

Website : www.vidyasagar.ac.in
E-mail :
vcconfidential@mail.vidyasagar.ac.in
vc@mail.vidyasagar.ac.in
susantachakrabortyzoology@gmail.com
susantachakraborty@yahoo.com
Mobile : 9433270591 / 9748919812
Telefax : (03222) 275329

Foreword

I feel proud and privileged to write a few lines about my observation on the Academic and Research activities of a very prominent Department of Vidyasagar University i.e. the Department of Commerce. All through my professional career spanning a period of more than 33 years, as a Teacher, as a Dean, Faculty of Science and as a Vice-Chancellor, I have developed a good impression of the evolution of this Department which started its academic journey in the year 1987 with the involvement of faculties like Professor Durga Shankar Pandey, Dr. Tarapada Ghosh, Dr. Kartick Chandra Paul, Dr. Manipada Dutta and others. I am really confident to certify that this department as to be one of the best departments in West Bengal in the field of Commerce and Management. I have no doubt in mentioning that the Department of Commerce under the Faculty of Arts and Commerce has been doing commendable job in not just doing but also promoting research. I have seen the department regularly organising conferences, publishing departmental journal and offering certificate courses. This edited book which is being published by a reputed publishing house of the country is a testimony to the same for which I appreciate the efforts of all the faculty members and especially the four Professors who are the editors of this book, from the core of my heart. I also look forward to even better academic contributions in the near future.

Though I am not an academician from the field of Commerce and Management, I understand that everybody is very closely connected with the financial system of a country and we are not an exception. This system which has been ever-changing and has been undergoing serious rapid transformation in recent times through sky-rocketing technological advancement, stringent regulatory changes, financial innovations etc. needs a continuous evaluation. This edited book which is a collection of good research outputs on various issues pertaining to the performance of financial institutions in India like banks, insurance companies, non-banking financial institutions and mutual funds is a very timely release for all. The book covers many other pertinent issues which is a concern for everybody including governments and policymakers.

I am very confident that the readers will get to understand the deep insights shared by the chapter contributors about the assessment of financial institutions in the background of the added complexities in the fast-changing financial landscape. This academic contribution gives me gratification as it has given academicians and researchers the platform to share their experiences through empirical research about the ground realities. I wish the department the very best in all the future endeavours in its academic journey.

(Professor Susanta Kumar Chakraborty)

Preface

The Indian financial sector has undergone remarkable transformation over the past few decades. From the days of post-independence Swadeshi ideology to the globalization era of the 1990s, and now in the age of digital disruption, financial institutions in India have evolved in both scale and complexity. This book is an exploration of that evolution, focusing particularly on the performance of financial institutions in India, the challenges they face, and the opportunities that lie ahead.

This book aims to provide a comprehensive analysis of how Indian financial institutions have performed in recent years. It also addresses a wide range of topics, the most important of which are the functioning of initial public offerings, external commercial borrowings, mutual funds, insurance, banking and non-banking sectors, and green bonds etc. Some of the contributions made by researchers evaluate the performance of banking sector as well as insurance sector with a comparison between the public and private sectors. The contributors have also explored the effect of digitization of banking services on the society as a whole. Besides this, a good number of studies deals with the performance of IPOs and mutual funds etc. The contributors of this edited book, however, also explore a number of other significant topics. The research on green bonds, digital marketing, and dividend payment decision and firms' financial performance are among the relevant ones.

The diverse array of subjects in the book will undoubtedly create interest among the researchers and academic fraternity related to the fields of commerce, management and economics. We hope that this book will serve as a useful resource for all stakeholders seeking to bridge the gap between academic research and practical insights.

Contents

Performance of NSE Listed IPOs after the Mandatory ASBA Mechanism: An Empirical Study

Shubhadip Kushari[1], Wilson Peter Minz[2] and Goutam Bhowmik[3]

ABSTRACT: An IPO is an opportunity for unlisted companies that want to develop, diversify, and grow with better future business prospects. An investor holding shares through an IPO can view it as a speculative chance in the short term or an opportunity to receive substantial dividends with capital appreciation in the long run. After SEBI implemented the Application supported by Blocked Amount (ASBA) mechanism mandatory for applying IPO (from January 1, 2016), the process of IPO listing became considerably easier and faster than before. Therefore, the present study aims to evaluate the listing day performance as well as to analyse short run and long run performance. To evaluate the IPOs performance, secondary data has been collected from January 2016 to November 2023, for the IPOs which have been listed over the period 2016 to November 2020. Wilcoxon signed rank test has been used to compare short run and long run performance. Out of 118 IPOs, 81 IPOs generated a positive return on the listing date. Moreover, five companies have generated more than 100% returns. In the short run 78, 74, 74 IPOs have showed a positive return by the end of first month, third month and sixth month respectively. Whereas, in case of long run performance, 81, 70, 70 IPOs have showed a positive return by the end of one year, second year and third year. Wilcoxon signed rank test reveals that the long run performance was found to be better than the short run performance. Therefore, the present study will provide a comprehensive knowledge about the short and long run performance of IPOs after the mandatory of ASBA.

Keywords: ASBA, IPO, Listing Day, Short Run and Long Run Performance, Wilcoxon Signed Rank Test.

JEL Classification: O16, E22.

---

[1] Research Scholar, Department of Commerce, University of Gour Banga, West Bengal, India. E-mail: shubhadipkushari25@gmail.com

[2] Research Scholar, Department of Commerce, University of Gour Banga, West Bengal, India.

[3] Professor, Department of Commerce, University of Gour Banga, West Bengal, India.

Introduction

The Indian stock market is one of the oldest in Asia, having been in existence since 1875, although it remained mainly outside the global integration process until the late 1980s. After China and Hong Kong, the Indian stock market has risen to become Asia's third largest. India's stock market is an emerging market and divided into two parts: the primary market and the secondary market. When a firm issues its shares to raises the necessary capital in the market for the first time, this market is referred to as the primary market and the procedure is known as an initial public offering (IPO). After the introduction of Applications Supported by Blocked Amount (ASBA) by SEBI (w.e.f. 1st January 2016) for applying IPO, the process of IPO listing is much easier and faster than before. It reduces the turnaround time for listing IPO and make the process of refunding faster. If an investor applies through ASBA, his or her application money will be deducted from his or her bank account only if his or her application is selected for allotment. An IPO requires a minimum investment upto ₹ 15,000 to participate. Thats why regular investors are pouring money into it. The second most important factor is listing gain; which everybody loves to enjoy. It makes no difference to any investor what the company does or who is in the management. The investor simply intends to gain from the listing. The most common term for an investor in an IPO listing is under-pricing or overpricing. When the listing day closing price is greater than the issue price, is known as under-priced, but when the listing day closing price is less than the issue price, is known as overpriced.

Some investors invest their money in anticipation of listing gains, while others may want to hold it for a long time. Many investors think the IPO market can never fail, especially when the market is getting close to all-time highs. Despite in the IPO process, the listing gain and short run gain are crucial indications. They do not reflect the effect of capital market asset creation. The capital market is, by definition, intended for long-term assets. As a result, any study of IPO would be incomplete unless it examines the long-term performance of the shares issued through an IPO. Therefore, the present study aims to evaluate the listing day performance along with analyse and compare short and long run performance of IPOs after implementation of ASBA mechanism.

Literature Review and Research Gap

A brief review of relevant literature is given below chronologically. Murthy & Singh (2014) analysed short term performance of IPOs in Indian market for a sample of 89 IPOs during the period of 2006–09. 30 days data were taken to analyse short term returns and logistic regression model used to test the hypothesis. The findings revealed that-most of the IPOs have significant returns on the day of listing but thereafter they do not give much return in the short run. Shah & Mehta (2015) explored listing day performance along with return on Market Adjusted Anormal Return (MAAR) pertaining to 113 IPOs in India during January, 2010 to December, 2014 as well as analysed the impact of various factor on under-pricing of IPOs. Results revealed that on average, significantly positive return on the listing day. MAAR of all sample IPO companies was 7.19%. Furthermore, among the four factors oversubscription was the only factor for under- pricing of IPOs. Murthy *et al.* (2016) examined the long run performance of 31 IPOs during the period of 2000 to 2003. logistic regression model has been used to test the hypothesis. Study revealed that long run variables have no relationship with short run variables.

Malhotra & Premkumar (2017) explored the long-run performance of IPOs that went public between 2004 and 2008, as well as the factors that may have an impact on the price reaction of an IPO by the firms. The findings revealed that majority of IPOs underperformed in the long run, with a positive association between the number of shares offered at the time of the IPO's subscription. Hawaldar *et al.* (2018) analysed listing day performance and post listing market performance among the book- built based IPOs and Fixed-price based IPOs that went to public between 2001 to 2011. The findings depict that, as compared to fixed-price IPOs, book-built IPOs are underpriced by a smaller margin. Furthermore, although book-built IPOs have negative cumulative average abnormal returns (CAARs) for up to five years and beyond, negative CAARs associated with fixed-price IPOs turn positive after one and a half years and remain positive thereafter. Dhuria & Kumar (2018) studied the price behaviour of book- built IPOs in India during the financial year 2017–18. Market adjusted abnormal return (MAAR) was used to examine price behaviour. The findings revealed that the Indian IPO market remained underpriced over the study period. Bakshi *et al.* (2019) explored the determinants of listing gains in Indian market. A sample of 50 companies that went to public between 8th September 2017 to 18th September 2018 were selected in the study. Result revealed that out of four factors (Subscription size of issue, market sentiments, promoters holding and industry performance) only subscription size of the issue was influencing listing gain. Ganatra & Dave (2020) explored investor satisfaction with IPOs investments using the ASBA mechanism. Structure questionnaires were used to obtain data from 400 sample respondents of Ahmedabad city. The study's concluded that have an impact on the investor's level of satisfaction. Khan *et al.* (2021) investigated stock performance on the day of listing and compared short run performance to long run performance among 26 listed IPOs that went public in 2016. Among the 26 IPOs, 20 had a positive return on listing date. In the long run, IPO traders on the stock exchange are thought to be more promising than short-term traders. Dave (2022) addressed the factors that determine the listing gain of IPOs. This study used a total of 64 IPOs that went public in 2021 as a sample. It was discovered that the issue size, lot size, issue price, subscription in the QIB, HNI, Retail, and Employee categories, as well as the grey market premium and opening price of the Sensex on the day of listing, had a statistically significant influence on listing gain. Biswas & Joshi (2023) studied the comparative performance of a list of IPOs that were launched in 2018. The findings revealed that market performance for IPOs is not always due to basic efficiency. Further, the nature of equity ownership does not influence the market performance significantly.

The above review showed that most of the studies have been conducted on the listing day performance or short run performance and long run performance. Moreover, some studies have also conducted to identify the factor influencing listing gain. However, few studies have been conducted to compare the long-term and short-term performance of IPOs, but there have been no comprehensive studies on the entire IPOs population after the ASBA mechanism became mandatory. Therefore, the present study aims to evaluate short run and long run performance of IPOs as well as compare short run and long run performance of IPOs after the ASBA mechanism became mandatory.

Objectives and Hypothesis of the Study

The main objectives of the study are:

- To evaluate the performance of IPOs on listing day.
- To analyse short run and long run performance of IPOs.
- To compare short run and long run performance of IPOs.

The hypothesis is:

- H_0: There is no significant difference between the short run and long run returns during the period 2016–2020.

Research Methodology

Empirical research design has been used to assess the post listing performance of IPOs. Return on short run performance is evaluated using closing prices of one, three, and six months, whereas long run performance is evaluated using closing prices of one, two, and three years. The listing gain or loss is calculated based on the closing price of listing day. Ranking of IPOs has been done at each stage (listing day, short run and long run) based on its performance (returns). The study covers the period from January 2016 to November 2020 and an additional three years have been taken in order to analyse the long-term performance of the IPOs for the said period. The reason behind of choosing the above mention time frame is to analyse the performance of IPOs after the mandatory of ASBA. The study is based on secondary data, which has been collected from the official website of NSE India. Issue price of IPO's, listing day closing price, closing price of the day has been gathered from 1 month, 3months, 6 months and 1 year, 2 years, 3 years from the date of listing. If a day occurs after the listing of IPOs on which the market is closed, the next day's closing price is used to determine performance. The sample consists of all Indian Companies which issue IPOs and were listed on the NSE between January 2016 and November 2020. The tools used in the study include Ranking technique, Wilcoxon signed rank test and bar diagram has been used for the present study.

Table 1: IPO listing in National Stock Exchange

Year	*Number of IPO Listed in NSE*
2016	27
2017	38
2018	24
2019	17
2020	13

Source: Collected from NSE website

Results and Discussion

This section provides a comparative result and interpretation of short run and long run performance of IPOs listed in National Stock Exchange (NSE) in India. Furthermore, Wilcoxon Signed Rank test has been performed to evaluate the difference in the short run and long run performance of IPOs.

Performance of IPOs on Listing Day

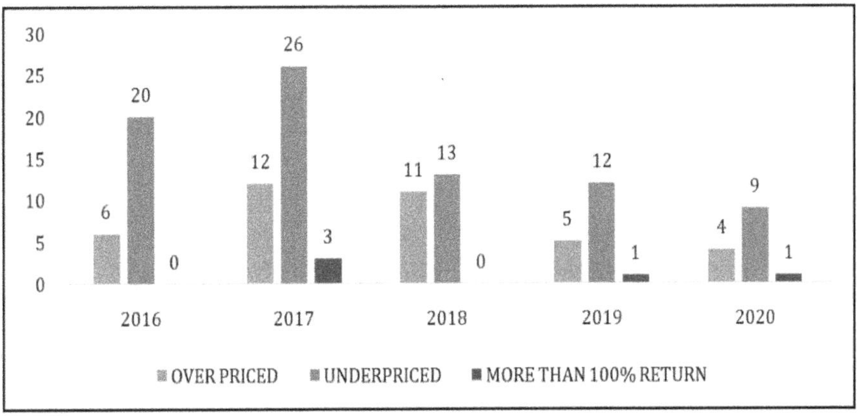

Chart 1: Performance of IPOs on Listing Day

Source: compiled and constructed by the authors

Chart 1 analyses the listing day performance of 118 IPOs that were listed between 2016 and 2020.Out of 118 IPOs, 80 IPOs generated a positive return on the listing date during 2016 to 2020. Furthermore, five companies generated more than 100% on their listing date.

Annexure table 1 depict that, out of 26 IPOs that were listed in the year 2016, 20 companies have shown a positive return in its listing date wherein, Advanced Enzymes has generated a highest return of 31.48% on its listing day. Out of the 38 IPOs that were listed in 2017, 26 companies were found to be underpriced on their listing date. Furthermore, out of 26 companies 3 companies provided more than 100% positive returns on their listing day wherein, Salasar Techno Engineering generated highest return of 143.06 %, followed by Astron Paper and Board and Aveneue Supermarts. On the other hand, 12 companies were found to be overpriced on their listing date. In the year 2018, 24 IPOs were listed in NSE, out of which 13 IPOs were found to be under-priced on their listing date. Wherein, Amber Enterprises provided the highest return of 45.48% among them. On the other hand, the remaining 11 IPOs were found to be over priced on its listing date. Out of 17 IPOs listed on NSE in 2019, 12 IPOs were found to generate positive returns on its listing date. The IRCTC Limited exhibits relatively higher returns of 123.46% in comparison to other listed IPOs in 2019. On the other hand, 5 IPOs were found to have-negative returns on its listing date. A total of 13 IPOs were listed in NSE up to November, 2020. 9 IPOs were under-priced on their listing date. The highest return of 111.44% was achieved by Happiest Minds Technologies, among the underpriced IPOs. The remaining 4 IPOs were overpriced on their listing date.

Progressive Growth of IPO Return's in Short Term Period

Chart 2 demonstrates the overall progressive growth of IPO returns in short term period, out of 118 IPOs, 78 IPOs were found to have a positive return over the period of one month and among 118 IPOs, 5 IPOs has been able to generate more than 100% returns in respect to its issue price. A total of 74 IPOs has generated positive returns by the end of third and sixth month. Whereas, 9 and 19 IPOs were able to provide more than 100% returns by the end of the third and sixth month respectively. Annexure table 2 exhibits short term progressive growth of IPO return's using buy and hold strategy by investors for the period of five years (2016–2020). Short term progressive growth has been measured by increase in returns compared to the issue price during the different time horizons like, 1 month, 3 month and 6 months.

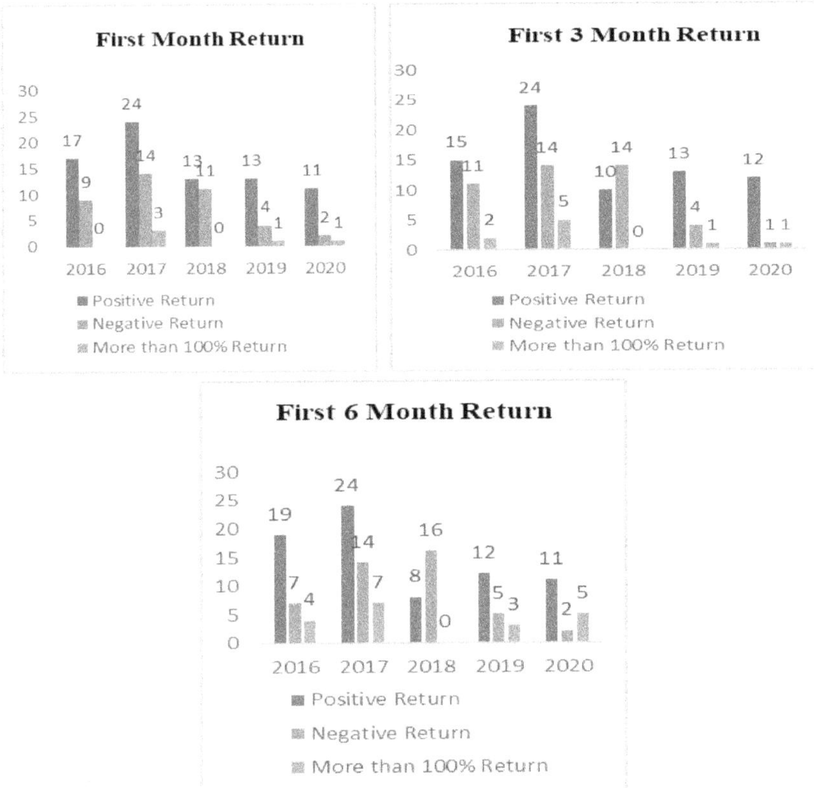

Chart 2: Overall Progressive Growth of IPO Returns in Short Term Period

Source: Compiled and constructed by the authors

Buy and hold for 1 month, 3months and 6 months in 2016:

It is evident from the table 2 that, out of 26 IPOs, 17 IPOs have generated positive returns within a month in respect to its issue price. The highest returns of 53.45% was achieved by Advanced Enzymes in this period.

Further, when the performance is explored over a period of 3 month it was observed, 15 IPOs generated positive returns. Moreover, out of 15 IPOs two generated more than 100% returns. However, it is notable that out 26 IPOs 3 IPOs showed a declining trend and 10 IPOs showed an increasing trend in its return during the third month in comparison to one month return.

Moreover, 19 IPOs were found to have a positive return over six month. In addition, 4 IPOs was found to generate more than 100% returns by the end of the sixth month. Furthermore, 17 IPOs were found to have an increasing trend in returns during its sixth month in comparison to third month return.

Whereas, 3 IPOs were found to have a declining trend in its return during the period of 6 month.

Buy and hold for 1 month, 3months and 6 months in 2017:

It is evident from the table 2 that, out of 38 IPOs, 24 IPOs were found to have a positive return within a month, 3 month and 6 months in respect to its issue price. Moreover, among 24 IPOs 3 IPOs namely, Astron Paper & Board, Avenue Supermarts and CDSL has generated more than 100% within a month.

For 3 months return, 5 IPOs generated more than 100% return. Compared to 1 month, it is notable that 18 IPOs showed an increasing trend in its return during the third month. However, 3 IPOs namely Astron Paper & Board, CDSL and Tejas Network has showed a declining trend in its returns during the same period.

Out of 24 IPOs that generated positive returns over the period of 6 months, 6 IPOs exceeded 100% return. 12 out of 14 IPOs that generated negative returns continued to do so in the first, third and sixth months compared to their issue price. In the sixth month, 18 IPOs showed an increase in their returns relative to the third month, while 6 showed a decrease.

However, 12 IPOs had been generating continuous negative return in its first, third and sixth months in respect to its issue price. During sixth month, 18 IPOs were found to have an increasing trend in its return in comparison of its returns in third month. On the other hand, six IPOs has showed a declining trend.

Buy and hold for 1 month, 3month and 6 months in 2018:

A total of 24 IPOs were listed in the year 2018. From the table 2 it can be depicted that out of 24 IPOs, 13 IPOs was able to generate positive returns over the 1-month period in respect to its issue price. HDFC AMC has provided a highest return of 53.25%.

10 IPOs were able to generate positive returns during the third month only. Furthermore, out of 24 IPOs, 5 IPOs showed an increasing trend by the end of third month compared to one month of returns. Whereas, 5 IPOs has showed a declining trend in comparison to the returns of first month.

Only 8 IPOs has been able to generate positive returns by the end of six month. Fine Organics has generated a highest return of 53.58%. In addition, it is notable that 9 IPOs has shown continuous negative returns during one, three and six-month period. Out of 24 IPOs, 4 IPOs showed an increasing trend in returns during sixth month compared to three months of returns. On the other hand, 4 IPOs were found to have a declining trend in returns by the end of sixth month.

Buy and hold for 1 month, 3month and 6 months in 2019:

It is evident from the table 2 that, 17 IPOs that were listed in 2019, 13 IPOs were found to have a positive return within a month and 3 months in respect to its issue price. Furthermore, IRCTC Limited has generated more than 100% returns during one-month and three-month period respectively with 185.53% and 204.42%

11 IPOs showed an increasing trend by the end of third month. On the other hand, 2 IPOs namely Ujjivan Bank and Xelmpoc Design and Tech has shown a decreasing trend

Moreover 12 IPOs was able to generate positive returns by the end of six month. India Mart Inter Mesh, Affle India and IRCTC Limited has shown more than 100% return. Moreover, Sterling & Wilson Solar and Prince Pipes has continuously provided a negative return for one, three and six months. 7 IPOs have demonstrated an upward tendency in return during the sixth month when compared to the return of third month. Whereas, 5 IPOs has shown decreasing trend in returns during the sixth month in comparison to the return of third month.

Buy and hold for 1 month, 3month and 6 months in 2020:

Out of 13 IPOs, 11 IPOs generated a positive return by the end of one month in respect to its issue price. Among 11 IPOs, 1 IPO namely Route Mobile has provided more than 100% return by the end of one month.

During the third month 12 IPOs were found to have a positive return. Route Mobile continued more than 100% return by the end of third month. In comparison of returns of third month with the first month, it was found out that 11 IPOs has showed an increasing trend in returns by the end of third month over one month. Mindspace Business Parks REIT has showed a declining trend in returns by the end of third month by 0.22%.

In sixth month, 11 IPOs was found to have a positive return in respect to its issue price. Out of 11 IPOS, 4 IPOs namely, Route Mobile, Happiest Minds Technologies, Likhitha Infrastructure, Gland Pharma and Rossari Biotech has provided more than 100% return. Moreover, 7 IPOs has shown an increasing trend in returns by the end of sixth month whereas 2 IPOs has showed a declining trend in comparison to third month.

Progressive Growth of IPO Return's in Long Run Period

Chart 3 demonstrates the overall progressive growth of IPO returns in long term period, out of 118 IPOs, 81 IPOs were found to have a positive return over the period of one year and among 118 IPOs, 25 IPOs has been able to generate more than 100 % returns in respect to its issue price. A total of 70 IPOs has generated positive returns by the end of second and third year. Whereas, 29 and 30 IPOs were able to provide more than 100% returns by the end of the second and third year respectively.

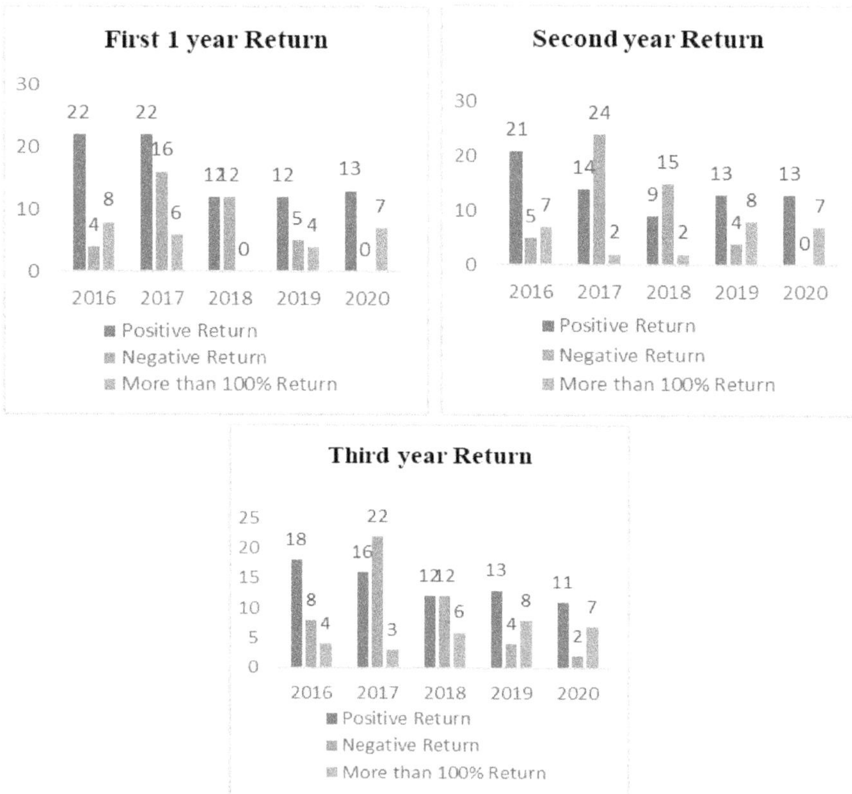

Chart 3: Overall Progressive Growth of IPOS Returns in the Long Run Period

Source: Compiled and Constructed by the authors

Annexure table 3 exhibits long term progressive growth of IPO return's using buy and hold strategy by investors for the period of five years (2016–2020). Progressive growth is expressed in terms of increase in returns. It is calculated by considering the closing price at the end of the trading day divided by the issue price and has been expressed in terms of percentage.

Buy and hold for 1 year, 2 year and 3 years for the IPOs listed in 2016

Out of 26 IPOs, 22 IPOs were found to have a positive return during the period of one year. Among 22 IPOs, 8 IPOs were able to generate more than 100% returns by the end of one year.

By the end of the second year, out of 26 IPOs, 21 IPOs has showed a positive return during the second year. Among 21 IPOs, 7 IPOs were able to generate more than 100% of returns by the end of the second year. While in comparison with second year return with first year IPOs return, 11 IPOs were found to have an increasing trend by the end of the second year. Whereas, 8 IPOs were found to have a declining trend by the end of second year.

Out of 26 IPOs, 18 IPOs were found to have a positive return by the end of the third year. Among 18 IPOs, 4 IPOs has generated more than 100% return. Furthermore, 3 IPOs namely, Precision Camshafts, Quick Heal and HPL Electric has showed a continuous negative outcome for the period of three years. While in comparison with third year return with second year, it was found out that only 4 IPOs has showed an increasing trend in return by the end of third year. Whereas, 14 IPOs has showed a decreasing tendency during the third year in comparison to second year return.

Buy and hold for 1 year, 2 year and 3 year for the IPOs listed in 2017

Out of 24 listed IPOs, only 12 IPOs were found to have a positive return. Wherein, 4 IPOs namely, IRCTC Limited, Affle India, Indian Mart and Inter Mesh and Neogen Chemicals has been able to generate more than 100% returns by the end of one year.

In the second year, 13 IPOs has been able to provide a positive return. Among 13 IPOs, 10 IPOs has been able to generate more than 100% returns by the end of the second year. Furthermore, 10 IPOs was found to have an increasing trend by the end of second year in comparison of returns of the third year's return.

Similarly in the third year 13 IPOs were found to have a positive return. wherein 8 IPOs were found to have more than 100% returns by the end of the third year. Furthermore, 5 IPOs were found to have an increasing trend in returns by the end of the third year in comparison to second year's return.

Buy and hold for 1 year, 2 year and 3 year for the IPOs listed in 2018

Out of 24 IPOs only 12 IPOs were found to have a positive return during its first year. Wherein, Aavas Financiers were found to have the highest returns of 94.77.

In the second year only 9 IPOs were able to generate a positive return by the end of the second year. Among 9 IPOs, 2 IPOs namely, Fine Organics and HDFC AMC has been able to generate more than 100% return. Out of 24 IPOs only 7 IPOs has showed an increasing trend during the second year in comparison to first year returns. Whereas, 2 IPOs namely Avas Financiers and RITES LTD. Has showed a declining trend in the second year.

In the third year only 12 IPOs has showed a positive return during the third year. Out of 12 IPOs 6 IPOs were able to generate more than 100% of returns by the end of third year. Furthermore, 11 IPOs has showed an increasing trend by the end of third year in comparison to second year return. Whereas, one IPOs namely, Garden Reach Shipbuilders has showed a declining trend during third year by 8.22%.

Buy and hold for 1 year, 2 year and 3 years for the IPOs listed in 2019

Out of 17 IPOs 12 IPOs has showed a positive return in respect to its issue price. Wherein, 4 IPOs namely, IRCTC Limited, Affle India Indian Mart Inter Mesh and Neogen Chemicals has been able to generate more than 100% return.

In the second year, 13 IPOs were able to generate higher return wherein, 8 IPOs has been able to generate more than 100% return by the end of second year. While in comparison with the returns of second year with the first year, it was found out that 11 IPOs has showed an increasing trend in the second year over first year returns.

In the third year 13 IPOs has been able to generate positive return wherein, 8 IPOs has been able to generate returns more than 100%. While in comparison with the returns of third year with the second year, it was found out that only 5 IPOs has showed an increasing trend by the end of the third year.

Buy and hold for 1 year, 2 year and 3 years for the IPOs listed in 2020

In 2020 all 13 listed IPOs were found to have a positive return by the end of one year. Wherein, 7 IPOs has been able to generate more than 100% of returns in respect to its issue price.

Similarly, in the second year all the IPOs were found to have a positive return in respect to its issue price. Wherein, 7 IPOs has been able to generate more than 100% returns by the end of second year. While in comparison of returns of second year with that of first year, it was found out of 13 IPOs, 3 IPOs has an increasing trend during the second year.

In the third year, out of 13 IPOs, 11 IPOs were found to have a positive return. Wherein, 8 IPOs were found to have more than 100% return in respect to its issue price. Whereas, 8 IPOs were found to have an increasing tendency in returns by the end of third year in comparison to second year's return.

Comparison of Short Term and Long-Term Returns

Wilcoxon Signed Ranks Test has been conducted in order to find out the significant difference between the short run and long run performance among 118 IPOs that were listed during 2016–2020.

Table 2: Rank of 118 IPOs Listed during 2016–2020

Ranks				
		N	*Mean Rank*	*Sum of Ranks*
Returns in Long Run	Negative Ranks	55[a]	47.76	2627.00
Returns in Short Run	Positive Ranks	63[b]	69.75	4394.00
	Ties	0[c]		
	Total	**118**		

a. Long Run < Short Run
b. Long Run > Short Run
c. Long Run = Short Run
Source: Compiled and constructed by the author by using SPSS

The table 2 shows the result of Wilcoxon Signed Rank Test. The mean rank in short and long run period is categorized as positive and negative ranks. Positive ranks indicate that the return in the long run is better when compared to short run and vice-versa. The above table reveals that 63 companies are performing better in the long run over short run whereas 55 companies are earning better returns in the short run over a long run period.

Table 3: Results of Wilcoxon Signed Ranks Test

Hypothesis	*Z*	*P-Value*	*Decision*
H_0: There is no significant difference between the short run and long run returns during the period 2016–2020	–2.373[b]	.018	Reject the H_0

a. Wilcoxon Signed Ranks Test
b. Based on negative ranks
Source: Compiled and constructed by the author by using SPSS

The table 3 determines the existence of significant difference between the short term and long-term returns for the period of five years. The result of Wilcoxon signed rank test reveals that the mean of long run returns and short run returns are unequal $F (55,63) = -2.375$, $p = .018$ (which is lesser than 5% level of significance). Hence, null hypothesis has been rejected and so concluded that there is a significant difference between the short run and long run returns of the IPOs listed during the year 2016–2020.

Findings and Concluding Observations

The major findings of the study can be summarised below:

- Out of 118 IPOs, 81 IPOs generated a positive return on the listing day during 2016 to 2020. Out of 81 IPOs, 5 IPOs has generated more than 100% return in its listing day.

- Though highest number of negative returns on the listing date was witnessed in the year 2017, highest number of IPOs were recorded for generating more than 100% return in the same year.
- In respect to short run performance of IPOs, 78, 74 and 74 IPOs showed positive return by the end of first month, third month and sixth month respectively. Moreover, 5, 9 and 19 IPOs have been able to generate more than 100% returns by the end of first, third and sixth month respectively.
- Long run performance revealed that 81, 70 and 70 IPOs generated positive return by the end of first year, second year and third year respectively.
- Furthermore, 25, 29 and 30 IPOs have been able to generate more than 100% return during first year, second year and third year respectively.
- Wilcoxon Signed Rank Test revealed that there is significant difference between the short run and long run performance of IPOs made during 2016–2020.

The above findings clearly demonstrate that about 68% IPOs were found to be under-priced and the listing price (market value) of IPOs were higher than the initial offering price. However, listing gains can be tempting for investors who want to make quick profit but it involves some risk. The investors must consider one major factor that some IPOs which showed high listing gains did not able to sustain their value in the long run. Therefore, the retail investors must consider the fundamentals, valuation and growth potential of the company before investing into a particular IPOs for long run.

References

[1] Bakshi, A., Medhi, P. and Mitra, S. (2019). Determinants of listing gains in IPO in Indian market. *Prestige International Journal of Management and Research*, 12R (1–2) 134–141.

[2] Biswas, S. and Joshi, N. (2023). A performance based ranking of initial public offerings (IPOs) in India. *Journal of Decision Analytics and Intelligent Computing, 3*(1), 15–32.

[3] Dave, R. (2022). A research study on factors influencing listing gains of IPOs. *Journal of Asiatic Society of Mumbai,* XCV (20), 14–17.

[4] Dhuria, A. and Kumar, V. (2018). Pricing of initial public offerings in India: a study based on BSE. *Journal of Management Research and Analysis,* 5 (3), 126–130.

[5] Ganatra, R.P. and Dave, M.D. (2020). Investor Satisfaction with Respect to Investment in IPO through ASBA in Ahmedabad city. *Research guru,* 13 (4), 94–99.

[6] Hawaldar, I. T., Naveen Kumar, K.R. and Mallikarjunappa, T. (2018). Pricing and performance of IPOs: Evidence from Indian stock market. *Cogent Economics & Finance, 6*(1), 1–20.

[7] Khan, M.A., Zeeshan, K., Ahmad, F., Alakkas, A.A. and Farooqi, R. (2021). A study of stock performance of select IPOS in India. *Academy of Accounting and Financial Studies Journal, 25*(6), 1–11.

[8] Malhotra, M. and Premkumar, N. (2017). Long run performance of initial public offerings in India. *The Business and Management Review, 9*(1), 206–214.

[9] Murthy, K.B. and Singh, A.K. (2014). Short run performance of IPO market in India. *International journal of Financial management, 4*(2), 11–22.

[10] Murthy, K.V., Singh, A.K. and Gupta, L. (2016). Long-run performance of IPO market in India. *International Journal of Financial Management, 6*(1), 17–27.

[11] Shah, S.N. and Mehta, D.H. (2015). Initial performance of IPOs in India: Evidence from 2010–2014. *Samvad, 9*, 77–86.

[12] Accessed through www.nseindia.com

Annexure

Table 1: Listing Day Performance of IPOs during 2016 to 2020

Year of Listing	*Name of the Company*	*Listing Gain*	*Rank*
2016	Narayana Hrudayalaya	34.78	24
2016	Precision Camshafts	–4.6	94
2016	TeamLease Services	20.34	41
2016	Quick Heal	–20.92	118
2016	HealthCare Global	–21.56	119
2016	Bharat Wire Ropes	1.22	72
2016	Infibeam	3.18	66
2016	Equitas Holdings	22.91	34
2016	Thyrocare Technologies	38.74	20
2016	Ujjivan Financial Services	10.26	57
2016	Parag Milk Foods*	14.88	50
2016	Mahanagar Gas	23.59	33
2016	Quess Corp	58.71	13
2016	L&T Infotech*	–1.75	89
2016	Advanced Enzymes	31.48	28
2016	Dilip Buildcon	14.95	48
2016	SP Apparels	7.74	59
2016	RBL Bank	33.07	26
2016	L&T Technology Services	1.05	74
2016	GNA Axles	18.38	44
2016	ICICI Prudential Life Insurance	–10.91	110
2016	HPL Electric	–6.29	98
2016	Endurance Technologies	37.06	22
2016	PNB Housing Finance	14.99	47
2016	Varun Beverages	3.26	65
2016	Sheela Foam	41.37	19
2016	Laurus Labs	12.24	54
2017	BSE Limited	32.66	27
2017	Music Broadcast	11.98	55
2017	Avenue Supermarts	114.58	5

Year of Listing	*Name of the Company*	*Listing Gain*	*Rank*
2017	CL Educate	–15.92	116
2017	Shankara Building Products	37.49	21
2017	S Chand & Company	0.9	76
2017	IRB InvIT Fund	–0.2	82
2017	HUDCO*	20.92	40
2017	PSP Projects	–5	95
2017	Indigrid InvIT Fund	–1.36	88
2017	Tejas Networks	2.53	69
2017	Eris Lifesciences	–0.25	83
2017	CDSL	75.57	7
2017	GTPL Hathway	0.97	75
2017	AU Small Finance Bank	51.3	15
2017	Salasar Techno Engineering	143.06	1
2017	SIS India	–7.11	101
2017	Cochin Shipyard*	22.26	36
2017	Apex Frozen Foods	21.2	39
2017	Bharat Road Network	1.68	71
2017	Dixon Technologies	63.73	11
2017	Matrimony.com*	–8.16	104
2017	Capacit'e Infraprojects	37.02	23
2017	ICICI Lombard	3.06	67
2017	SBI Life Insurance	1.08	73
2017	Prataap Snacks	25.87	32
2017	Godrej Agrovet	29.49	29
2017	MAS Financial Services	42.57	18
2017	Indian Energy Exchange	–1.26	87
2017	GIC*	–4.13	92
2017	Reliance Nippon Life Asset Management	12.86	53
2017	Mahindra logistic	0.12	79
2017	The New India Assurance*	–9.11	106
2017	Khadim India	–8.15	103
2017	HDFC Standard Life Insurance	18.83	42
2017	Shalby	–3.39	91

Year of Listing	*Name of the Company*	*Listing Gain*	*Rank*
2017	Future Supply Chain Solutions	3.37	64
2017	Astron Paper & Board	141.5	2
2018	Apollo Micro Systems	60.64	12
2018	Newgen Software	3.02	68
2018	Amber Enterprises	45.48	17
2018	Galaxy Surfactants	14.9	49
2018	Aster DM Healthcare	–4.45	93
2018	HG Infra Engineering	–0.83	85
2018	Bharat Dynamics*	–8.93	105
2018	Bandhan Bank	27.16	31
2018	Hindustan Aeronautics*	–6.76	99
2018	Sandhar Technologies	–2.97	90
2018	Karda Constructions	–20.67	117
2018	Mishra Dhatu Nigam*	0.06	80
2018	ICICI Securities	–14.4	115
2018	Lemon Tree Hotels	27.95	30
2018	IndoStar Capital Finance	2.47	70
2018	RITES Ltd*	15.3	46
2018	Fine Organics	5.08	61
2018	Varroc Engineering	7.28	60
2018	TCNS Clothing	–7.94	102
2018	HDFC AMC	65.09	10
2018	CreditAccess Grameen	0.01	81
2018	IRCON International	–12.57	112
2018	Aavas Financiers	–5.68	97
2018	Garden Reach Shipbuilders	–12.46	111
2019	Xelpmoc Design and Tech*	–9.32	107
2019	Chalet Hotels	4.18	63
2019	MSTC*	–5.04	96
2019	Embassy Office Parks REIT	4.89	62
2019	Rail Vikas Nigam*	0.26	78
2019	Metropolis Healthcare	9.07	58
2019	Polycab India	21.71	37

Year of Listing	*Name of the Company*	*Listing Gain*	*Rank*
2019	Neogen Chemicals	22.58	35
2019	IndiaMART InterMESH	33.81	25
2019	Affle India	17.27	45
2019	Spandana Sphoorty Financial	–0.96	86
2019	Sterling & Wilson Solar	–6.9	100
2019	IRCTC Limited*	127.42	3
2019	Vishwaraj Sugar	0.58	77
2019	CSB Bank	53.9	14
2019	Ujjivan Bank	51.08	16
2019	Prince Pipes	–14.3	114
2020	SBI Cards	–9.8	108
2020	Rossari Biotech	74.51	8
2020	Mindspace Business Parks REIT	10.44	56
2020	Happiest Minds Technologies	123.46	4
2020	Route Mobile	86.09	6
2020	CAMS	13.95	51
2020	Chemcon Speciality Chemicals	71.88	9
2020	Angel Broking	–9.87	109
2020	UTI AMC	–14.04	113
2020	Mazagon Dock Shipbuilders	18.59	43
2020	Likhitha Infrastructure	13.75	52
2020	Equitas Small Finance Bank	–0.61	84
2020	Gland Pharma	21.3	38

Source: Compiled and constructed by the authors

Table 2: Short Run Performance of IPOs during 2016 to 2020

Year of Listing	*Name of the Company*	*1-month Return*	*Rank*	*3-month Return*	*Rank*	*6-month Return*	*Rank*
2016	Precision Camshafts	–14.57	105	–20.78	109	–21.61	103
2016	TeamLease Services	15.26	50	4.68	69	29.11	53
2016	Quick Heal	–31.56	118	–19.78	108	–25.33	105
2016	HealthCare Global	–15.92	107	–15.76	104	1.4	74
2016	Bharat Wire Ropes	–9.67	97	–2	76	–10	91
2016	Infibeam	18.77	45	61.22	20	113.33	13

Year of Listing	*Name of the Company*	*1-month Return*	*Rank*	*3-month Return*	*Rank*	*6-month Return*	*Rank*
2016	Equitas Holdings	27.68	34	57.86	24	66.64	29
2016	Thyrocare Technologies	34.6	24	24.46	51	41.67	41
2016	Ujjivan Financial Services	75.02	10	105.81	9	104	19
2016	Parag Milk Foods*	17.07	46	47.81	32	23.72	57
2016	Mahanagar Gas	21.7	41	56.81	26	87.14	23
2016	Quess Corp	67.13	11	94.59	14	113.97	12
2016	L&T Infotech*	–6.39	90	–12.17	96	–4.49	82
2016	Advanced Enzymes	53.45	14	145.97	6	99.99	20
2016	Dilip Buildcon	5.11	64	–5.55	85	24.82	56
2016	SP Apparels	21.72	40	11.92	63	57.16	31
2016	RBL Bank	29.42	30	61.67	19	111.87	14
2016	L&T Technology Services	–0.85	80	–7.66	90	–9.03	90
2016	GNA Axles	20.46	43	–13.21	99	–6.62	87
2016	ICICI Prudential Life Insurance	–7.6	93	–10.15	93	11.05	69
2016	HPL Electric	–19.03	109	–50.27	117	–37.77	114
2016	Endurance Technologies	14.92	51	27.4	50	72.4	26
2016	PNB Housing Finance	10.99	59	27.97	48	70.5	27
2016	Varun Beverages	–5	88	–9.22	92	10.6	70
2016	Sheela Foam	30.23	27	50.48	28	84.3	24
2016	Laurus Labs	12.35	55	23.97	54	41.53	42
2017	BSE Limited	10.51	60	24.41	52	32.7	49
2017	Music Broadcast	4.58	65	8.27	66	19.98	64
2017	Avenue Supermarts	148.56	4	173.51	4	257.54	4
2017	CL Educate	–8.98	96	–15.34	101	–30.44	110
2017	Shankara Building Products	53.28	15	95.46	13	230.45	5
2017	S Chand & Company	–15.9	106	–28.51	113	–29.1	108

Year of Listing	*Name of the Company*	*1-month Return*	*Rank*	*3-month Return*	*Rank*	*6-month Return*	*Rank*
2017	IRB InvIT Fund	–2.8	84	–5.79	86	–10.98	93
2017	HUDCO*	13.17	53	33.58	40	37.08	45
2017	PSP Projects	29.67	29	57.36	25	114.76	11
2017	Indigrid InvIT Fund	–8.89	95	–4.03	79	–5.56	86
2017	Tejas Networks	27.3	35	20.58	56	50.23	35
2017	Eris Lifesciences	0.87	78	–4.35	80	31.73	52
2017	CDSL	150.7	3	129.36	7	140	9
2017	GTPL Hathway	–16.21	108	–17.24	106	–4.79	84
2017	AU Small Finance Bank	51.62	17	62.23	18	95.41	21
2017	Salasar Techno Engineering	86.39	9	163.89	5	187.22	8
2017	SIS India	–3.29	85	3.4	72	49.07	37
2017	Cochin Shipyard*	30.14	28	30.43	44	23.03	58
2017	Apex Frozen Foods	93.09	7	367.57	1	299.71	2
2017	Bharat Road Network	–13.27	103	–4.56	82	–11.39	94
2017	Dixon Technologies	50.78	18	98.26	10	95.22	22
2017	Matrimony.com*	–14.05	104	–6.94	89	–17.76	100
2017	Capacit'e Infraprojects	34.92	23	60.32	22	18.08	65
2017	ICICI Lombard	3.31	68	18.19	58	20.05	62
2017	SBI Life Insurance	–8.25	94	–1.36	75	–2.86	80
2017	Prataap Snacks	25.12	37	29.61	47	43.54	40
2017	Godrej Agrovet	15.58	49	32.8	42	51.95	34
2017	MAS Financial Services	28.45	32	35.8	39	32.7	49
2017	Indian Energy Exchange	–5.65	89	–2.95	78	–0.99	76
2017	GIC*	–12.74	102	–15.35	102	–21.67	104
2017	Reliance Nippon Life Asset Management	1.21	75	4.31	71	–4.21	81
2017	Mahindra logistic	3.12	69	10.01	65	32.05	51

Year of Listing	*Name of the Company*	*1-month Return*	*Rank*	*3-month Return*	*Rank*	*6-month Return*	*Rank*
2017	The New India Assurance*	–29.83	117	–7.81	91	–13.06	96
2017	Khadim India	–11.36	99	–6.17	87	10.21	71
2017	HDFC Standard Life Insurance	31.52	26	48.78	30	70.45	28
2017	Shalby	–3.57	86	–11.71	95	–30.12	109
2017	Future Supply Chain Solutions	2.9	70	6.91	68	–1.29	77
2017	Astron Paper & Board	181.4	2	113.4	8	108.4	17
2018	Apollo Micro Systems	16.82	47	–12.58	98	–53.24	117
2018	Newgen Software	–0.61	79	–2.33	77	–2	79
2018	Amber Enterprises	28.07	33	30.93	43	16.04	67
2018	Galaxy Surfactants	0.97	77	–5.28	84	–14.14	97
2018	Aster DM Healthcare	–12	101	–4.97	83	–8.16	89
2018	HG Infra Engineering	22.96	38	11.94	62	–10.93	92
2018	Bharat Dynamics*	–4.65	87	–11.05	94	–25.33	105
2018	Bandhan Bank	35.05	22	39.69	35	52.09	33
2018	Hindustan Aeronautics*	–7.34	91	–30.54	114	–35.82	112
2018	Sandhar Technologies	19.59	44	15.41	61	–7.35	88
2018	Karda Constructions	3.97	67	–6.69	88	–11.42	95
2018	Mishra Dhatu Nigam*	60.17	12	35.83	38	26.72	54
2018	ICICI Securities	–28.9	115	–41.75	115	–48.77	116
2018	Lemon Tree Hotels	29.29	31	30.09	46	25	55
2018	IndoStar Capital Finance	–1.65	83	–21.83	110	–36.26	113
2018	RITES Ltd.*	39	21	33.54	41	44.59	39
2018	Fine Organics	2.23	73	36.58	37	53.58	32

Year of Listing	*Name of the Company*	*1-month Return*	*Rank*	*3-month Return*	*Rank*	*6-month Return*	*Rank*
2018	Varroc Engineering	2.57	71	–15.66	103	–25.34	107
2018	TCNS Clothing	–7.44	92	–15.9	105	–0.45	75
2018	HDFC AMC	53.25	16	27.53	49	22.62	59
2018	CreditAccess Grameen	–21.16	112	–12.17	96	–4.93	85
2018	IRCON International	–27.04	114	–4.52	81	–16.39	98
2018	Aavas Financiers	–19.86	110	2.55	73	38.51	44
2018	Garden Reach Shipbuilders	–23.05	113	–19.62	107	–16.82	99
2019	Xelpmoc Design and Tech*	11.67	56	7.05	67	3.03	73
2019	Chalet Hotels	1.12	76	24.41	52	12.07	68
2019	MSTC*	–11.63	100	–27.42	112	–21.21	102
2019	Embassy Office Parks REIT	7.16	61	21.76	55	32.92	48
2019	Rail Vikas Nigam*	15.79	48	38.68	36	35.53	46
2019	Metropolis Healthcare	5.86	62	18.59	57	45.43	38
2019	Polycab India	11.4	57	15.65	60	33.55	47
2019	Neogen Chemicals	39.35	20	66.84	17	75.26	25
2019	IndiaMART InterMESH	22.31	39	96.34	11	109.65	16
2019	Affle India	13.69	52	87.35	16	124.36	10
2019	Spandana Sphoorty Financial	–0.88	81	48.65	31	21.84	60
2019	Sterling & Wilson Solar	–20.79	111	–63.39	118	–70.9	118
2019	IRCTC Limited*	183.53	1	204.42	3	284.55	3
2019	Vishwaraj Sugar	13.17	53	49.25	29	5.42	72
2019	CSB Bank	2.51	72	–14.05	100	–30.69	111
2019	Ujjivan Bank	42.03	19	4.59	70	–20.27	101
2019	Prince Pipes	–1.15	82	–42.33	116	–38.85	115
2020	SBI Cards	–29.66	116	–22.42	111	16.5	66
2020	Rossari Biotech	88.44	8	89.86	15	107.14	18

Year of Listing	*Name of the Company*	*1-month Return*	*Rank*	*3-month Return*	*Rank*	*6-month Return*	*Rank*
2020	Mindspace Business Parks REIT	11.05	58	10.83	64	20	63
2020	Happiest Minds Technologies	95.36	6	95.93	12	229.76	6
2020	Route Mobile	114.6	5	205.64	2	342.87	1
2020	CAMS	5.62	63	45.47	34	49.31	36
2020	Chemcon Speciality Chemicals	25.24	36	47.15	33	21.65	61
2020	Angel Broking	1.7	74	15.8	59	–4.62	83
2020	UTI AMC	–10.83	98	0.2	74	–1.55	78
2020	Mazagon Dock Shipbuilders	21.41	42	51.03	27	38.86	43
2020	Likhitha Infrastructure	31.79	25	61	21	208.54	7
2020	Equitas Small Finance Bank	4.24	66	30.3	45	65.61	30
2020	Gland Pharma	54.65	13	59.3	23	110.62	15

Source: Compiled and constructed by the authors

Table 3: Long Run Performance of IPOs during 2016 to 2020

Year of Listing	*Name of the Company*	*1year Return*	*Rank*	*2 year Return*	*Rank*	*3 year Return*	*Rank*
2016	Precision Camshafts	–15.54	91	–36.72	93	–69.41	107
2016	TeamLease Services	6.16	73	158.29	20	234.16	16
2016	Quick Heal	–21.42	95	–4.77	74	–45.9	96
2016	HealthCare Global	3.23	79	32.64	57	0.92	69
2016	Bharat Wire Ropes	115	24	147	21	30.33	53
2016	Infibeam	119.59	21	267.36	13	–5.09	72
2016	Equitas Holdings	55.86	42	37.09	53	23.5	56
2016	Thyrocare Technologies	59.98	40	42.93	49	2.66	68
2016	Ujjivan Financial Services	65.12	38	92.19	34	49	47
2016	Parag Milk Foods*	12.51	66	63.05	43	13.26	62
2016	Mahanagar Gas	134.82	18	97.04	32	95.91	31

Year of Listing	*Name of the Company*	*1year Return*	*Rank*	*2 year Return*	*Rank*	*3 year Return*	*Rank*
2016	Quess Corp	183.88	9	237.73	14	51.74	45
2016	L&T Infotech*	8.21	70	146.61	22	113.52	27
2016	Advanced Enzymes	72.77	36	15.63	64	–15.71	79
2016	Dilip Buildcon	138.11	16	286.51	12	84.22	33
2016	SP Apparels	56.12	41	25.39	60	–13.28	78
2016	RBL Bank	142.04	13	178.78	17	45.42	49
2016	L&T Technology Services	–9.74	89	93.53	33	81.79	36
2016	GNA Axles	46.5	45	75.7	40	27.44	54
2016	ICICI Prudential Life Insurance	16.41	62	–0.07	71	37.31	52
2016	HPL Electric	–26.76	100	–71.81	113	–79.21	109
2016	Endurance Technologies	132.43	20	133.23	26	121.65	26
2016	PNB Housing Finance	80.71	34	17.45	63	–25.07	89
2016	Varun Beverages	13.29	65	72.82	42	149.96	23
2016	Sheela Foam	140.23	15	97.11	31	81.69	37
2016	Laurus Labs	23.93	56	–9.04	77	–13.21	77
2017	BSE Limited	5.38	75	–27.02	89	–35.04	90
2017	Music Broadcast	9.49	69	–7.81	75	–79.88	110
2017	Avenue Supermarts	348.03	4	395.7	6	540.84	6
2017	CL Educate	–62.25	116	–75.79	115	–93.79	118
2017	Shankara Building Products	292.41	6	0.39	70	–51.88	99
2017	S Chand & Company	–41.52	110	–78.91	116	–91.81	117
2017	IRB InvIT Fund	–21.61	96	–37.15	94	–68.62	106
2017	HUDCO*	–4.33	84	–35.67	91	–62.17	104
2017	PSP Projects	140.52	14	141.88	24	54.83	42
2017	Indigrid InvIT Fund	–3	82	–14.24	81	0.3	70
2017	Tejas Networks	6.91	72	–43.52	96	–81.09	111
2017	Eris Lifesciences	13.61	64	–15.45	82	–22.47	86
2017	CDSL	88.09	30	47.48	45	81.68	38

Year of Listing	*Name of the Company*	*1year Return*	*Rank*	*2 year Return*	*Rank*	*3 year Return*	*Rank*
2017	GTPL Hathway	–40.56	107	–67.38	109	–58.97	102
2017	AU Small Finance Bank	78.53	35	83.42	37	73.83	41
2017	Salasar Techno Engineering	172.59	10	28.01	58	83.89	34
2017	SIS India	34.09	52	–0.46	72	–9.07	75
2017	Cochin Shipyard*	5.03	77	–18.56	84	–18.46	84
2017	Apex Frozen Foods	133.77	19	17.54	62	54.49	43
2017	Bharat Road Network	–24.83	99	–64.1	107	–84.34	113
2017	Dixon Technologies	54.78	43	44.3	48	432.31	9
2017	Matrimony.com*	–45.06	112	–44.36	97	–42.32	94
2017	Capacit'e Infraprojects	–8.7	88	–17.28	83	–52.62	100
2017	ICICI Lombard	27.83	54	82.11	38	92.14	32
2017	SBI Life Insurance	–22.56	98	18.66	61	16.99	59
2017	Prataap Snacks	9.85	68	–8.79	76	–36.04	91
2017	Godrej Agrovet	16.66	61	5.61	69	14.36	61
2017	MAS Financial Services	5.27	76	45.01	46	78.15	39
2017	Indian Energy Exchange	–6.67	86	–12.24	80	18.09	58
2017	GIC*	–65.36	117	–70.05	111	–86.68	115
2017	Reliance Nippon Life Asset Management	–35.6	104	32.88	56	13.1	63
2017	Mahindra logistic	22.81	57	–9.14	78	–11.03	76
2017	The New India Assurance*	–44.21	111	–62.31	105	–71.41	108
2017	Khadim India	–21.99	97	–71.93	114	–85.08	114
2017	HDFC Standard Life Insurance	35.66	49	99.14	30	131.05	25
2017	Shalby	–40.69	109	–61.85	104	–57.54	101
2017	Future Supply Chain Solutions	0.34	81	–26.51	88	–84.12	112

Year of Listing	*Name of the Company*	*1year Return*	*Rank*	*2 year Return*	*Rank*	*3 year Return*	*Rank*
2017	Astron Paper & Board	116.2	22	–23.8	86	3.8	67
2018	Apollo Micro Systems	–55.64	115	–71.65	112	–51.44	98
2018	Newgen Software	17.96	60	–4.29	73	19.02	57
2018	Amber Enterprises	–12.78	90	74.37	41	200.32	19
2018	Galaxy Surfactants	–29.91	101	11.16	66	53.29	44
2018	Aster DM Healthcare	–18.55	92	–11.82	79	–24.61	88
2018	HG Infra Engineering	–5.57	85	–20.65	85	9.57	65
2018	Bharat Dynamics*	–33.01	103	–62.37	106	–17.21	80
2018	Bandhan Bank	31.39	53	–42.51	95	–7.84	74
2018	Hindustan Aeronautics*	–40.65	108	–56.78	102	–18.77	85
2018	Sandhar Technologies	–20.63	94	–58.72	103	–36.54	92
2018	Karda Constructions	7.97	71	–28.67	90	234.86	15
2018	Mishra Dhatu Nigam*	53.78	44	91.72	35	112.72	28
2018	ICICI Securities	–54.15	114	–46.61	98	–24.12	87
2018	Lemon Tree Hotels	40.09	48	–68.04	110	–37.5	93
2018	IndoStar Capital Finance	–37.45	106	–51.42	100	–47.04	97
2018	RITES Ltd*	60.35	39	45	47	47.65	48
2018	Fine Organics	82.77	32	138.44	25	276.41	14
2018	Varroc Engineering	–51.4	113	–80.13	117	–61.05	103
2018	TCNS Clothing	0.63	80	–53.96	101	–18.25	83
2018	HDFC AMC	88.87	29	116.33	27	165.73	22
2018	CreditAccess Grameen	22.42	58	39.56	51	50.77	46
2018	IRCON International	–20.57	93	–83.18	118	–90.49	116
2018	Aavas Financiers	94.77	27	76.03	39	230.04	18
2018	Garden Reach	43.73	46	84.03	36	75.81	40

Year of Listing	*Name of the Company*	*1year Return*	*Rank*	*2 year Return*	*Rank*	*3 year Return*	*Rank*
	Shipbuilders						
2019	Xelpmoc Design and Tech*	–3.71	83	347.8	7	449.02	8
2019	Chalet Hotels	21.63	59	–36.3	92	–5.3	73
2019	MSTC*	–37.08	105	145.92	23	139.67	24
2019	Embassy Office Parks REIT	11.43	67	8.43	68	23.89	55
2019	Rail Vikas Nigam*	–7.63	87	42.37	50	82.63	35
2019	Metropolis Healthcare	42.97	47	176.81	18	175.16	21
2019	Polycab India	35.51	50	160.78	19	377.41	11
2019	Neogen Chemicals	102.37	25	317.35	9	617.07	4
2019	IndiaMART InterMESH	115.42	23	645.28	2	287	13
2019	Affle India	172	11	458.85	4	642.52	3
2019	Spandana Sphoorty Financial	–32.34	102	–26.14	87	–43.59	95
2019	Sterling & Wilson Solar	–67.96	118	–65.81	108	–63.99	105
2019	IRCTC Limited*	318.14	5	1607.36	1	1029.45	2
2019	Vishwaraj Sugar	81.25	33	213.67	15	40	51
2019	CSB Bank	15.05	63	36.62	54	15.1	60
2019	Ujjivan Bank	5.54	74	–46.89	99	–18.24	82
2019	Prince Pipes	67.53	37	293.31	11	232.78	17
2020	SBI Cards	35.38	51	10.78	67	–3.62	71
2020	Rossari Biotech	192.88	8	100.27	29	108.01	29
2020	Mindspace Business Parks REIT	4.46	78	35.36	55	11.27	64
2020	Happiest Minds Technologies	797.53	1	504.22	3	460.27	7
2020	Route Mobile	457.04	2	301.01	10	348.2	12
2020	CAMS	142.73	12	101.08	28	104.67	30
2020	Chemcon Speciality Chemicals	27.63	55	27.53	59	–17.34	81
2020	Angel Broking	348.3	3	403.43	5	550.07	5

Year of Listing	*Name of the Company*	*1year Return*	*Rank*	*2 year Return*	*Rank*	*3 year Return*	*Rank*
2020	UTI AMC	95.39	26	39.51	52	44.1	50
2020	Mazagon Dock Shipbuilders	85.83	31	325.41	8	1376.62	1
2020	Likhitha Infrastructure	213.13	7	212.96	16	430	10
2020	Equitas Small Finance Bank	90.15	28	50.15	44	196.36	20
2020	Gland Pharma	136.03	17	14.41	65	8.67	66

Source: Compiled and constructed by the authors

Financing Through Foreign Loans in India: To What Extent External Commercial Borrowings are in Desired Direction?

Arnab Roy[1] and Archita Ghosh[2]

ABSTRACT: Foreign loan is considered as an important source of economic growth and External Commercial Borrowings is the most important component in India's external debt. Existing studies however show that external debt when used for unproductive purposes can exert negative impact on the growth of an economy. This paper, with the use of some industry level data, a disaggregated analysis of ECB inflows finds that although ECB inflows have been rising over time, these have never been too high. Maturity-wise trend of ECBs reflect that majority of ECBs availed for medium-term followed by long term loans. An analysis of end-use inflows of ECBs reveals that a high share of ECBs is availed for productive purposes but this share has been drastically falling over time and a major amount is being used for unproductive purposes like repayment of loans etc. and raising concern for future state of India's external sector.

Keywords: ECB, External Debt, Productive, Unproductive.

Introduction

In the age of globalization external debt/foreign loan is considered as an important tool to promote economic growth. When an economy in its way to growth and development lacks enough domestic resources for investment, it has to borrow from foreign sources. However, there is a debate among the economists on the impact of such foreign loans. Neo Classical economists argue that external debt has a positive impact on investment and economic growth. Again, some economists with contradicting view opine that external debt creates problems like accumulation of debt leading to unsustainability of the same, inability of a country to meet debt obligations, inability of a country to raise foreign loans in its own currency etc. and thus leads to de-acceleration of economic growth.

India since ages resorts to such foreign loans for its development. According to the Balance of Payments Accounts of India foreign loans constitute of External Assistance, External Commercial Borrowings (ECB), Non-Resident Indians'

---

[1] State Aided College Teacher, Sovarani Memorial College, India.
E-mail: arnabray.roy343@gmail.com

[2] Professor, University of Kalyani, India. E-mail: archita@klyuniv.ac.in

Deposits, Banking Capital and Short-term Loan. External Assistance is availed by the Governments, while all others are primarily received by the private sector except that part of the ECB, which is availed by the public sector corporates. ECB is a part of medium and long-term external debt which is used in India to enhance access of foreign money for commercial purposes by Indian companies and Public Sector Undertakings. ECBs are mainly used to finance the Indian companies for enhancement of existing stocks of capital, modernization and new investment which will help the companies to expand their profit.

Over the years, Indian companies have been increasingly dependent on ECB. The cost of funds borrowed from external sources at times works out to be cheaper as compared to the cost of Rupee funds. The international market is a better option in case of large requirements, as the availability of the funds is huge compared to domestic market. Inflows of ECB constitute a major portion of inflows of total foreign loans in India, which is about 41.71% in 2019–20. This implies that private Indian companies are relying heavily on External Commercial Borrowings to enhance their growth. But what is important is that for the loans like ECB the country has to bear a burden of interest payment, which can be huge amount when measured in terms of a depreciated home currency. Interest payments on external debt as percentage of exports of goods, services and primary income in India were 2.33 as of 2014. Its highest value over the past 39 years was 19.53 in 1990, while its lowest value was 1.51 in 2010.

A loan becomes viable only when the consequent increase in productivity surpasses its cost of interest payment. The firms are mainly supposed to take this loan to enhance their productivity and growth. However, it has often been seen that firms do not use the loans for the stipulated purpose for which the loan has originally been taken. In this study we attempt to examine how the Indian corporate sector uses ECBs. Objectives of the present study are

1. To look at the overall trend of External Commercial Borrowings in India;
2. To analyze the maturity-wise and purpose-wise trends in External Commercial Borrowings;

The data is sourced from various balance sheets published by the Reserve Bank of India (RBI) for the External Commercial Borrowings and the annual reports published by 19 companies that have received ECBs consistently for at least three consecutive years.

Types, Routes and Rules for External Commercial Borrowings in India

ECBs according to RBI are commercial bank loans, buyers' and suppliers' credit, securitized instruments such as Floating Rate Notes and Fixed Rate Bonds etc. and external loans from Multilateral Financial Institutions such as International Finance Corporation (Washington), Asian Development Bank (ADB), Australian

Foundation Investment Company (AFIC), Continuous Discharge Certificate (CDC), etc. There are two types of routes through which India avails ECBs - automatic route and approval route. Availing of ECB for investment in industrial sector and for investment in infrastructure sector is allowed under automatic route which can be done without the prior approval of the Reserve Bank or the Government of India. Sectors such as export and import which required specific permissions of the government before taking a loan come under the approval route.

In the Master Circulars of RBI on External Commercial Borrowings and Trade Credits in different times, various rules for ECBs have been specified.

Amount and Maturity under Automatic and Approval Route

ECBs up to $20 million or equivalent with minimum average maturity of three years and ECBs above $20 million up to $500 million or equivalent with minimum average maturity of five years are allowed under the automatic route.

Under approval route ECBs can be availed with a minimum maturity period of three years. However, a few trades related credits can have a maturity of minimum one year.

End Use of ECBS

(a) ECBs can be availed only for investment such as import of capital goods, new projects, modernization/expansion of existing production units etc. in real sectors, i.e., industrial sector including small and medium enterprises (SME) and infrastructure sector.

(b) Utilization of ECB proceeds is permitted in the first stage acquisition of shares in the disinvestment process and also in the mandatory second stage offer to the public under the Government's disinvestment programmed of PSU shares.

(c) "Prepayment of ECB up to USD 100 million is permitted without prior approval of RBI, subject to compliance with the stipulated minimum average maturity period as applicable for the loan".

Impact of ECBs on an Economy: Theories and the Empirical Findings

External debt will have favorable effect on economic growth because it will increase capital inflow, i.e., low-cost international funds can improve inflow of more money and when used for growth related expenditures will accelerate the pace of economic growth. On the other hand, when external debt accumulates beyond a certain limit, it may contract economic growth by hampering investment. There are also other disadvantages like increase in default risk, bankruptcy risk, and a plethora of interest rate and market risks related to having more debt on a company's balance sheet. Having more debt may increase the actual cost of borrowing, i.e. the interest rate paid on the debt. With public companies, the ratings agencies will judge the additional debt burden and possibly lower the company's rating, which automatically boosts borrowing costs. This could have a downward spiraling effect on the company as its borrowing costs go up, but suddenly less capital is available to draw due to the lower credit rating. In case of a liquidity crunch, this can dramatically increase the risk of bankruptcy.

The existing literature also shows contradictory results on the impact of foreign loans. The studies can be divided into two groups – one group deals with the impact of external debt on the aggregate economy and the other group attempts to find out the impact of external loans on different sectors/industries/firms of a country. We have reviewed literature on both these groups.

In the first group, Sulaiman (2012) for Nigeria also found positive impact during 1980 to 2008. However, his results showed that if the available funds (internal and external) are not well utilized into viable project that will benefit the economy, investment will decline. Dauda (2012) for Malaysia and Said (2013) for Tanzania also found a consistent positive relationship between external debt and economic growth. Arslan (2014) also found a positive impact of external debt in Pakistan. Korkmaz (2015) also found a positive impact for Turkey in the period 2003–2013. Therefore, it was said that borrowing is a necessity in case of emergency but not a solution to all economic problems of the country. Mehrizi (2011) for Iran for the period 1974 to 2007 and Ali (2012) for Pakistan during 1970 to 2010 found negative impact on economic growth. Ahmed (2013) in case of Iraq for the time period 1980 to 2014 and Ngangnchi (2014) for Cameroon for time period 1980–2013 find that there is a negative impact of external debt on economic growth.

Qayyum (2017) investigated empirically the impact of foreign aid and external debt on economic growth for 60 developing countries that utilized both foreign aid and external debt to fulfill their requirements of additional capital. This analysis covers the period from 1984 to 2010. He found that foreign aid has a positive impact on growth whereas external debt poses a negative impact.

Bakht (1991) investigated the impact of external debt on investment, employment and value added in 51 small and cottage manufacturing industries in Bangladesh in the 1980's found that the private manufacturing investment and value added had been stagnated but not declined in absolute terms during the eighties and there was a declining trend in GDP. However, employment shows a relatively upward rise.

From the existing studies it is evident that in conformity of the theories the empirical literature also finds that the effect of external debt on the growth of a country can either be positive or negative depending on the situations of different countries or industries availing external debt. The negative impact can be seen mainly for those countries that borrowed loans to serve the purpose of interest payments and not for productivity growth. Excessive borrowings too had a negative impact on GDP of a country.

Trends and Composition of External Commercial Borrowings in India

A detailed analysis of the trends as well as composition of External Commercial Borrowings is an important tool for examining the role it plays in the production process and hence on GDP of a recipient country. Trend analysis is important for examining whether the net inflows of External Commercial Borrowings are getting very high over time with the possibility of unsustainability of such finances.

Trends of Aggregate External Commercial Borrowings

In table 1 below we have presented the decadal picture of gross ECB inflows as percentage of gross capital inflows and gross loans and that of gross loans as percentage of gross capital inflows since economic reforms started.

Table 1: Trends of External Commercial Borrowings in India in the Post-Reform Period

	1991–1992	*2001–2002*	*2011–2012*	*2015–2016*	*2016–2017*	*2017–2018*	*2018–2019*	*2019–2020*
Gross ECB as percentage of Gross Capital Inflow	13.51	6.21	6.80	6.12	3.27	3.82	5.22	6.44
Gross ECB as percentage of Gross loans	33.46	23.16	23.11	21.90	14.98	16.71	30.07	41.71
Gross loans as percentage of Gross capital Inflow	40.35	26.81	29.44	24.53	21.98	22.86	17.35	15.49

Source: Own calculation based on RBI data

In the above table we observe that in 1991–92, i.e., the year when the external sector reform started, gross ECB claimed a significant share in gross capital inflow. Thereafter the share halved within a decade and that trend is continuing in recent times also. But in recent times it increased to 33.82% with gradually showing its importance in foreign loans. So overall we find a huge rise in the importance of

ECBs in total foreign loans. Now if we consider Gross Loans as percentage of Gross Capital Inflow, then we can see that percentage of Gross Loans also has a huge turnaround from the financial year 1991–92 to 2001–02 with a decrease in almost 13.54 percentage points. After 2001–02, there was a slight increase in loan percentage in 2011–12, but again it has been decreasing since 2015–16 till 2019–2020. The emphasis in the post-reform period on inviting foreign investments more than foreign loans is the reason behind such a decline in importance of foreign loans in India's capital inflows

In figure 1 below we present the annual trend of net inflows of ECBs. Net inflows are defined as the gross ECBs availed by India minus repayment. India's loans to other countries are not included in this calculation of net ECBs. From the diagram we observe that the net ECB inflows in India declined during the years 1991–92 and 1992–93. Thereafter till 1996–97 it had been increasing at a high rate probably due to liberalization of policies which might have increased the scope for overseas borrowings by corporates. In 2003–04 and thereafter, the country observed increase in domestic industrial activity, increased demand for funds, favorable global rates of interest and liberalization of policies on ECBs. This resulted in the continuous increase in inflows of ECBs.

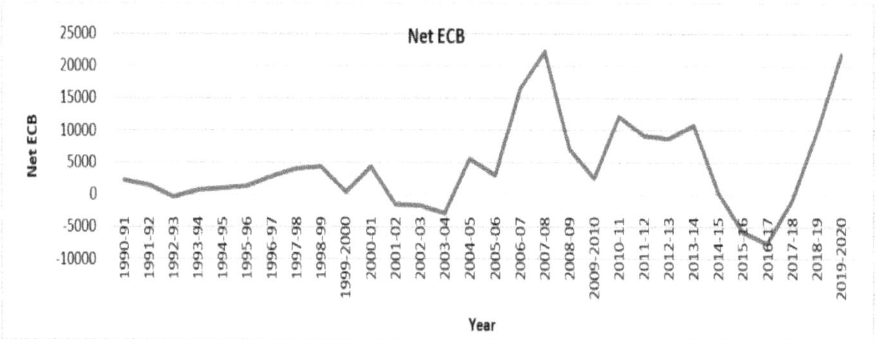

Figure 1: Trend of External Commercial Borrowing in the Post Reform Period
Source: RBI Database

Composition of External Commercial Borrowings

ECBs can be sub-divided maturity and end-wise. This classification of ECB will help us presume about the impact of ECBs on the real economy.

Maturity-Period Wise Trend of External Commercial Borrowings

Foreign capital with longer maturity period poses less threat of reversal. A study of the trend in ECBs maturity-wise is thus very useful for analyzing the probable degree of uncertainty it may cause to an economy. We can define maturity or maturity period as the final payment date of a loan or other financial instruments, at which point the principal and all remaining interests is due to be paid. In table 2 below we present the trend of maturity-wise inflows of ECBs. We have considered five maturity periods such as less than 3 years, 3–5 years, 5–7 years, 7–9 years and more than 9 years.

Table 2: Maturity-wise Trend of External Commercial Borrowings (shares in per cent)

Year	*Less than 3 years*	*3 to 5 years*	*5 to 7 years*	*7 to 9 years*	*More than 9 yeas*
2004	1.70	19.34	33.40	3.54	42.02
2005	6.58	40.60	30.17	10.73	11.92
2006	1.26	53.45	23.58	4.89	16.82
2007	0.16	29.46	38.14	12.19	20.05
2008	0.58	12.56	36.17	12.66	38.03
2009	0.32	31.30	25.59	16.79	26.00
2010	0.01	24.88	31.32	17.37	26.42
2011	0.06	17.07	30.05	22.63	29.74
2012	0	12.70	28.65	24.75	33.90
2013	1.63	23.85	29.72	13.72	31.08
2014	5.24	24.14	27.18	12.72	30.72
2015	5.76	14.17	50.02	14.47	15.58
2016	10.79	32.48	21.21	5.98	29.54
2017	10.46	34.84	17.30	6.39	27.01
2018	5.44	42.49	24.32	9.75	18.00
2019	4.58	41.54	26.62	8.38	18.88
2020	2.29	44.01	21.09	7.61	25.00

Source: Own calculation based on data provided in RBI database

It is seen from the table that majority of the ECBs is for medium-term, i.e., from 3 to 7 years followed by the long-term loans with a maturity period of more than 7 years. Short term borrowings, i.e., borrowings with a maturity period of less than 3 years are consistently lower than those with higher maturity periods till 2015. However, during the period 2016 and 2017, the share of short-term debt has increased compared to other years. We cannot say that ECBs of a particular maturity is constantly increasing or decreasing over the years from 2004 –2020. In figure 2 below we present the above findings graphically.

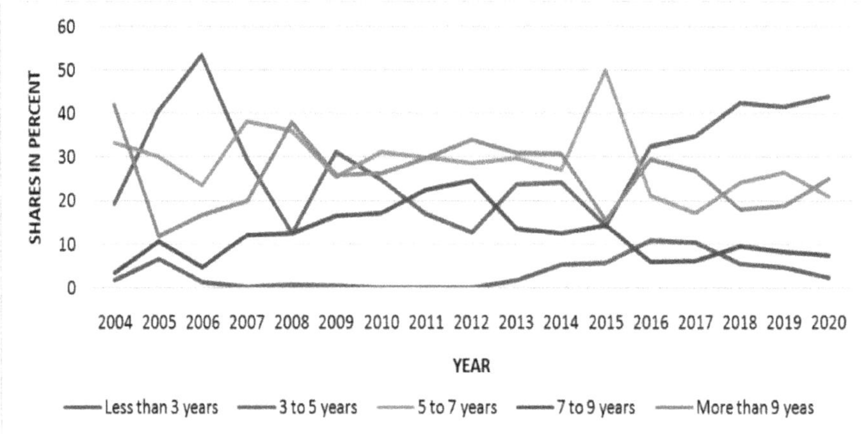

Figure 2: Maturity-wise Trend of External Commercial Borrowings (shares in per cent)

Source: Own calculation based on data provided in RBI database

End-Use Wise Trend of External Commercial Borrowings

External debt may be borrowed for supplementing investments to new projects or modernization or repayments of previous loans. So, there are many possible cases for which external loan are required to enhance funds for different projects or for solving other purposes as well. The shares of ECBs availed for different purposes in different years from the period 2004–2020. We have clubbed some items to get end-uses like infrastructure (road + telecommunication + ports + power), modernization plus import of capital goods (purchase of which is basically for modernization) etc. We added Import of Capital goods and Modernization because we can consider both as a measure for enhancing efficiency in production.

Analyzing from the data, we can find that the combined inflow for Import of Capital Goods and Modernization was highest till 2014. From 2004 to 2011, we can see that more than 40% of ECB was taken for this purpose and after 2011 there is a decreasing trend in ECBs on this account. Among these in 2008 the highest amount of ECBs (73.44%) was availed for Import of Capital Goods and Modernization. For infrastructure ECB borrowings also increased in year compared to 2015 but decreased compared to 2013 and 2014 and started to increase from 2018 onwards. For repayment of earlier loans ECB inflow has increased quite drastically compared to the previous years. We can state that for the last couple of year inflow of ECB for productive purposes had drastically fallen and majority amount are now being used to pay for earlier loan or for other payments.

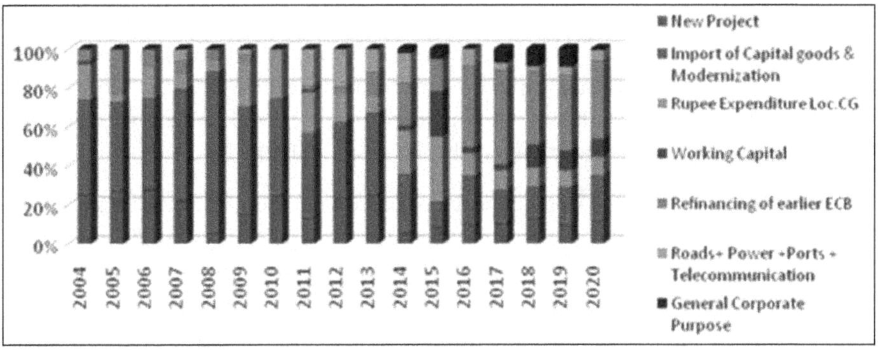

Figure 2A: Trend of External Commercial Borrowings Used in Different Purposes 1
Source: Own calculation based on data provided in RBI database

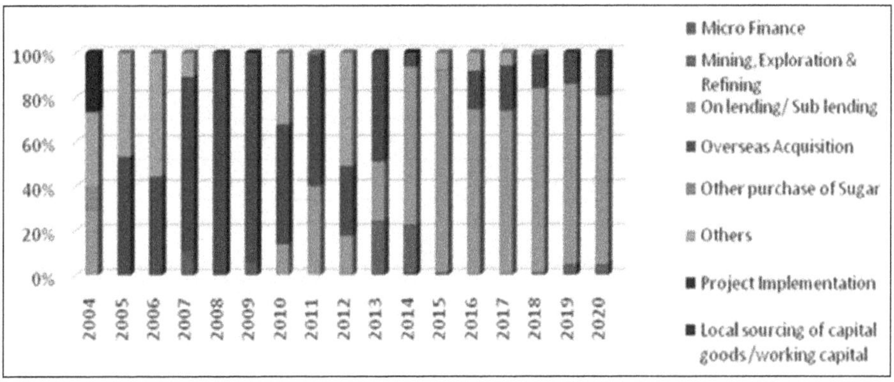

Figure 2B: Trend of External Commercial Borrowings used in Different Purposes 2
Source: Own calculation based on data provided in RBI database

In the above figures we depicted the purpose wise classification of ECB used in different years from 2004 to 2020.

Industry-wise classifications of External Commercial Borrowings

External debt or foreign debt is the total debt a country owes to foreign creditors. Debtors can be private commercial banks or governments or firms/industries or any other financial institutions. We are considering some of the major firms/industries that avail External Commercial Borrowings for different purposes such as modernization of existing capital stock, import of new capital goods, investment in new projects, refinancing of earlier loans. There are approximately more than 200 industries in India that availed external commercial borrowings during the period 2012–13 to 2019–20, but all the industries do not avail ECB in a regular pattern. Some industries do take external debt in regular way in order to expand their existing stocks of capital or for any other purposes. Major industries are chosen on the basis of their continuity in availing external loans in different years. We have selected 19 such industries (16 availing ECB through automatic route and 3 through approval route) that availed External Commercial Borrowings in regular manner from the year 2013 to 2020. These 19 industries together constitute more than 55% of ECBs from 2013 to 2020.

In this sub-section we shall depict the scenario of end-use of the ECBs availed by these 19 industries. In table 4 below we present the shares of ECBs availed by these selected industries together for different purposes. In the table the total share of ECB is calculated by considering the total amount of every use by 19 industries taken into considerations divided by the total amount of ECB availed by these 19 industries multiplied by 100.

Table 3: Share of Total ECBs Availed for Different Purposes by Major 22 Industries Together (2004–20)

Purposes	*Share of ECB*
New Project	8.62
Modernization	9.97
Import of Capital Goods	34.48
Refinancing of Earlier ECB	27.70
Rupee Expenditure Loc.CG	9.65
Overseas Acquisition	0.49
Working Capital Purpose	4.69
General Corporate Purpose	0.07
On-lending/Sub-lending	3.66
Others	0.67

Source: Own calculation based on RBI data

From the above table we find that most of the companies borrowed ECB mainly for improvement and enhancement of existing capital or goods and for repayment of earlier loans which was taken earlier for different activities. Maximum amount of ECB is for Import of Capital Goods (34.48%) and Refinancing of Earlier ECB (27.70%). If we combine Import of Capital Goods, Modernization and New Project then the total ECB availed for them were 53.07% which is quite high than the percentage of ECB availed for refinancing of earlier loans. ECB inflow for refinancing has increased to a major extent relative to productivity level.

ECB inflow for refinancing has increased to a major extent relative to productivity level. Thus it can be concluded that these industries availed ECB mainly to serve the purpose of efficiency in their production. Some of the industries did avail

ECB for refinancing but the amount for enhancing efficiency of their existing stocks or for some new capital employment is much higher.

Table 4: Share of Total ECBs Availed for Different Purposes by Major Industries Together

Industry	*Purpose*	*Shares (in percentage)*
	Automatic Route	
Medreich Limited	New Project	47.69
	Modernization	52.31
Dream Plast India Pvt. Ltd	Import of Capital Goods	100
JSW Steel Limited	Modernization	39.94
	Import of Capital Goods	21.67
	Overseas Acquisition	9.79
	Refinancing of earlier loans	28.60
Cashpor Micro Credit	Micro Finance	100
Aditya Birla Nuvo Limited	Refinancing of Earlier ECB	79.31
	Rupee Expenditure Loc.CG	20.69
	Modernization	39.70
Hindustan Petroleum	Refinancing of Earlier ECB	36.08
Corporation Ltd.		
	Working Capital Purpose	24.22
Arjuna Granites Export Pvt. Ltd.	New Project	100
Daido India Pvt. Ltd	Import of Capital Goods	37.06
	General Corporate Purpose	62.94
Greatship India Ltd.	Import of Capital Goods	27.65
	Refinancing of Earlier ECB	72.35
BPCL	Working Capital	100
Global United Shipping India Private Limited	Import of Capital Goods	100
Amneal Pharmaceuticals Co (I) Pvt. Ltd	Modernization	100
Koyama Precision Works India Pvt. Ltd.	New Project	100

Industry	*Purpose*	*Shares (in percentage)*
Indian Oil Corporation Limited	Refinancing of earlier ECB	64.80
	Rupee Expenditure Loc.	13.90
	Working Capital	21.30
Renault India Pvt. Ltd.	New Project	100
TBEA Energy (India) Pvt. Ltd.	New Project	37.40
	Modernization	16.53
	Working Capital	33.00
	General Corporate Purpose	13.07
	Approval Route	
Reliance Industries Limited	Import of Capital Goods	38.17
	Refinancing of Earlier ECB	41.27
	Rupee Expenditure Loc.CG	20.56
Air India Ltd.	Import of Capital Goods	85.82
	Working Capital	14.18
Rural Electrification Corporation Limited	Refinancing of Earlier ECB	17.86
	On-lending/Sub-lending	82.14

Source: Own calculation based on RBI data

From the above table we can state from the time period 2013 to 2020, among the 19 industries most of the industries availed ECB mainly to increase their production level and efficiency of their existing stocks. Import of new capital has increased to a great extent and ECB for modernization of old capital also taken to enhance the efficiency level of that firm. ECB for Refinancing for payment of earlier loans by some industries have been availed. Availing of ECB for repayment neither increases production level nor enhance efficiency. But overall, most of the industries availed ECB just to increase their efficiency level of production.

Summary and Conclusion

External Commercial Borrowings is one of the important components of foreign capital coming to India. This study has attempted to carry out a detailed analysis of the trends in absolute inflow of ECB as well as the trends in maturity-wise and purpose-wise inflows. We observe that net ECB inflows in India show an overall rising trend till 2013–14 though with some irregular fluctuations. We have also seen that the majority of the ECBs borrowed is for medium-term, i.e., from 3 to 7 years followed by long term loans with maturity more than 7 years.

Short term borrowings, i.e., borrowings with a maturity period of less than 3 years are consistently lower than those with higher maturity periods till 2015. However, from 2014 onwards such borrowing shows an increasing trend. This raises a matter of concern as a high share of short-term debt in foreign capital increases the vulnerability of a country to any external financial crisis.

In case of purpose wise inflows of ECB, we find that combined inflow of ECB for Import of Capital Goods and Modernization is much higher than other purposes. However, in the recent year inflow of ECB for productive purposes has drastically fallen and majority amount are being used to pay for earlier loan or for other payments. It has been found that during the period 2013–2020 more than 200 industries availed ECBs; however, only 19 industries availed ECBs over a continuous period. These industries together have taken more than 40 per cent of ECBs for non-productive purposes like Refinancing of Earlier ECB and on-lending/sub-lending. This fact sheds doubt on the effectiveness of ECBs in promoting growth of these companies. This finding leads us to suggest that the policy makers should take every caution for approving external commercial borrowings in Indian economy.

References

[1] Ahmed, Younis Ali and S.T. (2013). The Impact of External Debt on Economic Growth: Empirical Evidence from Iraq. *International Journal of Science and Research, 4* (8), 1–11.

[2] Bhattacharya, Z.B. (1991). Investment, Employment and Value Added in Bangladesh Manufacturing Sector in 1980s: Evidence and Estimate. *JSTOR,* Vol. 19 (No. 1/2), 1–19.

[3] Gujrati, D.N. (2013). *Basic Econometrics.* India: McGraw Hill Education (India) Private Limited.

[4] Haider, U.Q. (2012). Foreign Aid, External Debt and Economic Growth Nexus in Low-Income Countries: The Role of Institutional Quality. *The Pakistan Development Review,* Vol. 51 (No. 4), 97–115.

[5] Korkmaz, S. (2015, July 3–5). Relationship between External Debt and Economic Growth. *Proceedings of the 2nd European Academic Research Conference on Global Business, Economics, Finances and Banking.* Zurich, Switzerland.

[6] Mehrizi, M.S. (2011). External debt and economic growth in Iran. *Journal of Economics and International Finance,* Vol. 3(5), 322–327.

[7] Muhammad Arslan, R.Z. (2014). The Role of External Debt on Economic Growth: Evidence from Pakistan Economy. *Journal of Economics and Sustainable Development,* Vol. 5 (No. 24), 1–9.9.

[8] Muhammad Ilyas, H.K. (2010). Determinants of Manufacturing Value Added in Pakistan: An Application of Bounds Testing Approach to Cointegration. *Pakistan Economic and Social Review,* Vol. 48 (No. 2), 209–223.

[9] Mustafa, R.A. (2012). External Debt Accumulation and Its Impact on Economic Growth in Pakistan. *JSTOR,* Vol. 51, (No. 4), 79–95.

[10] Ngangnchi, F.H. (2014). External Debt, Domestic Investment and Economic Growth in Cameroon: A system Estimation Approach. *Journal of Economics Bibliography, 1* (1), 1–14.

[11] Said, F.K. (2013). Impact of External Debt on Economic Growth: A Case Study of Tanzania.

[12] Advances in Management & Applied Economics, 3 no. 4.

[13] Wahiba, N.F. (2014). External Debt and Economic Growth in Tunisia. *Journal of Knowledge Management, Economics and Information Technology, IV* (6), 1–12.

Is Digital Banking Unmixed Blessing to the Society?

Priya Gupta[1] and Samir Ghosh[2]

ABSTRACT: India's digital payments system is a success story in the making. A multitude of causes, such as the government's commitment towards digitalization, the rise in e-commerce, and the increase in internet and smartphone penetration, have contributed to the growth of the digital ecosystem in India. Therefore, the study tries to understand the perception and trust of users of digital payments and their experience with online fraud. We find that the degree to which past-experience with online fraud deters usage of digital payments varies with the purpose of the transaction.

Keywords: ATM, Credit Card, Debit Card, Phishing.

Introduction

Digital banking started taking shape in India during the late 1990s. ICICI bank was the first one to introduce this service to their retail customers. However, it gained popularity in 1999 with reduced internet charges and increased awareness. Digitally-enabled banks allow users to access all banking services 24×7 without the need to personally visit the bank branch – all one needs is a mobile phone or a computer. Plastic money (Credit Cards, Debit Cards and Smart Cards); internet banking including electronic payment services, online investments, online trading accounts, electronic fund transfer and clearing services, branch networking; telephone banking; mobile applications and wallet are some of the recent products and services acting as the drivers to the growth of banking sector.

Digital banking fraud is a type of fraud that targets online or mobile banking systems. It involves a range of fraudulent practices, such as stealing personal information, gaining unauthorised access to accounts, and making fraudulent transactions. Hackers and cybercriminals use different methods to commit digital banking fraud, including phishing, malware, and social engineering tactics. As digital banking becomes more popular, fraudsters are becoming more

[1] UGC-Senior Research Fellow, Department of Commerce, Vidyasagar University, India. E-mail: rscf_priyagupta@mail.vidyasagar.ac.in

[2] Professor, Department of Commerce, Vidyasagar University, India.
E-mail: samirghoshvu@gmail.com

sophisticated in their tactics, making it increasingly difficult for banks and their customers to identify and prevent fraudulent activities.

Traditional Banking vs. Digital Banking

The key differences between traditional and digital banking are given below.

Point of difference	Traditional banks	Digital banks
Presence	Physical presence via branch network	Online presence
Transaction time	Time-consuming as customers need to visit the branch	Quick and easy
Accessibility	Transactions can be done only during bank working hours	Transactions can be done anytime and anywhere at customers' convenience
Costs	Higher overhead costs due to branch network	Reduced overheads as there are no physical branches

Source: Compiled by researchers

Different Types of Frauds in Digital Banking

Many people rely on digital channels to access banking facilities online. For instance, when we want to check the status of a bank account, transfer funds, or carry out any other task, you might prefer to use a Mobile Banking App/Net Banking rather than visiting the bank. Digital Banking has undoubtedly made our lives easier, but with its growing usage, there has also been a sharp increase in bank frauds in the country.

1. **Vishing i.e., Phone Call Scam:** Hackers use a phone call to get out sensitive information like our login details, username, transaction passwords, card PINs, OTPs, CVVs, URNs, grid card values, or personal data like date of birth. Often, hackers place themselves as bank representatives and trick us to give our personal and financial information. We must not provide any of our personal or banking information over the phone when we receive a call asking for the same.
2. **Phishing i.e., Email Scam:** Phishing is to receive an email from a well known institution like a bank or a trusted website to provide some personal information. We must be aware and not click on such emails. Note that our banker would never request our personal information, such as our password, login details, or OTP, among other such information.
3. **Spear Phishing i.e., Targeted Email Scam:** It seems to have an e-mail from a reliable source and often originates from a colleague, boss, close friend, or

relative. If we click on attachments or malicious links in the email, hackers can easily access sensitive information stored on our device. Always avoid clicking on such fishy emails.

4. **Skimming i.e., ATM Scam:** For committing this fraud, scammers usually hide a small gadget called a skimmer in the card slots of ATMs or merchant payment terminals, which can read and record our card information. Hackers even use a carefully placed camera to record our PIN. It is advisable to stay alert whenever we visit an ATM booth to prevent such banking fraud.
5. **SIM Swap i.e., Mobile Number Scam:** Under SIM swap, a fraudster gets a new SIM card from our mobile service provider in our name using our registered mobile number. The frauder conducts financial transactions from our bank account by receiving the OTP and alerts needed. We must immediately report to our mobile service provider if our phone or SIM card is lost or has stopped working.
6. **Smishing i.e., SMS Scam:** Smishing scammers use toll-free phone numbers and message links to target us. We may receive a message stating that our accounts need to be updated with a link directing us to sign up for some new scheme. By clicking on such phishing links sent in the message, our confidential details may get compromised. To save yourself from smishing, you must not click on any link without knowing its source.
7. **Website Spoofing i.e., fake Website Scam:** Building a fake website to commit fraud is called website spoofing. Phishers use names, pictures, logos, and even website codes to make spoof sites appear authentic. We are urged to enter our detail on such fake websites. One must enter detail on a website only after checking the presence of 'HTTPS' in the URL.
8. **Finger print fraud:** Hackers duplicate the fingerprint in Adhar card of customer to withdrawal of money from personal account; it will be safe to block M. Adhar.
9. **Malware Attack i.e., Gadget Virus Attack:** A malware attack is malicious software developed by cyber criminals that can cause damage to the operating system of our smart device. Through this software, fraudsters can access our confidential banking information and use it to remove money from our bank account. It would be best to keep your devices secure with malware protection software.

Reasons of Frauds of Digital Banking

Digital banking fraud has been on the rise, with fraudsters becoming more sophisticated in their methods to exploit vulnerabilities in online and mobile banking systems. Here are the five main reasons behind the increase in digital banking fraud. By understanding these reasons, individuals and financial services institutions can take steps to protect themselves from these threats and create a safer online banking environment:

Technology Advancement

1. **Online banking:** Online banking allows customers to access their accounts and perform transactions from anywhere at any time. However, this convenience also presents risks, such as phishing attacks, account takeover and malware that can steal login credentials.
2. **Mobile banking:** Mobile banking has become increasingly popular due to its ease of use and convenience. However, mobile devices are also more vulnerable to cyber-attacks and financial crime than desktop computers. To combat these risks, mobile banking apps should implement strong authentication measures, such as biometric verification, and users should be educated on best practices for securing their mobile devices.
3. **ATMs:** ATMs are convenient for accessing cash, but they are also vulnerable to fraud like skimming and hacking. Criminals can steal credit card information through skimming or installing malicious software on ATMs. The consequences of ATM fraud can be severe, including cleared bank accounts and financial losses. Security measures like maintenance, transaction monitoring, and education are important to combat ATM fraud.
4. **Digital payment systems:** Digital payment systems, such as PayPal, have made online transactions more accessible and convenient. However, they also present new opportunities for fraudsters to exploit.

Weak Cyber Security

1. **Lack of strong authentication protocols:** Many online banking systems still rely on weak authentication protocols, such as passwords or PINs, which are vulnerable to brute-force attacks and social engineering tactics. As a result, financial institutions need to invest in stronger authentication methods, such as biometric authentication and multi-factor authentication (MFA), to better secure online banking systems.
2. **Use of weak passwords:** Weak passwords, such as "password123," are easily guessed by fraudsters, leaving accounts vulnerable to unauthorised access. Organisations are implementing stronger authentication strategies such as two-factor authentication (2FA) to protect their users' online accounts.
3. **Phishing and Social Engineering Attacks:** Phishing attacks use fraudulent emails, texts, or phone calls to trick users into giving away their login credentials or other sensitive information. Social engineering attacks exploit human emotions to gain access to sensitive information.

Field Study

The responses were collected from 630 respondents residing in and around Kolkata. The respondents are mostly male and educated. Most of them are either salaried employees, working in the government or private sector. This may be due to the online nature of the survey, and circulation limited to the social circles of the authors.

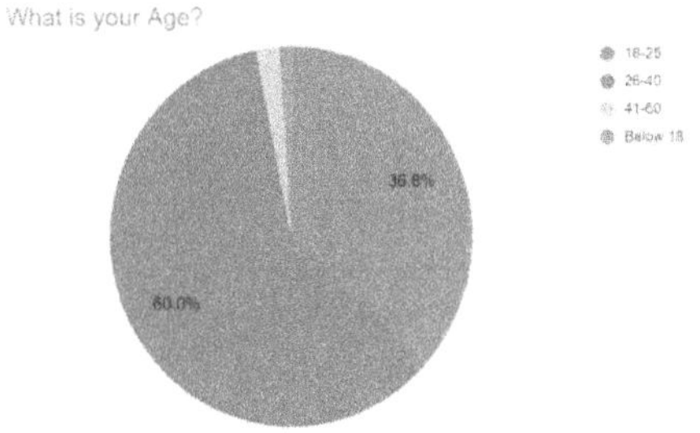

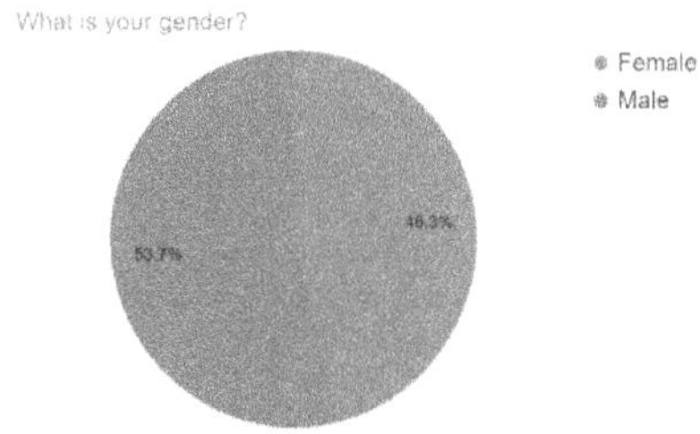

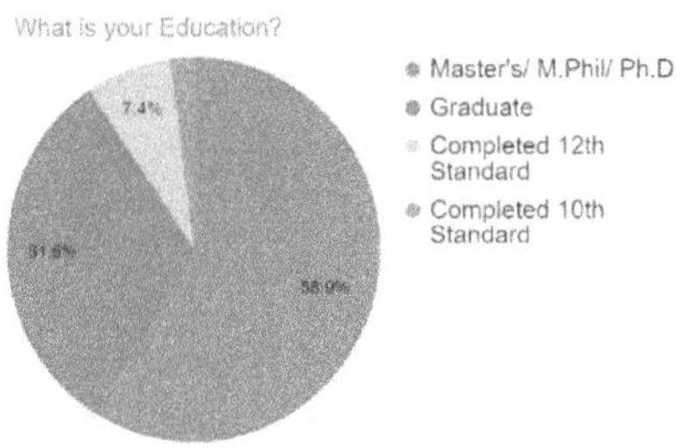

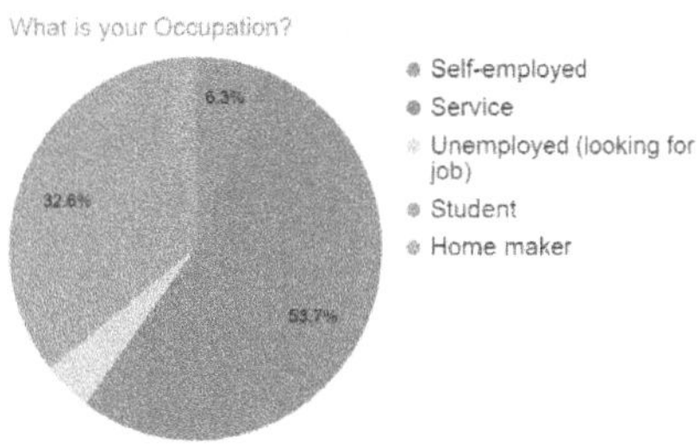

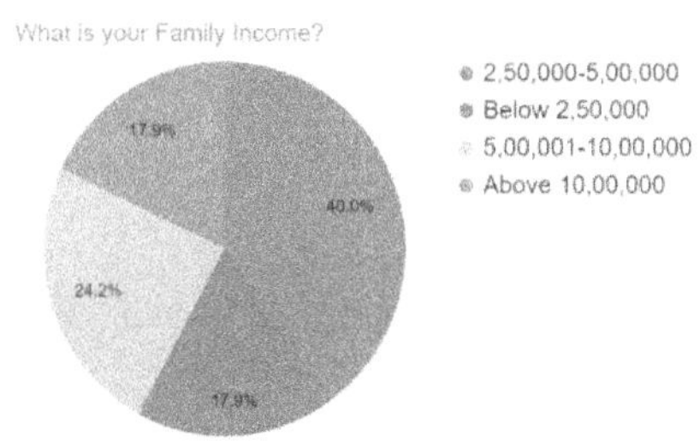

Awareness as well as usage regarding various digital payment instruments were high in the sample. It is important to keep this in mind while interpreting how payment behaviour is affected by other variables. Our respondents, being from the relatively well-off sections of society, were much more aware and comfortable with cards and UPI, rather than AEPS and USSD code-based payments. Digital mode was preferred for online shopping, paying utility bills, and purchasing durables (mostly medium to high value transactions). A combination of cash and digital modes was preferred for purchases of grocery and gold, which are starkly different in terms of transaction value. Being solely dependent on cash was relatively less preferable for all purposes.

The perception of cash and digital payments are recorded on four parameters viz., 'convenience', 'cost of payment', 'safety', and 'privacy/anonymity'. It is observed that on an average, digital payments perform better than cash on all four fronts. Confidence in digital payment systems is assessed on four parameters, with regards to banks (preference for depositing money in a bank, as well as trust in one's own bank), the central bank and in other participants like payment aggregators. Respondents seemed more confident in the RBI and banks, as compared to other service providers.

Technical issues, followed by low acceptance and lack of trust were identified as the major hindrances with digital payments. The experience of online fraud is divided into four categories based on their potential intensity of impact of the fraud. Out of 630 respondents that answered the question, 532 have had some experience of online fraud. Out of 411 respondents who had experienced the incident personally, a majority (279) reported no change in the nature of payments and only 26 mentioned that either they had completely switched to cash or had reduced the use of digital mode of transaction. Respondents were also asked if they reported the incident to the concerned authority after they experienced the fraud personally. Most of the respondents did not report the incident, especially if they had not faced any losses.

Protection Ways from Frauds

The best way to avoid fraud is to stay vigilant, but at the same time, you must follow some of the best practices to safeguard yourself from digital fraud in banking.

- Never share User ID, Password, OTP, PIN or any other confidential data
- Lost or stolen Credit Cards/Debit Cards should be blocked immediately
- Never use open public Wi-Fi
- Don't reply to fishy emails or text messages
- Avoid visiting unsafe websites & unreliable links
- Never allow anyone to remotely access your laptop or PC

References

[1] Aladwani, A.M. (2001). Online Banking: A Field Study of Drivers, Development Challenges, and Expectations. *International Journal of Information Management,* 21 (2001), 213–225.

[2] Harris, L. and Spence, L.J. (2002). The ethics of Banking. *Journal of Electronic Commerce Research,* 3(2), 59–66.

[3] Chavan, J. (2013). Internet Banking—Benefits and Challenges in an Emerging Economy. *International Journal of Research in Business Management (IJRBM),* 1(1), 19–26.

[4] Dheenadhayalan, V. (2010). Automation of Banking Sector in India. Yojana, 32–40.

[5] Ingle, A. and Pardeshim R. (2012). Internet Banking in India: Challenges and Opportunities, *IBMRD's Journal of Management and Research*, Vol. 1, pp. 13-18.

[6] Surulivel, S.T. (2010). A Study on the Impact of Technology on the Performance of Indian Banking Industry (Doctoral Thesis). Viewed on November 30, 2017 http:// hdl.handle.net/10603/5600

[8] Gupta, Nitin (2017). The Effect of Electronic Payment on Customer Satisfaction, *IJARIIE*, Vol. 3, Issue 3.

[9] Khurana, Sunayna (2010). Service Quality Gap And Customers' Satisfaction of Private Sector Banks: an Empirical Study", *International Journal of Electronic Customer Relationship Management*; Issue Volume 4, Number 1.

[10] Mukherjee, A. and Nath, P. (2003). A Model of trust in online relationship banking", International Journal of Bank Marketing, Vol. 21, No. 1.

Exploring the Untapped Potential of Shariah-Based Banking in the Indian Financial Landscape

Samyabrata Das[1], Asim Kumar Roy[2] and Iqbal Abdul Latif[3]

ABSTRACT: Islamic banking, which has its roots in Shariah law, can provide an alternate type of banking founded on moral and ethical standards. The worldwide proliferation of Islamic financial services has shown enormous potential for developing nations. Despite this, India has made little progress in the field of Islamic financial services. Within this context, the study endeavours to comprehend the idea and tenets of Islamic Banking and Finance. Furthermore, the study attempts to evaluate the potential for Islamic banking in the Indian scenario. This article examines the suggestions made by several committees and groups for Islamic banking within the Indian context. The article also identifies the barriers to the acceptance of Islamic banking in India.

The introduction of Islamic banking without a robust base may result in controversy and contention. Nonetheless, with the support from the government, regulatory bodies, and stakeholders Islamic banking can bring numerous benefits to India.

Keywords: Ethical, Islamic Banking, Islamic Finance, Shariah

JEL Code: G10, G20.

Introduction

Islamic banking, which has its foundation in Sharia law, has grown significantly across the globe and provides a substitute financial system based on moral and ethical standards. Its potential in India, a secular democracy with a majority non-Muslim populace, has drawn interest and scepticism, nevertheless. India has made less progress in Islamic Financial Services, even though there is much potential. India boasts a centuries-long history of trade and business, with Islamic influences evident in many facets of the country's economic structure.

[1] Associate Professor, Department of Commerce, New Alipore College, Kolkata, India. E-mail: samyabrata1@gmail.com

[2] Associate Professor, Department of Commerce, Dr. Kanailal Bhattacharyya College, Howrah, India. E-mail: asimkr.roy@gmail.com

[3] Assistant Professor, Department of Chemistry, New Alipore College, Kolkata, India. E-mail: iqbal.a.latif@gmail.com

Despite this historical link, Islamic banking has not yet been formally introduced in India. Because Islamic finance is built on the notion of risk-sharing rather than interest, it has begun to gain popularity in many countries, including the United States and the United Kingdom. The term "Halal Banking" refers to Islamic banking. The term "Ethical Banking" is sometimes used as well. Islamic countries adhere to a Shariah-compliant banking architecture. Both receiving and providing interest (RIBA) are, forbidden (Haraam) in Islam. As such, Islamic banking is a type of interest-free banking that encourages profit-loss sharing. Islamic banking has expanded fast on a global scale, including sizable markets in the Middle East, Southeast Asia, and some regions of Africa. However, Islamic finance is still a relatively new notion in India. Islamic finance in general and Islamic banking in particular have been extensively embraced by both Muslim and Western countries. Despite the rise and faith in Islamic banking, there are still some nations like India that have not integrated Islamic banking into their economies. It is surprising since the field of Islamic finance, according to many experts, can offer huge opportunities for existing as well as potential investors. However, the Reserve Bank of India (RBI) initiated talks regarding the viability of Islamic banking within the nation's regulatory structure after realising the importance of financial inclusion and diversity.

Review of Literature

Below is a synopsis of the relevant literature. According to Haque *et al.*, Islamic banking can attract capital from GCC nations, address the issue of financial inclusion, aid in infrastructure finance, and benefit the real estate sector. According to Fasih (2012), unlike making money from money, which typically places the burden on only one party, the Islamic model stimulates labour and rewards risk-taking, putting all partners on equal footing. According to Khan & Hussin (2013), Islamic banking in India has the potential to flourish alongside the traditional banking sector. For this, Indian regulators, Islamic finance academics, and industry advocates must consider the steps that must be taken to create Islamic banking in India. According to Munuswamy *et al.* (2013), it is safe to assume that both Muslims and non-Muslims in India are unaware of the benefits of Islamic finance. They are, nonetheless, eager to invest after learning about the rewards. Badruddin (2015) opined that NBFCs and mutual funds are two sectors in India where Islamic finance concepts can be introduced without many impediments. It is also stated that the introduction of Islamic banking will result in the inclusion of certain segments of the population who are currently excluded from mainstream banking owing to their religious beliefs. Beg (2016) observed that India has been sceptical of Islamic banks. The reason behind this is most likely political rather than economic. Although there is some Islamic financing in India, it is not widespread, and India is missing out on large investments. India is geographically positioned and can attract massive investment from the Gulf countries. As noted by Tabash (2017), five factors are hindering the development of Islamic banking: the regulatory framework, a dearth of Islamic finance professionals and scholars, a lack of understanding of Islamic finance offerings, a lack of standardisation, and a lack of cooperation and coordination among Islamic financial institutions. Komijani & Taghizadeh-Hesary (2018) observed a bright future for Islamic banking and finance in Asia and stated that the combination of substantial political backing, a huge investor base, and attractive tax breaks would act as incentives to expand Islamic finance in Asia. Shahid & Raj (2019) conducted a SWOT analysis of Islamic Banking in India and opined that India should allow Islamic banking because the strengths and opportunities outweigh the weaknesses and threats. According to Gupta (2020), the BR Act offers adequate flexibility to enable certain components of Islamic banking, given required notifications from the Central Government and RBI. However, significant 'political will' on the part of the Government and RBI would be required, as the topic of Islamic banking has been met with political opposition due to its religiosity in a normally non-religious context. Siddiqui *et al.* (2021) claimed that people who did not have a suitable job or an adequate income, primarily Muslims, chose the Islamic financial system. Higher financial inclusion will follow from an extended formal implementation of Islamic finance in India. Parameshwara & Aneesh (2022) noted the regulatory and legal framework of India, lack of political will, secular nature, opposition from some public etc. as major challenges before the introduction of Islamic banking in India. Sayeed (2023) stated that Islamic banks play a crucial part in the development of Islamic principles by linking economic value with social and ethical ideals. He opined that the R.B.I. must view Islamic banking as a viable tool for addressing social and economic issues. According to Ahmad *et al.* (2024), of the 195 countries in the globe, more than 105, or roughly 53.84% of the total, have already adopted Islamic banking, pointing to a global trend in this direction. The authors noted that the widespread belief that Islamic banking serves only Muslims acts as a barrier to its adoption in India.

Objectives of the Study

The objectives of this study are:

(a) To comprehend the concepts and doctrines of Islamic Banking and Finance;
(b) To look into different products related to Islamic Finance; and
(c) To evaluate the future of Shariah-based Banking in India.

Research Methodology

The paper is primarily based on secondary data gathered from numerous websites and journals, books, reports and magazines. The study is exploratory in nature. The study seeks to comprehend the concepts and doctrines of Islamic banking and finance. It also researches Islamic financial products. Finally, the study aims to assess the prospects for Islamic banking in the Indian context. This article looks at the ideas given by several committees and groups for Islamic banking in India. It also provides insight into a momentous decision made by the Kerala High Court. The article explores the huge opportunities associated with Islamic banking while outlining the challenges to its development in India.

Discussion

The fundamentals of Islamic banking, the main areas of Islamic finance, the state of Islamic banking and finance worldwide, and Shariah-based banking in India are all covered in this section.

Islamic Banking Principles

1. Religion and economics are intertwined.
2. Interest on money should not be received or paid.
3. Gambling, lotteries, and other speculative activities should not be funded.
4. The transactions should rely solely on the mutual sharing of profit/loss/risks by all parties involved which may also include the Bank as a partner.
5. Investment in industries such as alcohol, porn, pork, weapons, defence, gambling etc. are prohibited in Islam.
6. Transactions need to have physical assets supporting them.

Major Segments of Islamic Finance

The Islamic Banking and Finance industry can be divided into four major segments: Islamic Banking, Islamic Insurance, Islamic Capital Markets and Islamic Non-Bank Financial firms. Existing 'halal' Islamic finance products include Mudarabah, Murabaha, Musharaka, Takaful, Ijarah, Qard Hasan, Bai'salam, Sukuk, Istisna, and Islamic credit cards.

- *Mudarabah:* This is a contract between the bank and the customer in which the bank finances the project costs and the customer supplies labour. The profit earned by the project/enterprise is split between the two parties.
- *Musharaka:* It is a partnership deed between the bank and several customers/ partners where all parties contribute to the capital investment, and profits are divided in the same proportion.
- *Istisna:* It is a contractual agreement under which goods will be manufactured and sold to a certain party in the future and the resulting profit is shared by all parties.
- *Murabahah:* This is a contract between the bank and the customer, compare-able to a hire purchase agreement. Here, the bank purchases the asset rather

than financing it and rents it to the customer. When the rent recovered exceeds the cost of the asset, it might be given to the customer.

- *Ijara:* This kind of arrangement involves the bank purchasing an asset and leasing it to its clients.

Global Scenario of Islamic Banking and Finance

The founding of the Accounting and Auditing Organisation for Islamic Financial Institutions (AAOIFI) in 1991 and the Islamic Financial Services Board (IFSB) in 2002 marked significant turning points for the Islamic banking industry. These entities strive to establish uniform protocols and ensure the soundness and consistency of Islamic banking establishments. Regulating frameworks, however, differ across nations. Malaysia, for example, is renowned for its extensive Islamic banking laws. Nonetheless, Malaysia features a dual banking system with coexisting Shariah-based and conventional banks. The Gulf Cooperation Council (GCC) countries have invested much in and supported the development of regulatory frameworks that are favourable to Islamic banking. The Governments also played a crucial part in creating a robust regulatory structure of Shariah-based banking in GCC. The United Kingdom has positioned itself as a centre for Islamic banking in the West, implementing regulatory changes to provide financial products that comply with Shariah-based banking.

Table 1 presents the Global IFSI by Sector and Region.

Table 1: Breakdown of the Global IFSI by Sector and Region (USD billion) (2022)

Region	*Islamic Banking Assets*	*Ṣukūk Outstanding*	*Islamic Funds Assets*	*Takāful Contributions*	*Total*	*Share (%)*
Gulf Cooperation Council (GCC)	1342.9	356.6	24.1	16.7	1740.4	53.6
South-East Asia (SEA)	307.2	411.4	32.8	6.0	757.4	23.3
Middle East and South Asia (MESA)	478.3	57.8	62.9	5.9	604.9	18.6
Africa	49.6	2.9	1.9	0.8	55.2	1.7
Others	71.2	1.0	14.9	0.6	87.7	2.7
Total	2249.2	829.7	136.6	30.0	3245.5	100.00
Share (%)	69.3	25.6	4.2	0.9	100.00	XXXXX

Source: IFSB Secretariat Workings

It is observed from Table 1 that the share of Islamic Banking Assets is more than other Islamic financial instruments. Gulf Cooperation Council (GCC) enjoys the lion's share of Islamic Banking Assets followed by Middle East and South Asia (MESA).

Shariah-based Banking in India

Several multinational banks with operations in India, including Citibank, Standard Chartered, and HSBC, provide Islamic banking and finance services in West Asian countries. Non-Islamic countries such as China, the United Kingdom, the United States, and Germany also offer Islamic banking services. The Anand Sinha Committee (headed by the Deputy Governor of the RBI Mr. Anand Sinha) was set up by the RBI to investigate Islamic financial products in 2005, making it a crucial year for Islamic banking in India. The objective of this committee was to examine the feasibility of bringing more people under the umbrella of the banking system through Islamic banking instruments. The Committee observed that modifications in the existing banking regulations and taxation systems would have to be done before thinking about implementing Islamic banking in India. Interest-free banking was suggested by the Raghuram Rajan Committee (formed by the Planning Commission in 2008 under the headship of Mr. Raghuram Rajan) to promote financial inclusiveness. In 2008, the Ministry of Minority Affairs solicited bids for rebuilding the National Minority Development Finance Corporation (NMDFC) on Shariah principles. SEBI, the capital market regulator, approved India's first Shariah-compliant mutual fund scheme and venture capital fund in 2009, while the Kerala Government declared the establishment of an Islamic NBFC. The 'BSE-TASIS Shariah 50 Index' was first released by the BSE and TASIS in the year 2010. Kerala State Industrial Development Corporation (KSIDC), a wholly-owned subsidiary of the Kerala state government, entered into an arrangement with the Al Barakah group in 2010 to provide Shariah-compliant financing to the Muslim population. KSIDC owned 11% of the proposed Islamic financial institution. Subramanian Swamy, the leader of the Janata Party, opposed the Kerala Government's directive, claiming that such actions by government entities breached the secular ideal inherent in the Indian Constitution. As a result, it was stayed for violating Articles 14, 25, and 27. In February 2011, the Kerala High Court dismissed Subramanian Swamy's appeal and upheld the establishment of an Islamic investment company. Finally, in 2012, the RBI revoked the licence of an Islamic NBFC. The Reserve Bank of India (RBI) suggested that Indian commercial banks implement interest-free banking in 2015. Islamic banking concepts, however, can be practised in India as an NBFC but not as a bank which is ironic. The current banking system permits banks to obtain loans and make deposits with the RBI at interest, which is in contradiction with Islamic banking.

Islamic banking can benefit the unorganised sector, which is frequently denied debt finance due to a lack of collateral. However, Islamic finance can help the sector by providing equity funding, which can help it grow.

Opportunity/Scope for Islamic Banking in India

In the Indian scenario, Islamic banking can serve a wide range of people's financial requirements while encouraging people to follow moral and ethical financial conduct and practices. The demand for financial products which are Shariah-compliant is on the rise because of the existence of a sizeable chunk of the Muslim population in the country. It is evident, therefore, that there exists an untapped latent market for Islamic banking in India. The huge opportunities of Shariah-based banking in the Indian scenario are summed up below.

1. Shariah-based Islamic finance and banking are ethical.
2. It has the potential to promote entrepreneurial activities. Entrepreneurs with lucrative ideas but no collateral would benefit from Islamic banks.
3. Obtaining equity capital is advantageous for the unorganised sector and agriculture.
4. It might be considered as an alternative to traditional banking, resulting in good competition. Alternatively, it can complement conventional banking.
5. It has the potential to enhance Foreign Direct Investment (FDI).
6. It may provide job opportunities for Islamic finance students and others interested in a career in this industry.
7. Because there is no interest requirement on the part of the borrowers, Islamic banking can help to eradicate poverty by reducing economic imbalances.
8. It can lower the rate of inflation by reducing the generation of artificial money (Saleem, 2007).
9. Islamic banking can appeal to a wide range of Indians, irrespective of their religious background, by being consistent with the Islamic principles of justice, openness, and social responsibility.

Impediments to Islamic Banking in India

In the Indian financial landscape, Shariah-based banking can flourish. However, there are many challenges as well. Among the obstacles, misconceptions about Islamic banking principles and the existing regulatory system are considered to be serious impediments. These impediments are summarised below.

1. There are several credit rating agencies for conventional financial institutions, but none for Islamic financial institutions. As a result, investors lose confidence.
2. The problems investors encounter in establishing whether a company is truly adhering to Shariah law are worsened by the lack of skilled Shariah specialists.

3. According to the Banking Regulation Act of 1949, all banks in India are supposed to operate on an interest-based basis. In India, Islamic banks are illegal from the legal viewpoint because these banks are based on the principle of 'no interest'.
4. Another problem is gaining the trust of investors. Investors have confidence in the traditional banking system. They feel that their deposits are safe because these deposits are protected by deposit insurance and credit guarantees. On the other hand, Shariah-based banks do not provide such guarantees.
5. The existing taxation system and accounting standards pose a serious threat to the implementation of Shariah-based banking in the country.
6. The general acceptability of Islamic banking is further impeded by misconceptions and fears about it such as the idea that it is closely associated with radical Islam.
7. The key hurdle is a suitable political environment, which is now working against the establishment of Islamic banking in India.

The Government of India, according to the opinion of the advocates for Islamic banking, should take steps to facilitate conventional banks to open Islamic banking windows. And, this measure will attract customers which will be beneficial for the development of an Islamic banking system in the country. According to a study that compared the performance of commercial banks with Islamic banks during the global financial crisis, the latter displayed more resilience than the former (IMF Survey Online, 2010).

Conclusion

Developing countries must look into new routes of finance to stimulate economic innovation. Islamic finance gives developing nations that opportunity. With a recent drive towards digitalization, India's financial system has improved a lot. However, the enormous prospective of Islamic financial services in India has yet to be realised. A fair environment with clear laws is essential in India to realise the potential advantages of Islamic Financial Services. Indians are still unfamiliar with the ideas of Shariah-based finance. The hunt for alternatives to conventional banking is expected to shift focus to Islamic banking. In India, this appears to be an impossible and unwelcome task. Without a solid foundation, the implementation of Islamic finance and banking will result in confusion and conflict. It will be impossible to adopt Islamic banking even on a modest scale without adequate regulations. Myths associated with Shariah-based banking in India act as a crucial barrier to its acceptance and implementation. To debunk misconceptions and promote a better knowledge of Islamic finance principles among financial institutions, policymakers, and the general public, education and awareness initiatives are critical. Finally, plans to establish Islamic banking in secular countries like India may confront a variety of political, legal and sociological challenges. However, the government's backing and support from the stakeholders for the implementation of Islamic banking would provide numerous benefits to India. India can leverage the revolutionary potential of Islamic banking to foster inclusive growth and financial stability by welcoming diversity and innovation in its financial industry.

The need for ethical financial services and the development of regulatory frameworks have been the driving forces behind the impressive expansion and resilience of the worldwide Islamic banking industry. Islamic banking is expanding into new areas as non-Muslim-majority nations come to understand its advantages. India should keep a close eye on these developments and make decisions about how it will implement Islamic banking into its financial services in the future.

Scope for Further Research

The following fields are open to further research:

1. Analysing the effective use of Islamic banking in other nations with comparable socioeconomic backgrounds through comparative studies might yield insightful information.
2. The operational effectiveness, profitability, and customer satisfaction levels of Shariah-based banks can be ascertained by conducting a comparative analysis of performance with regular banks in areas where both operate.
3. There can be research focusing on the identification and mitigation of the particular risks connected to Shariah-compliant banking in particular, as well as Shariah-compliant financial products in general.
4. It is possible to research the development of innovative financial products that comply with Shariah law and are suited for the Indian market.
5. Research on the potential role of public-private partnerships in the growth and promotion of Islamic banking in India should examine other nations' successful public-private partnership models.
6. Researchers may examine how India can strike a balance between secularism and the arrival of faith-based financial institutions.

References

[1] Ahmad, E., Azami, A.R. and Siraj, M.B. (2024). A Comprehensive Review of Non-Interest Banking in India: Requirements, Potential, and Hurdles. *International Journal of Advances in Engineering and Management*, 6(2), 39–44.

[2] Badruddin, A. (2015). Islamic Banking and Finance in India: A Kosher or Myth. *International Journal of Management, Innovation and & Entrepreneurial Research (IJMIER)*, 1(1), 1–6.

[3] Beg, S. (2016). Prospects, Problems and Potential of Islamic banking in India. *International Journal of Accounting and Financial Management Research*, *6*(3), 9–20.

[4] Fasih, F. (2012). Inclusive Growth in India through Islamic Banking. *Procedia—Social and Behavioral Sciences*, 37, 97–110.

[5] Gupta, A. (2020). 'Banking' in the Name of 'Faith': A Legal Perspective of Islamic Banking in India. *Nirma University Law Journal*, 10(1), 19–39.

[6] Haque, I., Lone, F.A. and Thakur, G.H. Islamic Banking in India: What More Needed? Journal of Islamic Economics, Banking and Finance, 5(3), 75–86.

[7] Khan, M.A. and Hussin, N. (2013). Islamic Banking in India: Developments, Prospects and Challenges. *International Journal of Research in Commerce & Management*, 4(1).

[8] Komijani, A. and Taghizadeh-Hesary, F. (2018). An Overview of Islamic Banking and Finance in Asia. *ADBI Working Paper 853. Tokyo: Asian Development Bank Institute.* Available: https://www.adb.org/publications/overview-islamic-banking-and-finance-asia

[9] Munuswamy, S., Soundararajan, G. and Ramasamy, R. (2013). Islamic Finance in India: A Study on the Perception of College Teachers in Chennai. *Journal of Islamic Economics, Banking and Finance*, 9(3), 131–148.

[10] Parameshwara and Aneesh (2022). Islamic Banking in India: Concept, Principles and Developments. Available at SSRN: https://ssrn.com/abstract=4153479 or http://dx.doi.org/10.2139/ssrn.4153479.

[11] Saleem, S. (2017). Role of Islamic Banks in Economic Development. *MPRA Paper No. 6449*, Available at SSRN: https://ssrn.com/abstract=989055. Accessed on 16.11.2023.

[12] Sayeed, I. (2023). The Rise of Islamic Banking in the Time of Economic Crisis. *EPRA International Journal of Economics, Business and Management Studies (EBMS)*, *10*(2), 10–16.

[13] Shahid, M. and Raj, J. (2019). Islamic banking in India: an overview. *Zenith International Journal of Multidisciplinary Research*, *9*(6), 246–252.

[14] Siddiqui, T., Naushad, M. and Farooque, M. (2021). A study on Islamic finance as an approach for financial inclusion in India. *Accounting*, *7*(2), 487–496.

[15] Tabash, M.I. (2017). Critical Challenges Affecting Islamic Banking Growth in India Using Analytical Hierarchy Process (AHP). Banks and Bank Systems, 12(3), 27–34. doi:10.21511/bbs.12(3).2017.02.

Do Credit Sales Impact Profitability Negatively?

Sk. Naushad[1] and Kalpataru Bandopadhyay[2]

ABSTRACT: Efficient receivable management is crucial for the financial health of businesses, particularly for SMEs facing unique challenges. This research paper aims to investigate the relationship between receivable management and profitability within the context of Indian SMEs, listed on the National Stock Exchange (NSE). The study is based on secondary data collected from ACE database for a period of 10 years from 2013 to 2022. This study explores the impact of receivable management on the firm's profitability employing fixed effect regression model. Accounts receivable days is taken as independent variables while return on assets (ROA) is taken as dependent variable. Further, growth in sales and financial leverage were also used as control variables. The findings reveal negative association between profitability measures (ROA) and the explanatory variable (accounts receivable days) in selected Indian SMEs.

Keywords: Accounts Receivable Management, Indian SMEs, Panel Data, Profitability.

Introduction

The relationship between working capital management and profitability is crucial for a business's financial health. Efficient management of current assets and liabilities ensures liquidity, allowing for smooth operations and positively impacting profitability. Key elements in this symbiotic connection include optimizing inventory levels, timely management of accounts receivable and accounts payable, and adapting to seasonal variations. Additionally, the cost of capital and the financing approach employed can influence profitability, as can the ability to navigate operational delays resulting from inadequate working capital. Ultimately, the judicious use of working capital as an investment, aligned with business cycles and industry demands, contributes to a higher return on investment and, consequently, enhanced profitability.

In order to manage the working capital properly, the components of working capital viz account receivable, cash, inventory and accounts payable, should be

---

[1] Research Scholar, Department of Commerce, Vidyasagar University, India.
E-mail: thesknaushad@gmail.com

[2] Professor, Department of Commerce, Vidyasagar University, India.
E-mail: bkalpa.0to1@gmail.com

managed efficiently. Accounts receivable, in particular, is a significant component of current assets, accounting for around 35% of total assets (Madishetti & Kibona, 2013). It plays a vital role in cash flow management and overall financial stability (Abdullah Al Mamun, 2018; Kehinde, 2011). Poor management of debtors has been identified as a cause of failure for approximately 20% of firms in the UK (Richard & Kabala, 2019). Consequently, accounts receivable management is critical to maintaining liquidity, profitability, and sustainability of a company (Adusei, 2017). Despite its importance, empirical research on the connection between accounts receivable management and profitability is relatively sparse. While there is extensive literature on working capital management and inventory management, accounts receivable management has not received comparable attention.

This study places special emphasis on Small and Medium Enterprises (SMEs), which encounter multiple hurdles in accessing external funding, particularly through formal channels (Beck & Demirguc-Kunt, 2006). Research by Beck, Demirguc-Kunt, and Maksimovic (2008), spanning 48 countries, reinforces that SMEs generally utilize less external financing compared to larger firms. As a result, SMEs depend heavily on efficient management of current assets and liabilities to ensure liquidity and smooth operations, which positively impacts profitability. This underscores the need to comprehensively study the financial landscape of the SME sector to unlock their potential and address issues related to receivable management and profitability. This study is distinctive in its exclusive focus on receivable management within SMEs, specifically in India, over the period from 2012 to 2022. It investigates the relationship between receivable management and profitability.

Theoretical Framework and Review of Earlier Studies

Receivable management refers to the set of policies, procedures, and practices employed by a firm for managing sales offered on credit. The management of accounts receivable is vital for monetary health of all businesses, no matter whatever the kind and size (Padachi, 2006). Effective accounts receivable management is a critical component of financial strategy for businesses, playing a pivotal role in defining overall profitability. By optimizing accounts receivable management, businesses can free up cash for operational needs, reduce reliance on external financing, and improve overall financial health. Accounts receivable emerges from the chronological gap between a sale and the actual receipt of cash (Altaf & Shah, 2018; Fabozzi & Peterson, 2003). In this context, accounts receivable can be seen as a form of trade credit extended to customers by the firm (Martínez-Sola *et al.*, 2013). The nature of this relationship between accounts receivable management and profitability is contingent upon the adoption of aggressive or conservative policies by firms (Garcia-Teruel & Martinez-Solano,

2007; Nazir & Afza, 2009; Tauringana & Afrifa, 2013). An aggressive policy, characterized by a shorter accounts receivable period, has the potential to enhance profitability by boosting cash flow, thereby increasing the firm's current asset levels and liquidity. This growth in creditworthiness safeguards firms from liquidity crises and financial distress (Arena & Julio, 2010). While Transactional cost theory, as proposed by Ferris (1981) regarding trade credit, suggests that firms can enhance operational efficiency by reducing transaction costs associated with a decrease in the accounts receivable period. Consequently, a reduction in accounts receivable period is anticipated to positively impact profitability (Nelson, 2002).

The literature on the association between the accounts receivable days and firm profitability presents conflicting perspectives. For example, a reduction in accounts receivable days is posited to bolster cash flows, acting as a safeguard during uncertain situations (Fabozzi & Peterson, 2003). Moreover, a shorter accounts receivable day is anticipated to decrease bad debts (Altaf & Ahmad, 2019), implying a potential negative correlation between accounts receivable days and firm profitability (Mathuva, 2010; Sharma & Kumar, 2011; Singhania *et al.*, 2014). Conversely, divergent opinions exist. Some scholars argue that adopting a longer ARP could positively impact firm profitability. They contend that an extended ARP offers more time for product quality verification (Smith, 1987). Additionally, granting extended trade credit can function as a sales promotion tool, contributing to increased sales and profitability (Altaf & Shah, 2017; Blazenko & Vandezande, 2003). Consequently, this perspective supports a positive relationship between ARP and firm profitability (Abuzayed, 2012; Raheman & Nasr, 2007).

Research Gap

Despite the momentous role that accounts receivable management plays in the financial health and sustainability of Small and Medium Enterprises (SMEs), there exists a notable gap in the current research landscape regarding the specific challenges, strategies, and best practices associated with accounts receivable management within this particular context. While extensive literature exists on global perspectives and larger corporate entities, there is a limited understanding of the unique dynamics and industry-specific nuances that characterize accounts receivable management practices among Indian SMEs. This research gap calls for an in-depth exploration and analysis that focuses specifically on the accounts receivable management practices of Indian SMEs, aiming to provide a comprehensive understanding of the relationship between accounts receivable management and profitability influencing effectiveness, efficiency, and overall financial performance in this critical aspect of business operations.

Objective of the Study

Based on the above discussions the primary objective of this study is to examine the relationship between account receivable management practices and profitability to provide insights for effective financial decision-making among businesses, with a specific focus on small and medium-sized enterprises (SMEs).

Hypothesis

In order to achieve the objective of finding the relationship between accounts receivable management and profitability of NSE listed SMEs the following hypotheses are set

- ***Null Hypothesis (H_0):*** There is no significant relationship between accounts receivable management and profitability of NSE listed SMEs.
- ***Alternate Hypothesis (H_1):*** There is a significant relationship between accounts receivable management and profitability of NSE listed SMEs.

Data and Methodology

Our empirical framework is modeled after the one initially employed by Deloof (2003). The focus is on establishing the relationship between accounts receivable management practices and the profitability of Indian SMEs listed on the National Stock Exchange (NSE) over a decade, spanning from the fiscal year 2013 to 2022. Data for this study was obtained from the financial statements of Indian SMEs listed on the NSE Emerge, with the sample drawn from the ACE Database. In pursuit of our objective, Profitability, measured by ROA, is designated as the dependent variable, while the Receivable Days serves as the independent variable. Additionally, factors such as growth in sales and leverage are incorporated as control variables.

Data set and Sample Design

According to information from NSE India, as of December 2023, there were a total of 200 MSMEs listed on the NSE Emerge. Among these, 170 were classified as SMEs, and their data was accessible through the ACE directory. The selection of the sample for our study was liable on the availability of complete financial data for SMEs in the ACE directory. However, out of the 170 enterprises initially identified, only 40 had a comprehensive set of data covering each year from 2013 to 2022. Therefore, the analysis was conducted on the financial data of these 40 firms, encompassing a ten-year period from 2013 to 2022. This resulted in a total of 400 firm-year observations.

Variables Used in the Study

To assess the impact of accounts receivable management on the profitability of Indian SMEs, the study incorporates the one dependent variable, one independent variable and two control variables. The choice of variables is influenced by previous studies on working capital management and accounts receivable management.

The dependent variable utilized in this study is Return on Assets (ROA). ROA is quantified as the ratio of Earnings Before Interest and Tax (EBIT) to total assets, serving as a proxy measure for profitability, as established by previous studies (Paul & Mitra, 2018; Nazir & Afza, 2009; Jana, 2018; Panda *et al.*, 2021; Altaf & Ahmad, 2019).

The independent variable employed in this study is the Accounts Receivable Days (RD). RD is computed by dividing accounts receivable by sales and then multiplying the result by 365 days. This variable serves as a proxy for accounts receivable management, as indicated by prior studies (Sharma & Kumar, 2011; Kumar & Ramanan, 2013; Bhatia & Srivastava, 2016).

Moreover, this study also incorporates annual sales growth and financial leverage as control variables, aligning with findings from prior research (Deloof, 2003; Nazir & Afza, 2009; Appuhami, 2008; BanosCaballero *et al.*, 2010; Akinlo, 2012; Chiou *et al.*, 2006).

This table explains the definition and symbol for variable used in this study

Table 1: List of Variables Examined in this Study

Dependent Variables	
Return on Assets (ROA)	EBIT/Total Assets
Independent Variables	
Receivable Days (RD)	Average Time a Customer Takes to Pay Back a Business for Products or Services Purchased
Control Variables	
Growth in Sales (GS)	$(Sales_1-Sales_0)/Sales_0$
Financial Leverage (LEV)	Total Debt/Total Assets

Source: Compiled by Authors

Model Specification

To achieve the research objective and to test the research hypothesis, we employed panel regression analysis. Panel data in this context comprise a time series for each member in the cross-sectional dataset, thereby enhancing the sample size and enabling the assessment of dynamics of change. Panel regression addresses a fundamental limitation of simple regression, which assumes the observation of static parameters within a sample. This constraint is overcome in panel regression, as it allows for the variation of parameters in a systematic or random manner across the dataset (Ismail, 2006). Additionally, panel data regression facilitates the control of unobservable heterogeneity by mitigating biases stemming from individual effects (Hsiao, 1985). Before applying panel regression, it is essential to conduct various pre-estimation and post estimation tests. In our study, the pre-estimation tests include examining multicollinearity, heteroscedasticity, and autocorrelation. Multicollinearity is assessed using the variance inflation factor (VIF), while the Modified Wald test and Wooldridge tests are employed for heteroscedasticity and autocorrelation testing, respectively. Additionally, a post-estimation technique, the Breusch-Pagan Lagrangian Multiplier Test, is utilized for model selection.

Under these circumstances, we tested the hypothesis using the following multivariate regression model with ROA as a dependent variable and receivable days as independent variable while keeping growth in sales and leverage as control variables:

$$ROA_{it} = ß_0 + ß_1(RD)_{it} + ß_2(GS)_{it} + ß_3(LEV)_{it} + \varepsilon_{it}$$

Where,

ROA_{it} = Return on assets of firm i at time t;

β_0 = Common y-intercept;

$\beta_1 - \beta_3$ = Coefficients of the explanatory variables concerned;

RD_{it} = Accounts Receivable Days of firm i at time t

GS_{it} = Sales growth of firm i at time t

LEV_{it} = Leverage of firm i at time t

e_{it} = Stochastic error term of firm i at time t

I = Entity (SME)

T = Time

Research Results and Discussions

In our research, we conducted two distinct types of data analysis: descriptive and quantitative. The descriptive analysis was employed to explain the characteristics of each relevant variable. In the realm of quantitative analysis, we utilized two methods. Initially, we employed the Pearson correlation to gauge the extent of association among the various variables under study. Subsequently, we employed regression analysis to estimate the causal relationship between the profitability variable, accounts receivable management variables and selected control variables. The analysis was conducted using the fixed effect regression method, with the aid of STATA software.

Descriptive Analysis

The descriptive analysis provides insights into the central tendency and variability of the key variables examined in the study. It includes the average and standard deviation, offering a summary of the distribution of values. Additionally, it highlights the maximum and minimum values, providing an outlook on the range of each variable.

Table 2 displays descriptive statistics for 40 Indian SMEs over a 10-year period spanning from 2013 to 2022, comprising a total of 400 observations.

Table 2: Descriptive Statistics

Variable	*Obs*	*Mean*	*Std. Dev.*	*Min*	*Max*
ROA	400	3.794	8.516	–45.500	37.154
RD	400	94.138	74.028	3.860	502.013
GS	400	14.821	48.943	–81.029	581.153
LEV	400	1.165	2.128	–3.128	7.629

Source: Computed by Authors

The mean Return on Assets (ROA) is approximately 3.8 percent, with a standard deviation of 8.5 percent, indicating a potential deviation of profitability values from the mean by up to 8.5 percent in either direction. The highest observed ROA is 37.15 percent, while the lowest is -45.5 percent.

On average, companies receive payments against sales within a period of 94 days, but the standard deviation is 74 days, suggesting considerable variation from the mean. The minimum accounts receivable days were 4, and the maximum was 502.

In terms of sales growth, the average is 14.8 percent with a standard deviation of 49 percent. The range is substantial, with the minimum and maximum growth rates at –81 percent and 581 percent, respectively, indicating non-uniform sales growth within the industry.

The average leverage is 1.165, with a standard deviation of 2.128. Some firms exhibit negative leverage, with the minimum at –3.128, while the maximum leverage is 7.63.

Quantitative Analysis

In our quantitative analysis, we employed two distinct methods. Initially, correlation was utilized to assess the degree of association among the various variables under scrutiny. This allowed us to identify the significant variables associated with profitability. Subsequently, regression analysis was employed to measure the degree of association between the different variables under consideration.

Correlation Analysis

In Table 3 Pearson's correlation analysis is used for data to see the relationship between variables of accounts receivable management and profitability.

Table 3: Correlation Matrix of ROA and Independent Variables

	ROA	*RD*	*GS*	*LEV*
ROA	1.0000			
RD	–0.3225	1.0000		
GS	0.3109	–0.3257	1.0000	
LEV	–0.3114	0.0882	–0.0222	1.0000

Source: Computed by Authors

If we analyze the relationship between the dependent variables and the independent variables then we can see that ROA, used as a measure of profitability, is negatively correlated with receivable days. This aligns with the perspective that a decrease in accounts receivable days is expected to enhance cash flows, serving as a protective measure in times of uncertainty. Additionally, a shorter accounts receivable period is predicted to reduce bad debts, suggesting a potential negative correlation between accounts receivable days and firm profitability (Mathuva, 2010; Sharma & Kumar, 2011; Singhania *et al.*, 2014). A positive association between Return on Assets (ROA) and growth in sales indicates that as a company experiences an increase in its sales, its profitability, as measured by ROA, tends to rise as well. This positive correlation suggests that the company is effectively translating its sales growth into higher returns on its assets. The above table also shows a negative correlation between ROA and Leverage as companies with higher leverage may incur higher interest expenses, which can impact their overall profitability. As a result, the negative relationship between ROA and leverage indicates that firms with lower levels of financial leverage may experience higher returns on their assets compared to those with higher leverage.

On the other hand, as there will always be multicollinearity in a multiple regression model so our results also exhibit relationship between the dependent variables. Multicollinearity is not the problem of existence of collinearity among independent variables, it is the problem of extent. So, we proceeded with VIF test to check the severity of multicollinearity in a regression analysis and found it to be less than 5 (as indicated in table 4) so we proceeded with our study.

Table 4: VIF Test Results

Variable	VIF	1/VIF
RD	1.13	0.887632
GS	1.12	0.894082
LEV	1.01	0.992251
Mean VIF	1.08	

Source: Computed by Authors

A shortcoming of the Pearson correlation is that they do not allow identifying the causes of consequences (Deloof, 2003). To provide a reliable indicator of association we have used regression analysis.

Regression Analysis

For the purpose of identifying the important variables influencing the dependent variable, we have used the regression analysis. In panel data regression, time-series and cross-sectional observations are combined and estimated. Panel data is more useful in studying the dynamics of adjustment and is better able to identify and measure effects that are simply not detectable in pure cross-section or pure time-series data. But before delving into the regression analysis, we thoroughly conducted additional pre-estimation tests. The earlier VIF results provided assurance that multicollinearity was not a concern, allowing us to proceed confidently. Subsequently, we applied the Modified Wald Test for Groupwise Heteroskedasticity to scrutinize the homogeneity of variances across groups or subgroups in the dataset.

In the context of the Modified Wald Test for Groupwise Heteroskedasticity, the null hypothesis posits homoskedasticity, signifying that the variance of the error terms is consistent across all groups or subgroups in the dataset. The Table 5 below shows the result of Modified Wald test for group-wise heteroscedasticity.

Table 5: Modified Wald Test for Heteroscedasticity

Chi2 (1)	*28679.94*
Prob> Chi2	0.0000

Source: Computed by Authors

The p-value of the table is less than 0.05. So, we reject the null hypothesis. So, in our case, there is a problem related to heteroskedasticity.

For testing first-order autocorrelation, we used the Wooldridge test. According to Drucker (2003), Wooldridge technique is technique which is a simple technique with few assumptions. Here the null hypothesis is that there is no autocorrelation in the model. Table 6 shows the results of the Wooldridge test for autocorrelation

Table 6: Wooldridge Test for Autocorrelation

F (1, 39)	*15.128*
Prob>F	0.0004

Source: Computed by Authors

The presented table indicates that the p-value is below 0.05. In light of this, the null hypothesis is rejected. Consequently, we infer that the model is afflicted by an autocorrelation issue.

While using panel data, one must decide whether to use a fixed effects model or a random effects model. The random effects model assumes a single common intercept term, and that the intercepts for individual companies vary from this common intercept in a random manner, whereas the fixed effects model assumes different intercept for individual companies. In order to choose the appropriate model, both the fixed effects and random effects estimators were used to estimate the coefficients in model stated in section 7.3. The results indicated that both the fixed effect model and random effect model are statistically significant. So, to select the more appropriate model the post estimation Hausman test was performed. In Hausman test the null hypothesis assumes that the random effects model is consistent. Since the p-value is less than 0.05. So, we reject the null hypothesis. Hence, the fixed effect model is more suitable for our data set. Since our data suffers from the problem of heteroscedasticity and auto correlation, robust standard error was used to address this problem and the results are shown in table 7.

Table 7: Fixed Effect Regression Results

		Prob>F=0.0000
ROA	Coef.	P>ItI
RD	–.0322933	0.001
GS	.0373294	0.001
LEV	–.699034	0.000
Cons	7.094474	0.000

Source: Computed by Authors

Through the Fixed Effect Model, we found a statically significant and negative relationship between accounts receivable management and profitability. A negative relationship between accounts receivable days and profitability implies that, on average, as the number of days it takes a company to collect its accounts receivable decreases, the profitability of the company increases. In other words, a shorter period for collecting accounts receivable is associated with higher profitability. The negative relationship between accounts receivable days and profitability can be attributed to various operational and financial factors like shorter accounts receivable days mean that a company is collecting payments from customers more quickly. This leads to improved cash flow, providing the company with more immediate funds to cover expenses, invest, or reduce debt which improves the profitability. The results also indicate a negative association between the leverage and profitability as SMEs are financially not very strong and they are dependent on external financing to a great extent which may force them to get debts on unfavourable conditions resulting in a negative impact on profitability.

Conclusion

The research has shed light on the complex relationship between accounts receivable days and profitability within the context of Indian SMEs. The key findings indicate a negative correlation between the efficiency of accounts receivable management and the overall profitability of the sampled companies. This insight contributes to a deeper understanding of financial dynamics and operational efficiency in the studied domain. The results also indicate a negative relationship between leverage and profitability. Since SMEs are often not financially robust and heavily reliant on external financing, they may be compelled to take on debt under unfavourable conditions, leading to a detrimental effect on profitability.

The observed negative relationship, highlights the importance of effective receivables management and debt management as strategic levers for enhancing financial performance. To mitigate the negative impact of accounts receivable on SME profitability, businesses should establish strict credit policies, improve invoicing and collection processes, and utilize technology for efficient tracking. Negotiating shorter payment terms, offering early payment discounts, and considering factoring or invoice discounting can enhance cash flow. Regularly reviewing accounts receivable, actively following up on overdue accounts, and maintaining strong customer relationships are also crucial. These strategies collectively help reduce bad debts, improve cash flow, and enhance overall profitability. Further, to mitigate the negative impact of leverage on the profitability of SMEs, it is crucial to facilitate access to affordable financing and Implementing government-backed loan programs for SME.

However, it is crucial to acknowledge the potential impact of industry-specific factors and external economic conditions on the identified relationship. Future research endeavours could explore these contextual nuances to provide a more comprehensive understanding of the dynamics at play.

References

[1] Abdullah Al Mamun, A. (2018). Receivables management of pharmaceutical industry in Bangladesh. *Journal of Business Studies.* 1(1). 34–46.

[2] Abuzayed, B. (2012). Working capital management and firms' performance in emerging markets: the case of Jordan. *International Journal of Managerial Finance.* 8(2). 155–179.

[3] Adusei, C. (2017). Accounts receivables management: Insight and challenges. *Journal of Finance & Banking Studies,* 6(1). 101–112.

[4] Akinlo, O. O. (2012). Determinants of working capital requirements in selected quoted companies in Nigeria. *Journal of African Business,* 13(1). 40–50.

[5] Altaf, N. and Ahmad, F. (2019). Working capital financing, firm performance and financial constraints. *International Journal of Managerial Finance,* 15(4). 464–477.

[6] Altaf, N. and Shah, F. (2017). Working capital management, firm performance and financial constraints. *Asia-Pacific Journal of Business Administration,* 9(3). 206–219.

[7] Altaf, N. and Shah, F., A. (2018). Investment and financial constraints in Indian firms: Does working capital smoothen fixed investment? *Decision,* 45(1), 43–58. https://doi.org/10.1007/s40622-018-0178-8.

[8] Appuhami, B.A.R. (2008). The impact of firms' capital expenditure on working capital management: An empirical study across industries in Thailand. *International Management Review,* . 4(1). 11–24.

[9] Arena, M. and Julio, B. (2010). Litigation risk and corporate cash holdings. *Working Paper.* Marquette University.

[10] Arunkumar, O.N. and Ramanan, T.R. (2013). Working Capital Management and Profitability: A Sensitivity Analysis. *International Journal of Research and Development – A Management Review (IJRDMR),* 2(1), 52–58.

[11] Banos-Caballero, S., Garcia-Teruel, P.J. and Martinez-Solano, P. (2010). Working capital management in SMEs. *Accounting & Finance.* 50(3). 511–527.

[12] Beck, T.A., Demirguc-Kunt and Maksimovi, V. (2008). Financing Patterns Around the World: Are Small Firms Different?". *Journal of Financial Economics.* 89(3). 467–487.

[13] Beck, T. and Demirguc-Kunt, A. (2006). Small and Medium-Size Enterprises: Access to Finance as a Growth Constraint. *Journal of Banking & Finance,* 30(11), 2931–2943.

[14] Bhatia, S. and Srivastav, A. (2016). Working Capital Management and Firm Performance in Emerging Economies: Evidence from India. *Management and Labour Studies.* 41(2). 71–87. https://doi.org/10.1177/0258042X16658733

[15] Blazenko, G.W. and Vandezande, K. (2003). The product differentiation hypothesis for corporate trade credit. *Managerial and Decision Economics.* 24(6–7). 457–469. https://doi.org/10.1002/mde.1113

[16] Chiou, J.R., Cheng, L. and Wu, H.W. (2006). The determinants of working capital management. *Journal of American Academy of Business.* 10(1). 149–155.

[17] Deloof, M. (2003). Does working capital management affect profitability of Belgian firms? *Journal of Business Finance & Accounting.* 30(3–4). 573–588.

[18] Drukker, D. (2003). Testing for serial correlation in linear panel-data models. *The Stata Journal,* 3(2), 168–177.

[19] Fabozzi, F.J. and Peterson, P.P. (2003). Financial management and analysis, (Vol. 132). John Wiley & Sons.

[20] Ferris, J.S. (1981). A transaction theory of trade credit use. *Quarterly Journal of Economics,* 94. 243–270.

[21] Garcia-Teruel, P.J. and Martinez-Solano, P. (2007). Effects of working capital management on SME profitability. *International Journal of Managerial Finance,* 3(2). 164–177.

[22] Hsiao, C. (1985). Benefits and limitations of panel data. *Econometric Reviews.* 4(1). 121–174.

[23] Ismail, I. (2006). Is economic value added more associated with stock return than accounting earnings? The U.K evidence. *International Journal of Managerial Finance.* 2(4). 343–352.

[24] Jana, D. (2018). Impact of working capital management on profitability of selected listed FMCG companies in India. *International Research Journal of Business Studies.* 11(1). 21–30.

[25] Kahinde, J.S. (2011). Effective working capital management in small and medium scale enterprises (SMEs). *International Journal of Business & Management,* 6, 271–279.

[26] Madishetti, S. and Kibona, D. (2013). Impact of receivables and payables management on the profitability of SMEs in Tanzania. *Journal of Economics and Management,* 2(3), 9–21.

[27] Martínez-Sola, C., García-Teruel, P. J. and Martínez-Solano, P. (2013). Corporate cash holding and firm value. *Applied Economics,* 45(2). 161–170. https://doi.org/10.1080/00036846.2011.595696

[28] Mathuva, D. (2010). The Influence of working capital management components on corporate profitability. *Research Journal of Business Management,* 4(1), 1–11. https://doi.org/10.3923/ rjbm.2010.1.11

[29] Nazir, M.S. and Afza, T. (2009). Working capital requirements and the determining factors in Pakistan. *IUP Journal of Applied Finance,* 15(4), 28–38

[30] Nelson, R.R. (2002). Technology. institutions and innovation systems. *Research Policy,* 31(2), 265–272.

[31] Padachi, K. (2006). Trends in working capital management and its impact on firms' performance: An analysis of Mauritian small manufacturing firms. *International Review of Business Research Papers.* 2(2). 45 –58.

[32] Panda, A.K., Nanda, S. and Panda, P. (2021). Working capital management. macroeconomic impacts and firm profitability: Evidence from Indian SMEs. *Business Perspectives and Research,* 9(1), 144–158.

[33] Paul, P. and Mitra, P. (2018). Analysis of the effect of working capital management on profitability of the firm: Evidence from Indian steel industry. *Asia-Pacific Journal of Management Research and Innovation.* 14(1–2). 32–38. https://doi.org/10.1177/2319510X18812142

[34] Raheman, A. and Nasr, M. (2007). Working capital management and profitability – case of Pakistani firms. *International Review of Business Research Papers*, 3(1), 279–300.

[35] Richard, E. and Kabala, B. (2019). Account receivable management practices of SMEs In Tanzania: A qualitative approach. *Business Management Review*, 22(2), 51–66.

[36] Sharma, A.K. and Kumar, S. (2011). Effect of working capital management on firm profitability: Empirical evidence from India. *Global Business Review*, 12(1), 159–173. https://doi.org/10.1177/097215091001200110

[37] Singhania, M., Sharma, N. and Rohit, J.Y. (2014). Working capital management and profitability: Evidence from Indian manufacturing companies. *Decision*, 41(3), 313–326. https://doi.org/10. 1007/s40622-014-0043-3.

[38] Smith, J.K. (1987). Trade credit and informational asymmetry. *The Journal of Finance*. 42(4). 863– 872. https://doi.org/10.1111/j.1540-6261.1987.tb03916.

[39] Tauringana, V. and Afrifa, G.A. (2013). The relative importance of working capital management and its components to SMEs' profitability. *Journal of Small Business and Enterprise Development*, 20(3), 453–469. DOI 10.1108/JSBED-12-2011-0029

[40] Smith, J.K. (1987). Trade credit and informational asymmetry. *The Journal of Finance*, 42(4), 863–872. https://doi.org/10.1111/j.1540-6261.1987.tb03916.

Estimation of Profit Efficiency of Private Sector Banks in India

Srabani Ghosh[1] and Gautam Mitra[2]

ABSTRACT: It is a common knowledge that the total profit of a business firm equals the amount by which the total revenue earned by the firm exceeds its total cost. Profit is thus a residual concept which may or may not be positive depending on whether the total revenue of the firm is greater than or less than the total cost. The profit function of a firm can be derived from the input-output relationship of a firm. Since, we have taken an output oriented framework, our objective has been to evaluate the performance of the private sector banks based on their ability to disburse advances and generate fee and commission based income. However, the disbursement of loans does not always translate into income generation due to the presence of non-performing and less performing assets. Apart from, meeting the regulatory requirements, commercial banks have to deploy funds in low performing asset because of their own limitation or due to external factors. In view of the above, the present chapter seeks to measure the profit performance of the observed banks in terms of profit efficiency.

Keywords: Global Financial Crisis, Profit Efficiency, Risk Management.

Introduction

It is a common knowledge that the total profit of a business firm equals the amount by which the total revenue earned by the firm exceeds its total cost. Profit is thus a residual concept which may or may not be positive depending on whether the total revenue of the firm is greater than or less than the total cost. The profit function of a firm can be derived from the input-output relationship of a firm. Since, we have taken an output oriented framework, our objective has been to evaluate the performance of the banks based on their ability to disburse advances and generate fee and commission based income. However, the disbursement of loans does not always translate into income generation due to the presence of non-performing and less performing assets. Apart from, meeting the regulatory requirements, commercial banks have to deploy funds in low performing asset because of their own limitation or due to external factors. In view of the above, the present article seeks to measure the profit performance of the observed banks in terms of profit efficiency.

[1] Associate Professor, Department of Commerce, Dr. Kanilal Bhattacharyya College, India. E-mail: contactsrabanideymphil@yahoo.com

[2] Professor, Department of Business Administration, The University of Burdwan, India.

1. How did the old & new private sector banks perform during 2004–05 to 2020–21 in terms of profit efficiency?
2. Did the financial crisis of 2007–2009 (Global meltdown) influence private sector bank in terms of profit efficiency.
3. How the environmental/contextual variables did related to bank performance (Profit Efficiency) during the in-sample period (2004–05 to 2020–21). In case of efficiency we have regress profit efficiency scores on the contextual variables.

The present paper has the four sections and proceeds as follows. Section I provides introduction with the extant literature, Section II includes the brief discussion of methodology applied for efficiency evaluation, data, description of the variables and period of analysis. Section III states the discussion and results, Section IV concludes.

Literature Review

Ahmed and Siddiqui (2020) investigated the relationship among risk management, profit efficiency using capital adequacy ratios in Pakistan banking sector using stochastic frontier analysis. In the second stage the efficiency scores are regressed with banks specific macroeconomic variables using panel data regression. Akhigbe & MC Nulty (2003), was estimated profit efficiency of small commercial banks in the United States from period 1990 to 1996. The data set included those banks having less than five hundred million dollar in total asset. The study applied stochastic frontier approach for estimating profit efficiency. For the purpose of comparison of small banks with large banks the article applied separate profit efficiency functions for small and large banks. They found that small banks are more profit efficient than large banks for the period under observations. Arbelo *et al.* (2020), examined in the framework of the Research-Based – View, the firm's performance using profit efficiency measure. They had applied a stochastic frontier model with random coefficients to evaluate the impact of corporate reputation on profit efficiency. Bos *et al.* (2009), estimated cost & profit efficiency of German savings and co-operative banks for the period 1993 to 2005. Further the study examined the impact of heterogeneity on bank efficiency levels, rank and the scales of efficiency distribution. The study found that heterogeneity influences optimal cost and profit level of banks and their ability to be efficient. Chaudhary (2014), has been reviewed the emergence of private sector banks and there gradual evolution to suit the needs of the economy. She attempted to compare the performance of private and public sector banks by considering networks, growth in balance sheet size, and growth in total set income, asset quality, efficiency of management and earnings. She explored a variety of internal and external banking characteristics predict profitability and efficiency. Her analysis indicated that high capital and loan to asset ratios lead to higher profitability. The study also reveals that everything remaining equal, implicit and explicit taxes affect the bank performance relatively, while favorable macro economic conditions impact on performance positively. Dsouza *et al.* (2022), studied the impact of banking efficiency on the profitability of the Indian banking sector. They evaluated the impact of efficiency (Cost to income ratio and Staff expenses to total expenses) on the profitability which was measured in terms of (ROA and Net interest margin). The results of the study revealed that the Cost to income ratio has a significant negative impact on the bank return, on assets and net interest margin ratio. The expenses to total expense ratio has a significant positive impact on the bank return on assets and a positive non significant impact on the bank net interest margin ratio. Duho *et al.* (2020), studied the impact of risk on pro fit efficiency and profitability of banks in Ghana. The study revealed that the banking sector in Ghana exhibits a variable return to scale property, suggesting that the average cost has been changed with output size. Jayaraman and Srinivasan (2014) measured efficiency of bank with the help of cost, revenue and profit models of DEA. According to study those banks which are closed to efficient frontier are ranked better compared to those which are away from the efficient frontier under Shannon index. Mathur (2021), evaluated the comparative performance of the selected public & Private sector banks in terms of profitability & efficiency. The present study considers 3 public sector banks and 2 private sector banks. According to the result of the study the private sector banks performed better compared to their public sector banks in terms of profitability and efficiency. Rakshit (2022), examined the effect of Cost, Revenue and Profit Efficiency on bank profitability in India's emerging economy from 1997 to 2017. The sample size of the study was seventy Indian Commercial banks. The results of the study revealed that a higher level of Cost, Revenue & efficiency significantly improves India's bank profitability. According to the study public sector banks are more cost efficient compared to private & foreign banks. On the other hand, the Macroeconomic and institutional variables had also played an important role in determining bank profitability. Singh & Thakur (2020), had estimated profit efficiency with the help of two stage analysis, Data Envelopment analysis and Bootstrap analysis. According to their study, the result revealed that the GDP growth rate growth rate and Capital Adequacy ratio were not significant, but Return on Assets, Ownership structure, number of branches and size of operations/business are significant determinants in bank efficiency.

Conceptual Framework

The profit function of a firm can be derived from the input-output relationship of a firm. In specific, a profit function of a firm is related to the technology set in the following manner.

Let us consider the technology set as

P_T = {(X, Y):X can produce Y}

Where P_T r epresents the technology set of the firm. X and Y represent the input and output vectors respectively. The technology set encompasses the input requirement set & the output set. Corresponding to the technology set, we can specify the profit function (in set theoretic format) as:

$\pi = \text{Max}\ \{(pY\text{-}wX): (X, Y) \epsilon P_T\}$

Where π represents the profit and p and w represent output & input price vectors respectively.

The profit function satisfies the following conditions:

1. It is non-increasing in w and non-decreasing in p.
   This implies that an increase in input price reduces profit and increased in output price increases profit.
2. Homogenous of degree 1 in (p and w)
   This implies that if P is replaced by λ P and w is replaced by λ W then New profit level will be λ * π where, π represent the profit level.
3. Convex and continuous in positive prices.

The Conditions for Profit Maximization

In the neo classical framework (with given input & output Prices), the total profit of the firm depends on the output level only due to the fact that the (input & output) prices remain constant during the period of analysis.

The two conditions of profit maximization are

(a) $\frac{\partial \pi}{\partial Y} = \frac{\partial R}{\partial Y} - \frac{\partial C}{\partial Y} = 0$

(b) $\frac{\partial^2 \pi}{\partial Y^2} < 0$

In the context of efficiency analysis framework, we allow for profit inefficiency i.e. observed profit can be lower than or equal to the potential level of output. The objective of an observed firm is to maximize total profit subject to the conditions that observed input uses/usage cannot be lower than the benchmark input uses/usage and the observed output level cannot be greater than the benchmark level of output. Notionally we can write,

Max π (= pY–wX)

Subject to

$X_0 \geq \lambda X,\ Y_0 \leq \lambda Y,\ \lambda \geq 0$

Under variable returns to scale, we need to add the condition $\sum_i \lambda_i = 1$

Estimation of Profit Efficiency-Description of Inputs, Outputs and Prices

We have applied quantity-based approach for evaluating profit efficiency in the present study. In the conventional profit efficiency model (the quantity-based approach) we have used deposits mobilized by the banks & the number of employees as the input indicators. Price of deposit is proxied by the interest expense per unit of deposit. Per unit employee expenses has been taken as price of employee. A total asset has been considered as output of bank and the gross income per unit of asset is considered as price of asset. Gross income includes interest income plus other income of the commercial banks.

Table 1: Input, Output and Prices

Profit Efficiency Model	*Inputs*	*Input Prices*	*Output*	*Output Prices*
Quantity Based	Deposit	Interest expenses per unit of deposit	Total Asset	Total Income/Total Asset
	Number of employees	Wages expenses per employee		

Source: Conceptualised by authors

Results & Discussions

Profit Efficiency Estimates: The Quantity Based Model

Table 2 presents the descriptive statistics of profit efficiency estimates for the period under observation. Four measures (Mean, Standard Deviation, Skewness and Kurtosis) are included. See diagram 1 for pictorial representation.

Table 2: Descriptive Statistics of Quantity Based Profit Efficiency Scores

Year	*Average*	*SD*	*Skewness*	*Kurtosis*
2005	0.391583	0.320495	1.321538	0.038827
2006	0.38539	0.244149	1.999446	3.377627
2007	0.358933	0.257063	2.009019	3.161221
2008	0.414785	0.231441	2.024504	3.495626
2009	0.582427	0.21566	1.185387	0.298178
2010	0.670757	0.167376	1.30798	0.402672
2011	0.760608	0.17777	0.468589	−1.74758
2012	0.329297	0.396583	1.157065	−0.65701
2013	0.824284	0.145953	0.164188	−1.76523
2014	0.83287	0.118692	0.33252	−1.64088
2015	0.803956	0.187651	−0.23889	−1.52633

Year	Average	SD	Skewness	Kurtosis
2016	0.812745	0.133057	0.453855	−1.52203
2017	0.78357	0.118602	0.881981	−0.37291
2018	0.746661	0.136281	0.938194	−0.1412
2019	0.722406	0.127222	1.173296	0.875722
2020	0.66109	0.176295	1.075021	0.260791
2021	0.731056	0.134686	0.597801	0.280289

Source: Author's calculation

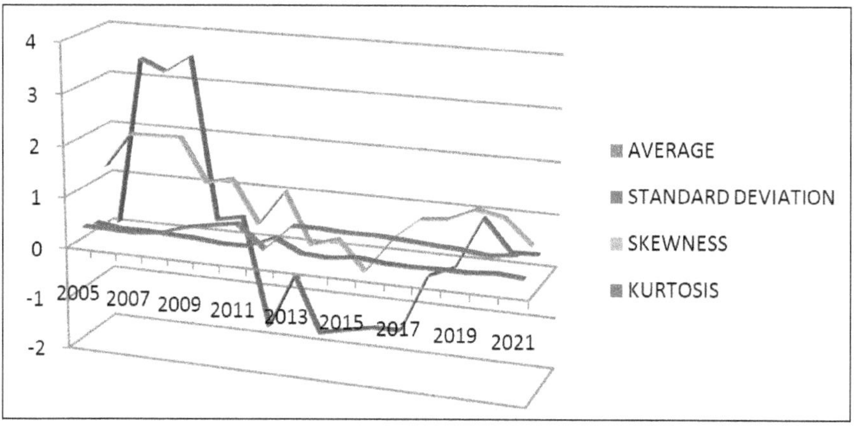

Diagram 1: Descriptive Statistics of Quantity Based Profit Efficiency Scores

Source: Table 2

Interpretation

The quantity based profit efficiency measures encompass seventeen financial years (2004–05 to 2020–21). For the first four years under observation (2004–05 to 2007–08) mean profit efficiency remained below 50%. Thereafter, profit efficiency improved during 2008–09 to 2010–11 from 58% to 68%. In 2011–12 profit efficiency remained very low (0.3293) due to a very bad performance by most of the private sector banks. There after profit efficiency improved and remained above 80% for the next four financial years (2012–13 to 2015–16). However, there was again a dip in profit efficiency for the last five observed years (2016–17 to 2020–21) as mean profit efficiency fluctuated between 0.78 and 0.73. Out of the aforementioned years (2016–17–2020–21) the last two years are witnessed of Covid outbreak. Volatility of mean efficiency (as proxied by standard deviation) remained high (low) during the year of low (high) mean efficiency. Except 2014–15, efficiency distribution had positive skewness for all other observed years. Kurtosis was negative for the period 2010–11 to 2017–18 and remained positive for the rest of the years.

Table 3: Descriptive Statistics of Quantity Based Scale Efficiency Scores

Year	*Average*	*Standard Deviation*	*Skewness*	*Kurtosis*
2005	0.697903	0.252764	–1.0875	–2.36732
2006	0.841949	0.203611	–2.10495	4.236277
2007	0.852122	0.211221	–2.27001	4.490274
2008	0.868679	0.181819	–2.27001	4.676373
2009	0.890149	0.142489	–1.88694	3.160225
2010	0.920708	0.112254	–2.08681	3.806803
2011	0.876069	0.1539	–1.00236	–0.72894
2012	0.844637	0.265967	–2.00008	3.564614
2013	0.924431	0.090646	–1.97023	4.94385
2014	0.96279	0.087475	–3.33543	11.58522
2015	0.903972	0.130103	–1.95669	4.293449
2016	0.921235	0.105264	–1.84676	2.746916
2017	0.92664	0.094297	–2.05638	4.545761
2018	0.914886	0.11242	–1.99889	3.891557
2019	0.919722	0.113419	–2.11552	4.233982
2020	0.883226	0.144458	–1.901	3.686651
2021	0.926599	0.108459	–2.36732	5.690037

Source: Author's calculation

Interpretation

In the above table between 2004–05 and 2009–10 mean scale efficiency had a secular improvement. There after mean scale efficiency exhibited a declining trend in the next two years. The mean scale efficiency remains above 90% with the exception of 2019–20 from 2012–13 to 2020–21.

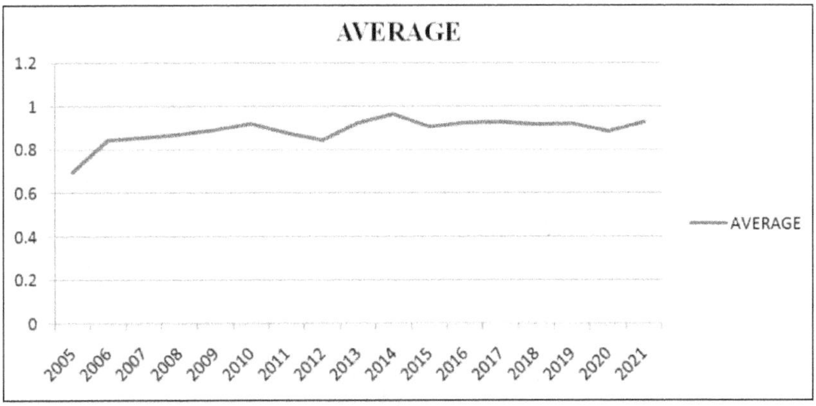

Figure 5.2: Averages of Scale Efficiency Scores

Source: Table 3

Table 4: Returns to Scale Exhibited by the Observed Banks (Quantity Based Profit Efficiency Model)

Year	*CRS*	*IRS*	*DRS*
2005	2	4	12
2006	2	16	–
2007	2	16	–
2008	2	16	–
2009	2	15	1
2010	2	16	–
2011	1	15	2
2012	10	8	–
2013	3	14	1
2014	2	15	1
2015	5	3	10
2016	3	15	–
2017	3	15	–
2018	2	16	–
2019	2	16	–
2020	2	14	2
2021	2	16	–

Source: Author's Calculation

Interpretation

Table 4 presents the return to scale statistics of the observed banks for the same period. During the period under observation, the number of banks exhibiting

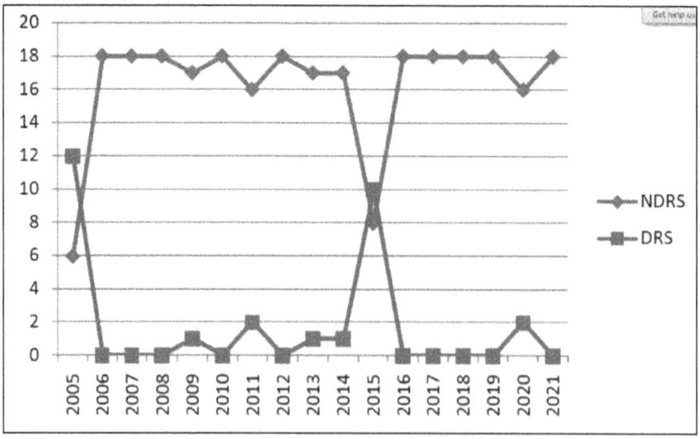

Diagram 3: Graphical Presentation

Source: Table 4

constant returns to scale varied from (5 to 2) except the year 2011–12 in which 10 out of 18 private commercial banks exhibited CRS. The number of banks exhibiting IRS varied from 4 to 16, except in 3 years (2004–05, 2011–12 & 2014–15). Most of the observed banks exhibited IRS. For ten out of the seventeen observed years no bank exhibited decreasing returns to scale. The proportion of the banks exhibiting DRS remains relatively high for 2004–05 and 2014–15.Diagram 3 provides a graphical presentation.

The Impact of Global Financial Crisis on Profit Efficiency

An important research question is included in our research study whether global financial crisis of 2007–08 and 2008–09 had any impact on private bank profit efficiency. For this we have compared the efficiency scores of the observed bank for two periods: 2004–05 to 2008–09 (Period 1) and 2009–10 to 2013–14 (Period 2). Note that the first two periods includes the two crisis years 2007–08 and 2008–09. For this purpose we have used paired t test. The table no. 5.7 below presented the results of paired t test.

Table 5: Impact of Global Meltdown (Using paired t test)

Particulars	*Mean*	*Standard Error*	*Standard Deviation*	*Lower Bound (95% confidence Level)*	*Upper Bound (95% confidence Level)*
Period 1 (2005–2009)	.4266236	.0277289	.2630596	.3715269	.4817204
Period2 (2010–2014)	.6835631	.0304265	.2886511	.6231063	.7440199
Difference	–.2569395	.0312789	.2967374	–.3190899	–.194789
Observed t	8.2145				
Degree of freedom	89				
Two sided test H_0:mean (diff) =0 against H_a: mean (diff)	Pr(|T|)> |t|) = 0.0000 implying the null hypothesis is to be rejected				
One sided test- H_0:mean (diff) =0 against H_a: mean (diff) > 0	Pr(T>t)= 1.0000 implying that null hypothesis is to be accepted				
One sided test- H_0:mean (diff) =0 against H_a: mean (diff) < 0	Pr(T<t)= 0.0000 implying that null hypothesis is to be rejected				

Source: Author's Calculation

From the above table, we find that mean profit efficiency of the commercial banks in period 2 have substantially higher than that in period 1. The null hypothesis that both period exhibits same mean efficiency is rejected on the basis of the results of t test.

On the other hand in order to assess the impact of global financial crisis on profit efficiency we have considered a ten year observation from 2004–05 to 2013–14. The period has been divided into two sub period 2004–05 to 2008–09 and 2009–10 to 2013–14. We have included period dummy (0 for first sub period and 1 for second sub period) in addition to the contextual variables used previously. We have been regressed quantity–based estimates on the contextual variable.

Table 6: Impact of Global Meltdown under Quantity Based Model

	Coefficient	*Std. Error*	*t-ratio*	*p-value*	
Const	–0.4405	0.0195	–22.56	<0.0001	***
Period Dummy	0.1918	0.0391	4.909	0.0001	***

Source: Author's calculation

The table 6 shows that the impact of period dummy is positive and statistically significant.

Regression of Pure Profit Efficiency on the Contextual Variables under Quantity Based Model

Table 7: Pure Profit Efficiency

Particulars	*Coefficient*	*Std. Error*	*t-ratio*	*p-value*	
Intercept	–1.51663	0.314665	–4.820	0.0002	***
Capital Adequacy Ratio	0.0098	0.0027	3.598	0.0022	***
NPA Ratio	0.0022	0.0109	0.2065	0.8388	
Log TA	0.2410	0.0634	3.803	0.0014	***

Source: Author's calculation

Interpretation

In table 7 we have presented the relationship of pure profit efficiency with Capital Adequacy ratio, Net NPA ratio and log of Total Asset in terms of Panel Data model. To be more specific a fixed effect Panel data model was selected on the basis of outcome of Hausman test. Since we are dealing with profit efficiency estimate, Return on equity has been dropped from the list of contextual variables.

Initially we have considered both fixed effect and random effect models. However, the application of Hausman test indicates that a fixed effect model is more appropriate in the present context. The table shows that the coefficients of all three contextual variables are positive. Further, the coefficients of both capital adequacy and log of total asset are statistically significant.

Table 8: Scale Efficiency

	Coefficient	*Std. Error*	*t-ratio*	*p-value*
Intercept	−0.490475	0.194160	−2.526	0.0218
Capital Adequacy Ratio	−0.00223362	0.00141819	−1.575	0.1337
NPA Ratio	−0.00793418	0.00779567	−1.018	0.3231
Log TA	0.102242	0.0401960	2.544	0.0210

Source: Author's calculation

In another Table 8 we have presented the relationship between scale efficiency and the aforementioned contextual variable. The table indicates that scale efficiency is positively related to bank size. However, the coefficients of the other two variables are not statistically significant.

Conclusion

The researchers have ranked the commercial banks in terms of profit efficiency and estimates scale efficiency. For estimating efficiency, we have considered quantity-based model in which the input and output prices faced by the observed banks are considered to be given and they can vary across firms. We have also considered the impact of contextual variables on profit efficiency results for quantity-based model. In the quantity-based model, the impact of capital adequacy and bank size are significant on the profit efficiency. However, the impact of net NPA ratio is not significant. On the scale efficiency only size is found to be significant.

References

[1] Akhigbe, A. and Stevenson, B.A. (2010). Profit efficiency in U.S. BHCs: Effects of increasing non-traditional revenue sources. *The Quarterly Review of Economics and Finance* 50.132–140.

[2] Ahmed, M. and Siddiqui, D.A. (2020). Profit Efficiency and Risk Management in the Banking Sector of Pakistan: A Comparative Analysis using Stochastic Frontier Approach. *Social Science Research Network.*

[3] Arbelo, A., Perez, A.M. and Gomez, P.P. (2020). Profit Efficiency as a Measure of Performance and Frontier Models: A Research Based View, *Business Research Quarterly, Sage Publications,* 24(2).

[4] Bos, J.W.B., Koetter, M., Kolari, J.W. and Kool, C.J.M. (2009). Effects of heterogeneity on bank efficiency scores. *European Journal of Operational Research* 195(1): 251–261.

[5] Chaudhary, G. (2014). Performance comparison of Private Sector Banks with the Public Sector Banks in India. *International Journal of Emerging Research in Management and Technology.* 3(2). 5–12.

[6] Duho, T, C.K., Onumah, R.A.O., Emmanuel, T.A. and Regina, M.O. (2020). Bank risk, Profit Efficiency& Profitability in a Frontier Market. *Journal of Economic & Administrative Sciences*, 36(4).

[7] Dsouza, S., Rabbani, R., M.,Howladar, T.I. and Jain, K.A. (2022). Impact of Bank Efficiency on the Profitability of the Banks in India: An Empirical Analysis Using Panel Data Approach, *International Journal of Financial Studies.*

[8] Jayaraman, A.R. and Srinivasan M.R. (2014). Performance Evaluation of Banks in India—A Shannon DEA Approach. *Eurasian Journal of Business and Economics,* 7(13). 5–68.

[9] Mathur, R. (2021). Profitability and Efficiency of Indian Banking (A Comparative Study of Selected Public and Private Sector Banks). *SIBM Pune Research Journal,* XXIII. 23–36.

[10] Rakshit, B. (2022). Assessing the effects of Cost, Revenue and Profit efficiency on Bank performance: Empirical evidence from Indian Banking. *International journal of Organizational Analysis.*

[11] Singh, P.K. and Thakur, K. (2020). Profit efficiency and determinants of Indian banks: A truncated bootstrap and Data Envelopment Analysis. *Cogent-economics and finance.* 8(1), 1–25.

A Comparative Financial Performance Analysis between Muthoot Finance Ltd. and Manappuram Finance Ltd.

Ram Ranjan Routh[1] **and Jaba Rani Patta**[2]

ABSTRACT: Gold has sentimental and social importance in India. In India gold has been used as collateral asset for money lending business for centuries. Nowadays organized gold loan business is one of the developing lending business segments for Non-Banking Financial Companies (NBFCs) and Banks in India. In the last decade, the organised sector has experienced record growth. Muthoot Finance Ltd. and Manappuram Finance Ltd provide gold loans on extremely easy terms and conditions to people of each segment of the society. So, the present study aims to compare the comparative study on financial performance of Muthoot Finance Ltd. and Manappuram Finance Ltd. over the ten years from 2014 to 2023. For this study financial ratios are used to evaluate financial performance of the two companies namely Muthoot Finance Ltd. and Manappuram Finance Ltd. who are in similar business operating under a parallel business environment. The study shows that Muthoot Finance Ltd. has performed better than Manappuram Finance Ltd.

Keywords: Financial Performance, Gold Loan, Manappuram, Muthoot, Non-Bank Financial Companies.

Introduction

The Non-Banking Financial Companies (NBFC) industry is witnessing steady growth, with the overall loan book consisting of retail and other wholesale loans (including infrastructure loans) projected to increase by approximately 13%. The Reserve Bank of India (RBI) has acknowledged NBFCs' efforts in reaching out to individuals who were previously underserved by the financial sector. To achieve the projected growth, NBFCs are expected to focus on new business areas such as unsecured loans and the Small and Medium-sized Enterprises (SME) segment, which offer higher growth prospects compared to traditional products. The NBFC-Retail sector's Assets Under Management are projected to grow at a rate of 12–14% in FY24.

---

[1] Assistant Professor, Department of Commerce, Kharagpur College, Kharagpur, West Bengal, India. E-mail: ramranjan.routh@gmail.com

[2] Assistant Professor, Department of Commerce, AKPC Mahavidyalaya, Bengai, Hooghly, India. E-mail: jabarani.routh@gmail.com

NBFCs are leveraging technology to enable faster paperless disbursals and expanding their reach to a wider audience. They are also concentrating on improving asset quality and profitability. Collaboration through technology is becoming common among NBFCs to offer a diverse range of products, benefiting smaller and mid-sized NBFCs to grow alongside established ones. Asset quality has shown improvement compared to the pre-pandemic period, as many NBFCs wrote off bad loans. Although new write-offs will be moderate compared to historical levels, the overall industry's Provision Coverage Ratio has been steadily improving over the last two years.

Gold has sentimental and a significant position in Indian society as a foundation of wealth and savings. However, evolving consumer preferences and globalization necessitate a comprehensive reassessment of the associated issues. India stands as one of the largest gold markets globally, with increasing affluence driving the demand for gold. In Q2 of FY23, global gold demand rose by 4% year-on-year to 453 tonnes, driven by a remarkable 49% surge in India's demand compared to Q2 FY22. The Indian gold industry contributes 1.3% to the national GDP and is mainly composed of small and medium enterprises. The domestic market is predominantly driven by cultural, wedding, and festive demand. In India gold has been used as collateral asset for money lending business for centuries. Nowadays organized gold loan business is one of the developing lending business segments for Non-Banking Financial Companies (NBFCs) and Banks in India. In the last decade, the organised sector has experienced record growth. Though there are many NBFCs in India that offer gold loans, Muthoot Finance, Manappuram Finance, and Muthoot Fincorp, all based in Kerala, handle about 95% of the gold loan market. In this context, the present study aims to compare the comparative study on financial performance of Muthoot Finance Ltd. and Manappuram Finance Ltd.

Review of Literature

The results from the notable studies that have been carried out are briefly mentioned below: Singh, A.B. & Tandon, P. (2012), in their study "A Study of Financial Performance: A Comparative Analysis of SBI and ICICI Bank". The study showed that SBI is performing well and financially sound as compared to ICICI bank, but in context of deposits and expenditure ICICI bank has better managing efficiency than SBI. R. Sowndharya and Dr.R.Shanmugam (2014), in their study "Analysis of Financial Performance of Non-Banking Financial Companies in India" in the Indian Journal of Applied Research this research paper includes Non-Banking Financial Companies, profitability, liquidity, leverage, Interest Coverage, Risk Indicator ratios. This study shows the selected NBFCs differ significantly in terms of profitability and leverage indicators. Karri, H.K.; Meghani, K.; & Mishra, B.M. (2015), in their study "A Comparative Study on Financial Performance of Public Sector Banks in India: An Analysis on Camel

Model". Bank of Baroda (BOB) and Punjab National Bank (PNB) were considered as sample size for the study. CAMEL model and t-test applied for data analysis purpose. Results showed that out of 14 ratios used in the CAMEL model the average figures of Bank of Baroda is the best for (6 ratios) followed by Punjab National Bank (5 ratios). Thus, it is recognized that Bank of Baroda is the best bank in the selected public sector banks. Chavali, K. & Rosario, S. (2018), in their study "Relationship between capital structure and profitability: A study of nonbanking Finance Companies in India" investigates the relationship between NBFCs' capital structure and their net profit, return on capital employed, return on equity, return on assets, and interest coverage ratio. The study found Non-Banking Finance Companies are vital to the financial system. Dutta, P., Jain, A., & Gupta, A. (2020), in their study "Performance analysis of non-banking finance companies using two-stage data envelopment analysis" performed a data envelopment analysis on Indian NBFC performance (DEA). The study found that a positive correlation was estimated between financial efficiency and profitability. There was no correlation between social effectiveness and voluntary disclosure rate. This article contributed to the academic literature by identifying new factors that influence voluntary disclosure. A large number of comparative studies of various companies have been conducted. The structured gold loan company is now one of the fastest-growing lending segments for Non-Banking Financial Companies (NBFCs) and banks in India. Though there are many NBFCs in India that offer gold loans, Muthoot Finance and Manappuram Finance, all based in Kerala, handle about 95% of the gold loan market. In this context, the present study is an attempt to understand the comparative study on financial performance of Muthoot Finance Ltd. and Manappuram Finance Ltd.

Objective of The Study

To analyse and compare the financial performance of Muthoot Financial Ltd. and Manappuram Finance Ltd.

Hypothesis

The following hypothesis has been formulated:

H0: There is no significant difference between the financial performance of Muthoot Finance Ltd. and Manappuram Finance Ltd.

H1: There is a significant difference between the financial performance of Muthoot Finance Ltd. and Manappuram Finance Ltd.

Database and Methodology

The study is mainly based on secondary data. Data are collected from the published annual reports of the selected companies and Ace Equity database. Listed two gold loan non-banking financial companies i.e., Muthoot Finance Ltd.

and Manappuram Finance Ltd. are considered as samples for the study. The study covered a period of ten years starting from the financial year 2014 to 2023.

Overview of Companies

Muthoot Finance Limited

As India's leading gold loan company, they have the largest loan portfolio and their focus has consistently been on extending financial services to segments of society that have remained underserved or overlooked. Their lending operations revolve around utilising 'Household Used Gold Ornaments' (HUGO) as collateral, eschewing any dealings in gold bullion—their commitment centres on comprehending the unique needs of individuals facilitating swift access to funds. They go the extra mile by offering secure, insured lockers for pledged gold, accompanied by a transparent disclosure of lending rates and associated loan charges at the outset, ensuring complete clarity and comprehension. Their ethos remains rooted in honesty, free from concealed fees or undisclosed additional charges. Their services embrace digital innovation and encompass online gold loans, convenient loan withdrawals, seamless renewals, interest payments, and loan repayments. Their user-friendly mobile app, iMuthoot, and the Muthoot online platform facilitate these services

Manappuram Finance Limited

Manappuram Finance Limited is a renowned Non-Banking Financial Company (NBFC) serving the credit requirements of people belonging to the lower socio-economic classes, particularly in rural and semi-urban areas of India. The Company offers a range of retail credit products and financial services. The Company has a diversified lending portfolio encompassing retail, microfinance, SME and commercial customers. It has been the second-largest gold finance NBFC in India. The Company offers credit against the security of used household gold jewellery (henceforth referred as gold loan). The Company's short-term gold loan product has been availed largely by customers who are requiring immediate funds and may not have access to other types of formal credit readily available. Their Micro finance subsidiary, Asirvad Microfinance Limited, an authorized and regulated NBFC-MFI by the Reserve Bank of India, provides microfinance loans and other financial services to low-income rural and semi-urban communities from its Branches spread across pan India. Their subsidiary, Manappuram Home Finance Limited, the Company provides loans to customers in the affordable housing market for home building, extension, purchase, and improvement. The third subsidiary, Manappuram Insurance Brokers Limited, offers life and non-life insurance products. via partnerships with numerous top insurance firms. The recently purchased Manappuram Comtech and Consultants Limited provides cost-effective and high-quality IT solutions with over two decades of experience.

Methodology

CAMEL Rating Model, Financial Ratio and Mean are used to analyze and compare the financial performance of listed selected gold loan non-banking financial companies in India. In India, the CAMEL rating model was introduced in 1995 on the recommendation of the former RBI governor, Mr. Padmanabhan. Under the CAMEL rating system, five metrics are used to rate every bank or financial institution-capital adequacy, asset quality, management quality, earnings quality and liquidity. Firm's Capital Adequacy Segment has been analyzed with the help of Capital Adequacy Ratio (CAR) and Asset Quality Segment is measured by Net NPA Ratio. Management Efficiency Segment is measured by Total Expenses/Total Revenue Ratio. Firm's Earnings Segment has been analyzed with the help of Return on assets (ROA), Return on Equity (ROE), Profit After Tax Margin (PATM) and Market value to Book value (M/B) and Liquidity Segment is measures by Current ratio.

Findings

In order to compare the financial performance of Muthoot Financial Ltd. and Manappuram Finance Ltd., we have calculated the capital adequacy, asset quality, management quality, earnings quality and liquidity which are depicted in the following:

Capital Adequacy Segment

Firm's Capital Adequacy Segment has been analyzed with the help of Capital Adequacy Ratio (CAR). This ratio indicates the risk-taking ability of banks. This ratio is an indicator of risk absorbing capacity by financial institutions on account of risky assets. The higher the ratio better is the financial health of the institution.

Table 1

Capital adequacy Ratio														
Company Name	2014	2015	2016	2017	2018	2019	2020	2021	2022	2023	MIN	MAX	Mean	Rank
Muthoot Finance Ltd	24.69	24.78	24.48	24.88	26.26	26.05	25.47	27.39	29.97	31.77	24.48	31.77	26.57	2
Manappuram Finance Ltd	27.68	25.64	24.00	26.12	26.96	23.81	21.74	29.02	31.33	31.70	21.74	31.70	26.80	1

Source: Computed by authors

From Table 1 it is found that the average Capital Adequacy Ratio (CAR) of Muthoot Finance is 26.57. They have the highest Capital Adequacy Ratio (CAR) in 2023 and lowest in 2016. But in case of Manappuram the average Capital Adequacy Ratio (CAR) is 26.80. CAR is highest in 2023 and lowest in 2020.

Manappuram Finance Ltd. has a higher Capital Adequacy Ratio (Mean 26.80%, Rank 1) and is followed by Muthoot Finance Ltd. (Mean 26.57%, Rank 2). Manappuram Finance Ltd. is having higher safety and risk absorbing capacity as compared to Muthoot Finance Ltd. According to Capital Adequacy segment Manappuram Finance Ltd. (Ranks 1) is better financial health compared to Muthoot Finance Ltd. (Rank 2)

Asset Quality Segment

Asset Quality Segment is measured by Net NPA Ratio. This ratio is an indicator of the quality of the assets of banks. It indicates the proportion of NPA of Net Advances. Lower the ratio better is the asset quality.

Table 2

Net non performing assets (%)														
Company Name	2014	2015	2016	2017	2018	2019	2020	2021	2022	2023	MIN	MAX	Mean	Rank
Muthoot Finance Ltd	1.57	1.88	2.46	1.69	3.76	2.35	1.93	0.88	2.99	3.79	0.88	3.79	2.33	2
Manappuram Finance Ltd	1.01	0.97	0.70	1.70	0.33	0.32	0.47	1.53	2.72	1.15	0.32	2.72	1.09	1

Source: Computed by authors

From the Table 2 it is found that the average Net NPA Ratio of the Muthoot Finance is 2.33. They have highest Net NPA Ratio in 2023 and lowest in 2021. But in case of Manappuram the average Net NPA Ratio is 1.09. Net NPA Ratio is highest in 2022 and lowest in 2019.

Manappuram Finance Ltd. maintains lower ratio (Mean 1.09%, Rank 1), and higher asset quality as compared to Muthoot Finance Ltd. (Mean 2.33%, Rank 2). According to Asset Quality Segment Manappuram Finance Ltd. (Ranks 1) is better asset quality compared to Muthoot Finance Ltd. (Rank 2).

Management Efficiency Segment

Management Efficiency Segment is measured by Total Expenses/Total Revenue Ratio.

Total Expenses/Total Revenue Ratio

Total Expenses/Total Revenue Ratio are very important in determining the management efficiency. The ratio gives stakeholders a clear view of how efficiently the firm is running. Lower the ratio, the company will be more profitable and efficient.

Table 3

Total expenditure/Total Income (%)														
Company Name	2014	2015	2016	2017	2018	2019	2020	2021	2022	2023	MIN	MAX	Mean	Rank
Muthoot Finance Ltd	21.94	25.54	25.46	25.74	23.84	22.07	20.94	17.19	17.03	20.01	17.03	25.74	21.98	1
Manappuram Finance Ltd	32.26	32.42	34.27	27.68	35.46	32.78	25.91	20.20	29.22	30.51	20.20	35.46	30.07	2

Source: Computed by authors

From Table 3 it is found that the average Total Expenses/Total Revenue Ratio (TE/TI) of Muthoot Finance is 21.98. They have the highest Total Expenses/Total Revenue Ratio in 2017 and lowest in 2022. But in case of Manappuram the average Total Expenses/Total Revenue Ratio is 30.07. Total Expenses/Total Revenue Ratio is highest in 2018 and lowest in 2021.

Muthoot Finance Ltd. (Mean Rs. 21.98%, Rank 1), have a lower ratio; it implies that management is efficiently and effectively working, which improves the profitability as compared to Manappuram Finance Ltd. (Mean 30.07%, Rank 2). According to Management Efficiency Segment Muthoot Finance Ltd. (Ranks 1) is more profitable and efficient compare to Manappuram Finance Ltd. (Rank 2).

Earnings Segment

Firm's Earnings Segment has been analyzed with the help of Return on assets (ROA), Return on Equity (ROE), Profit after Tax Margin (PATM) and Market value to Book value (M/B).

Return on Assets (ROA)

Return on assets indicates the effectiveness of the company's assets in increasing the shareholders' earnings. ROA is measured by dividing Earnings before interest & taxes (EBIT) by its total assets. It is an indicator of how profitable a company is managing its investment in assets. Higher the percentage is efficient, because the company is doing a good job using its assets to generate profit and lower is indicating inefficiency.

Table 4

Return on Assets (ROA)														
Company Name	2014	2015	2016	2017	2018	2019	2020	2021	2022	2023	MIN	MAX	Mean	Rank
Muthoot Finance Ltd	2.79	2.53	2.97	4.02	5.72	5.73	6.82	6.54	5.90	4.86	2.53	6.82	4.79	1
Manappuram Finance Ltd	1.92	2.45	2.91	5.82	4.99	4.92	5.96	6.89	4.97	4.51	1.92	6.89	4.53	2

Source: Computed by authors

From Table 4 it is found that the average Return on Assets (ROA) of Muthoot Finance is 4.79. They have the highest ROA in 2020 and lowest in 2015. But in case of Manappuram the average Return on assets (ROA) is 4.53. ROA is highest in 2021 and lowest in 2014. Muthoot Finance Ltd. (4.79%, Rank 1) having higher ratio and managing efficiently their assets to generate profit as compared to Manappuram Finance Ltd. (4.53%, Rank 2).

Return on Equity (ROE)

Return on equity measures a company's profitability revealing how much profit a company generated with the money that shareholders have invested. It is the relationship between profit after tax and net worth. Higher ratio indicates equities in increasing the value of shareholder's wealth by management.

Table 5

Return on Equity (ROE)														
Company Name	2014	2015	2016	2017	2018	2019	2020	2021	2022	2023	MIN	MAX	Mean	Rank
Muthoot Finance Ltd	19.53	14.39	15.19	19.52	24.88	22.45	28.29	27.79	23.56	17.63	14.39	28.29	21.32	1
Manappuram Finance Ltd	9.16	10.58	12.57	24.01	19.41	19.40	25.48	27.87	17.61	14.99	9.16	27.87	18.11	2

Source: Computed by authors

From Table 5 it is found that the average Return on Equity (ROE) of Muthoot Finance is 21.32. They have the highest ROE in 2020 and lowest in 2015. But in case of Manappuram the average Return on Equity (ROE) is 18.11. ROE is highest in 2021 and lowest in 2014.

Muthoot Finance Ltd. (21.32%, Rank 1) generates higher ROE, it implies higher efficiency in generating income on shareholder's wealth as compared to Manappuram Finance Ltd. (18.11%, Rank 2).

Profit after Tax Margin (PATM)

Table 6

PATM (%)														
Company Name	2014	2015	2016	2017	2018	2019	2020	2021	2022	2023	MIN	MAX	Mean	Rank
Muthoot Finance Ltd	15.83	15.54	16.65	20.60	28.37	28.67	34.63	35.26	35.68	33.03	15.54	35.68	26.43	1
Manappuram Finance Ltd	10.76	13.70	15.24	24.14	23.54	23.12	28.54	32.83	28.59	26.37	10.76	32.83	22.68	2

Source: Computed by authors

From Table 6 it is found that the average Profit After Tax Margin (PATM) of Muthoot Finance is 26.43. They have the highest PATM in 2022 and lowest in 2015. But in case of Manappuram the average Profit After Tax Margin (PATM) is 22.68. PATM is highest in 2021 and lowest in 2014. Muthoot Finance Ltd. (26.43%, Rank 1) generates higher PATM, it implies higher efficiency in generating profit as compared to Manappuram Finance Ltd. (22.68%, Rank 2).

Market value to Book value (M/B)

The market-to-book ratio seeks to evaluate whether a company's stock is over or undervalued by comparing the market price of all outstanding shares with the net assets of the company. The ratio determines the market value of a company relative to its actual worth. Investors and analysts use this comparison ratio to differentiate between the true value of a publicly-traded company and investor speculation. If the market value of a company is trading higher than its book value per share, it is considered to be overvalued. If the book value is higher than the market value, analysts consider the company to be undervalued. The market-to-book ratio is used to compare a company's net asset value or book value to its current or market value. A market-to-book ratio above 1, means that the company's stock is overvalued. A ratio below 1 indicates that it may be undervalued.

Table 7

Market Value to Book Value Ratio (MVBV)														
Company Name	2014	2015	2016	2017	2018	2019	2020	2021	2022	2023	MIN	MAX	Mean	Rank
Muthoot Finance Ltd	1.50	1.64	1.27	2.27	2.09	2.52	2.12	3.18	2.91	1.87	1.27	3.18	2.14	1
Manappuram Finance Ltd	0.73	1.04	1.07	2.49	2.43	2.41	1.51	1.83	1.21	1.17	0.73	2.49	1.59	2

Source: Computed by authors

From Table 7 it is found that the average Market value to Book value (M/B) of Muthoot Finance is 2.14. They have the highest M/B in 2021 and lowest in 2016. But in Manappuram the average M/B is 1.59. M/B is highest in 2017 and lowest in 2014.

Although both the company's market value is higher than the book value, still Muthoot Finance Ltd. (2.14%, Rank 1) generates higher M/B, it implies the company's stock is overvalued as compared to Manappuram Finance Ltd. (1.59%, Rank 2).

According to four sub parameters of Earnings segment as per Table 8 Muthoot Finance Ltd. (Rank 1) is having higher earnings capitalized and optimally using their assets, capital employed and shareholders' equity to generate higher level return, generating more profit and stock is overvalued as compared to Manappuram Finance Ltd. (Rank 2).

Table 8

Earnings Segment							
Sl. No.	*Company Name*	*Return on Assets*	*Return on Equity*	*Profit After Tax Margin (PATM)*	*Market Value to Book Value*	*Mean*	*Segment*
		Rank	*Rank*	*Rank*	*Rank*	*Rank*	*Rank*
1.	Muthoot Finance Ltd.	1	1	1	1	1	1
2.	Manappuram Finance Ltd.	2	2	2	2	2	2

Source: Computed by authors

Liquidity Segment

Liquidity means a firm's ability to meet claims and obligations as and when they become due. It refers to the capacity of meeting current liabilities. As current liabilities are met out of current assets, if the amount of current assets increases the liquidity position of the firm becomes improved. It is essential for smoothly conducting business activities. Liquidity Segment is measured by Current ratio. This ratio indicates the proportion of current assets in the current Liabilities. The NBFC with more liquid assets can meet its customer demand and emergencies. A higher ratio is desirable.

Table 9

Current Ratio														
Company Name	2014	2015	2016	2017	2018	2019	2020	2021	2022	2023	MIN	MAX	Mean	Rank
Muthoot Finance Ltd	1.83	1.89	1.75	1.54	1.96	1.98	1.91	2.31	2.81	3.35	1.54	3.35	2.13	1
Manappuram Finance Ltd	1.57	1.53	1.39	1.58	1.52	1.41	2.10	3.54	2.49	3.14	1.39	3.54	2.03	2

Source: Computed by authors

From Table 9 it is found that the average Current ratio of Muthoot Finance is 2.13. They have the highest Current ratio in 2023 and lowest in 2017. But in case of Manappuram the average Current ratio is 2.03. Current ratio is highest in 2021 and lowest in 2016.

Muthoot Finance Ltd. (2.13, Rank 1) is maintaining a higher ratio; it implies that Muthoot maintains adequate funds to meet its short-term obligations and has a sound liquidity position as compared to Manappuram Finance Ltd. (2.03, Rank 2). According to Liquidity Segment Muthoot Finance Ltd. (Ranks 1) is more liquid assets compared to Manappuram Finance Ltd. (Rank 2).

Overall Ranking

Table 10

Company Name	*Capital Adequacy*	*Asset Quality*	*Management Efficiency*	*Earnings*	*Liquidity*	*Overall Ranking of All Segments*	
	Rank	*Rank*	*Rank*	*Rank*	*Rank*	*Mean*	*Rank*
Muthoot Finance Ltd.	2	2	1	1	1	1.4	1
Manappuram Finance Ltd.	1	1	2	2	2	1.6	

Source: Computed by authors

According to eight sub parameters of 5 categories i.e., Capital Adequacy, Asset Quality, Management Efficiency, Earning and Liquidity segment as per Table 10 Muthoot Finance Ltd. Ranks 1 and Manappuram Finance Ltd. Ranks 2. Muthoot Finance Ltd. has top ranking in Management Efficiency Segment, Earnings Segment and Liquidity Segment. But Manappuram Finance Ltd. has top ranking in Capital Adequacy Segment and Assets Quality Segment. It implied that Manappuram Finance Ltd. is well capitalized and has greater capability to absorb negative shocks and lowest nonperforming assets. The management of Muthoot Finance is very efficient in terms of managing lower total expenses/total income ratio. Earnings of Muthoot as compared to Manappuram Are higher, which implies efficient use of assets, higher returns on shareholder's funds, earning higher profit and higher market value of share and also having sufficient funds to manage the short-term liquidity requirements.

Conclusion

The present study is an attempt to analyse and compare the financial performance of Muthoot Financial Ltd. and Manappuram Finance Ltd. The study covered a period of ten years starting from the financial year 2014 to 2023. CAMEL Rating Model, Financial Ratio and Mean are used to analyze and compare the financial performance of listed selected gold loan non-banking financial companies in India. Under the CAMEL rating system, five metrics are used i.e., capital adequacy, asset quality, management quality, earnings quality and liquidity. Firm's Capital Adequacy Segment has been analyzed with the help of Capital Adequacy Ratio (CAR) and the Asset Quality Segment is measured by Net NPA

Ratio. Management Efficiency Segment is measured by Total Expenses/Total Revenue Ratio and Asset Turnover Ratio. Firm's Earnings Segment has been analyzed with the help of Return on Assets (ROA), Return on Equity (ROE), Profit After Tax Margin (PATM) and Market value to Book value (M/B) and Liquidity Segment is measured by Current ratio.

The study shows that Muthoot Finance Ltd. has performed better than Manappuram Finance Ltd. Under the CAMEL rating system, it is found that Muthoot Finance Ltd. has top ranking in Management Efficiency Segment, Earnings Segment and Liquidity Segment. But Manappuram Finance Ltd. has top ranking in Capital Adequacy Segment and Assets Quality Segment. It implies that Manappuram Finance Ltd. is well capitalized and has greater capability to absorb negative shocks and lowest nonperforming assets. The management of Muthoot Finance is very efficient in terms of managing lower total expenses/total income ratio. Earnings of Muthoot as compared to Manappuram are higher, which implies that efficient use of assets, higher returns on shareholder's funds, earning higher profit and higher market value of share and also having sufficient funds to manage the short-term liquidity requirements.

From the above findings, it is recommended that Muthoot Finance Ltd. should change their credit appraisal mechanism to improve the qualities of assets and reduce their non-performing assets that can improve their financial health. Whereas Manappuram Finance Ltd. should improve the management efficiency and earning capacity by reducing their operational cost and efficient use of assets and also improve their funds to manage the short-term liquidity requirements. This study and its result are helpful to the policy makers when they decide on their regulatory framework in which these companies operate.

References

[1] Chavali, K. and Rosario, S. (2018). Relationship between capital structure and profitability: A study of nonbanking Finance Companies in India. *Academy of Accounting and Financial Studies Journal,* 22(1), 1–8.

[2] Dhanabhakyam, D. and Kavitha, M. (2012). Financial Performance of Selected Public Sector Banks in India. *International Journal of Multidisciplinary Research,* 2(1), 255–269.

[3] Dutta, P., Jain, A. and Gupta, A. (2020). Performance analysis of non-banking finance companies using two-stage data envelopment analysis. *Annals of Operations Research,* 295, 91–116.

[4] Karri, H.K., Meghani, K. and Mishra, B.M. (2015). A Comparative Study on Financial Performance of Public Sector Banks in India: An Analysis on Camel Model. *Arabian Journal of Business and Management Review (OMAN Chapter),* 4(8), 18–34.

[5] Singh, A.B. and Tandon, P. (2012). A Study of Financial Performance: A Comparative Analysis of SBI and ICICI Bank. *International Journal of Marketing, Financial Services & Management Research,* 1(11), 56–71.

[6] Singla, V. (2013). Analysis of Productivity of Indian Banks: A Comparative Study of Selected Private Banks. *International Journal of Computing and Business Research,* 4(2).

[7] Tandon, M., Anjum, B. and Julee (2014). A Study on Financial Performance of Selected Indian Banks. *International Journal of Research in Management,* Science & Technology, 2(3), 81–92.

[8] Shanmugam, R.S. (2014). Analysis of Financial Performance of Non-Banking Financial Companies in India. *Indian journal of Applied Research this research,* 4(12).

Factors Affecting Benefits Paid by Indian Public and Private Life Insurance Companies

Tusar Kanti Ghorai[1], Jagabandhu Mandal[2] and Arup Kumar Sarkar[3]

ABSTRACT: Human life is full of uncertainty and the idea of insurance was created for the security of human life. Now-a-days, insurance is not only a risk management mechanism but also an investment platform. In this backdrop, the study makes an enquiry into the benefits paid by the Life Insurance Companies in India. Some important parameters like Life Insurance Premium Income, Investment Income of Life Insurers, Commission Expenses of Life Insurers, Operating Expenses of Life Insurers, Benefits paid by Life Insurers, Profit After Tax and New Life Insurance Policy Issued by Life Insurers has been used to assess the insurance industry from 2001–02 to 2020–21. To come to the findings and conclusion the study has used different statistical and econometric tools and techniques such as Trend Analysis, ADF test for stationarity, Correlation Matrix and Granger Causality Test has been used to the study of factor effectiveness of variable. The study finds that after liberalization the benefit amount paid by the public insurance company significantly higher than private company but services of the private company and investment decision are significantly changes after 2010–11. The Effectiveness of the factors and correlation metrics of the maximum factor significantly determine benefit paid by Insurance Company. Pairwise Granger Causality Tests represent dependent independent relationship between Benefit paid by Insurance Company and Investment Income in case of Public is no causality between the variable. In case of Private Insurance Unidirectional causality runs from benefits paid by the Life Insurance to Investment Income. In case of public sector, Investment of the insurance company is not significantly determined but in case of private sector it is significantly determined.

Keywords: Benefit Paid by Insurance Company, Investment Income, Private Insurance, Public Insurance.

---

[1] State Aided College Teacher (Category-I), Department of Commerce, Uluberia College affiliated to the University of Calcutta, West Bengal, India. E-mail: tusarkantighorai2015@gmail.com

[2] Assistant Professor, Department of Economics, Subarnarekha Mahavidyalaya affiliated to the Vidyasagar University, West Bengal, India. E-mail: jmbandhu9@gmail.com

[3] Assistant Professor, Department of Commerce, Uluberia College Affiliated to the University of Calcutta, West Bengal, India. E-mail: arupvu86@gmail.com

Introduction

Insurance is the agreement through which an individual or organization receives financial preservation for losses from an Insurer. An organisation or institution that provides insurance services is called Insurer. Individual or organization that purchases insurance is called Policyholder. On January 19, 1956 the life insurance sector in India was nationalized and on September 1, 1956 Life Insurance Corporation of India (LIC) was created. Before economic liberalization LIC was the only institution in the insurance sector. As a result the LIC would have a monopoly on Indian insurance sector. But at the time of late 1990s when the door of insurance sector had opened for private company, the LIC need to compete with this private company. Currently LIC is the largest and only public sector company (holding almost 65% of market share) out of the 24 insurance companies operating in the Indian insurance sector.

Life Insurance business was started with the establishment of Oriental Life Insurance Company in the year 1818. But this company dissolved in 1834. In the year 1829, Madras Equitable was started life insurance business in Madras Presidency and in the Bombay Residency three companies ware started insurance business namely the Bombay Mutual (in 1871), Oriental (in 1874) and the Empire of India (in 1897).

In the year 1912, Indian Life Assurance Companies Act was passed for regulating the Indian life insurance business. In the year 1928 another act was passed namely the Indian Insurance Companies Act for collecting statistical information over both life and non-life insurance business in India. In the year 1938, the earlier act was synthesized and modified by the Insurance Act 1938 to protect the interest of policyholders and to regulate the function of insurers.

In the year 1993, the Govt of India setup Malhotra Committee for the purpose of betterment of insurance sector. And in 1994 this committee suggested to open the door of insurance sector for private companies. In 1999 IRDA (Insurance Regulatory and Development Authority) was formed as an autonomous body for developing and regulating the insurance sector as per the exhortation of Malhotra Committee report. And in the year 2000 it was incorporated as a statutory body. After liberalization the Indian insurance sector becomes more competitive due to entry of private company. Along with banking sector, the insurance sector plays an important role in the economic development of the country, providing long term fund in the infrastructure. The necessity of the present study is to measure the performance of life insurance sector in India after liberalization period.

Review of Literature

Puri and Gill (2017) make a study to know the customer satisfaction level from the service of LIC as public company and other four private life insurance company namely HDFC Life Insurance Co. Ltd., ICICI Prudential Life Insurance Co. Ltd., Bajaj Allianz Life Insurance Co. Ltd. and Aviva Life Insurance Company India Ltd. and also compare with them. The researchers collect primary data from 100 respondents at Amritsar and secondary data from various journals and magazines. The researchers find that all the respondents are aware of the status of the insurance company whether it is public or private. Respondents of LIC are more aware of the various plans offered by the LIC as compare to the respondents of private life insurance company. The study shows that the private live insurance companies used the social media mostly to inform the customer about their company. On the other hand television media is used mostly by the LIC to inform the customer about their company. Maximum number of Respondents of private life insurance company consults with their friends, relatives and a person who has a private life insurance policy. But maximum number of respondents of LIC took their own decision when they invest based on their faith in the company. The respondents of LIC are more satisfied with their policy which they have taken as compare to respondents of private life insurance company. As per the survey no one has a very bad feeling investing in LIC, maximum number of respondents has much better feeling after investing in LIC. But on the other hand some respondents of private life insurance have very bad experience after investment. 58% of LIC respondents are very satisfied with the grievance handling procedure of LIC. On the other hand, only 22% of private respondents are very satisfied with the grievance handling procedure of the company.

Mallick, Das and Nayak (2017) make a study to compare the insurance business of LIC with other five private life insurance companies namely Bajaj Allianz, SBI life, Birla sun life, Reliance life and ICICI prudential. The study cover the period from 2003–04 to 2013–14. After completion of study the researchers find that there is a increasing trend in LIC's number of offices, the rate of growth is about 57.33%. The number of offices of other five life insurance companies are increasing very high rate. The number of offices of private life insurance companies has grown from 226 to 4689 during the period of study. The study shows that the policies of LIC are sold by individual agent has decreased from 13,41,597 to 11,95,916 and the policies of LIC are sold by corporate agent has decreased from 602 to 149. And the policies of private life insurance companies are sold by individual agent has increased from 1,26,657 to 6,42,667 and the policies of private life insurance companies are sold by corporate agent has decreased from 996 to 370. The premium income of LIC has increased from Rs. 2,663.41 crores to 31,904.49 crores and the premium income of private life insurance companies has also increased from Rs. 2,881.61 crores to Rs. 20,780.83 crores. The market share of LIC's life insurance premium has decreased from 83.34% to 60.56% and the market share of entire private life insurance sector's life insurance premium has increased from 16.66% to 39.44%.

Padmaja and Shifaly (2018) they try to realise the investor's feeling to various insurance policies of LIC and to assess the investor's satisfaction level regarding services that LIC provides. They collect primary data from 76 policyholders of LIC at Machilipatnam and the data from some secondary sources like journals, magazines and company's website. The researchers find that majority of the investors (89%) chose LIC for investing their money focusing the safety of their investment. They found that all the investors has chosen LIC's insurance product as it is a public sector company. From the study it is observed by the researchers that the investors has some expectation for investing in LIC, like terms of the policy, premium charges, accessibility, rider benefits, interest & bonus, pre & post services and company image. But investors has given more priority on interest & bonus, premium charges and company image. The study shows that 87% of investors are aware about LIC and its policies, 56% of investors has expressed that there is an unreasonable delay in claim settlement, 46% of investors express that they has little complexity with LIC. And the researchers has observed that the investors has 100% positive perception on LIC.

Vijoy (2019) examine the financial performance of five private life insurance companies and one public life insurance company i.e. LIC. The study cover the period from 2012–13 to 2017–18 with the help of secondary data. After completion of the study the researcher find that the surplus of LIC is increasing year on year but others private life insurance company's surplus has fluctuated in different year. The LIC's profit after tax is increasing year on year. On the other hand among the private life insurance company ICICI Prudential Life Insurance Co. Ltd, HDFC Standard Life Insurance Co. Ltd's profit after tax is increasing year on year. But the profit after tax of Max Life Insurance Co. Ltd, Birla Sun-Life Insurance Co. Ltd and Kotak Mahindra Old Mutual Life Insurance Co. Ltd has fluctuated in different year. The operational expenses ratio LIC and two private life insurance companies namely HDFC Standard Life Insurance Co. Ltd. and ICICI Prudential Life Insurance Co. Ltd. is lower as compare to other three private life insurance company namely Birla Sun-Life Insurance Co. Ltd., Max Life Insurance Co. Ltd., and Kotak Mahindra Old Mutual Life insurance Co. Ltd.

Gairola (2016) make a study to examine the performance of private and public life insurers and also compare with them during post liberalization period from 2000–01 to 2015–16. The researcher find that the total premium income of

LIC is increasing year after year during the study period. And growth rate is highest in the year 2001–02 (42.79%). On the other hand total premium income of private insurers is increasing trend also during the period of study and rate of growth is highest in the year 2001–02 (4124.31%). During post liberalization period number of new policy business of LIC is fluctuating but on the other hand number of new policy business of private insurers is increasing continuously from 8.25 lakhs (in the year 2002–030) to 150.11 lakhs (in the year 2008–09) but from 2009–10 it is declining continuously. The market share of LIC is declining continuously from 99.46% (in the year 2001–02) to 69.77% (in the year 2010–11). As opposed to the market share of private insurers is increasing continuously from 0.56% (in the year 2001–02) to 29.90% (in the year 2010–11). From 2011–12 market share of LIC slightly increase and as opposed to market share of private insurers slightly decrease.

Sumathy and Kalyani (2019) make a study on the financial performance of LIC and other selected five private life insurance companies in India. The secondary data has been collected by the researchers for the period of 10 years from 2007–08 to 2016–17. The study has been made with the help of nine important parameters like Net Premium, Investment Income, Current assets, Current liabilities, Fixed Assets, Total Assets, Policy Liabilities, Shareholders fund & Capital Reserve and Net Profit. The study shows that on the basis of Net Premium collection, Investment Income, Fixed Assets, Total Assets, Net Profit LIC has highest mean value as compare to private life insurance companies. And on the basis of share holders fund LIC has least mean value as compare to private life insurance companies.

Patel and Dwivedi (2022) make a study to measure the profitability and long-term soundness of three private life insurance companies namely HDFC Life insurance Co. Ltd., ICICI Prudential Life Insurance Co. Ltd. and SBI Life Insurance Co. Limited. The secondary data has been collected by the researchers for the period from 2010–11 to 2019–20. The study has been made with the help of some important profitability and long term soundness ratios. The researchers find that in terms of profitability HDFC life has performed well as compare to SBI Life Insurance Company Ltd. and ICICI Prudential Life. And in terms of long-term soundness SBI Life has performed better as compare to HDFC Life and ICICI Prudential Life.

Parida (2022) examine the financial performance of LIC and three private insurance companies in India namely Bharti AXA Life insurance Company Ltd., HDFC Life insurance Co. Ltd., and Max life insurance Co. Limited. The researcher has collected secondary data for the period of 10 years from 2010–11 to 20199–20. The study has been made with the help of some important ratios though CAMEL Model. The researcher has used Mann-Whitney U test also to test whether there is any significant difference in the financial performance of public and private life insurance companies. They find although LIC's financial performances in most of the cases are not so good as compare to private life insurance companies. But as per Mann-Whitney U test result there exist similarity in the financial performance of public and private life insurers.

The earlier studies on measuring the financial performance of public and private life insurance companies in India have considered lesser number of insurance companies. In this study, we have considered whole insurance industry. Most of the earlier studies have taken few accounting years but in our study we have taken 20 years after post liberalization period. In the earlier studies, the factor analysis and causal analysis are not applied but in this study we have applied those analyses.

Objectives of the Study

- To analyze the trend and factors effectiveness of benefits paid by LIC and private life insurers.
- To examine the causality between the Benefits Paid and Investment Income of LIC and Private Life Insurers.

Data and Methodology

The study period is of twenty years ranges from 2001–02 to 2020–21. For the study data has been collected from some secondary sources like various journals, magazines, annual report of IRDA and websites. There are numbers of parameter are used for this study like Life Insurance Premium Income, Investment Income of Life Insurers, Commission Expenses of Life Insurers, Operating Expenses of Life Insurers, Benefits paid by Life Insurers, Profit After Tax and New Life Insurance Policy Issued by Life Insurers has been used to assess the insurance industry both public and private insurance. The methodology section is divided into various analytical stages, each employing specific econometric and statistical tools to analyze the data comprehensively:

Trend Analysis

Trend Analysis is performed to visualize and understand the long-term movement Life Insurance Premium Income, Investment Income of Life Insurers, Commission Expenses of Life Insurers, Operating Expenses of Life Insurers, Benefits paid by Life Insurers, Profit After Tax and New Life Insurance Policy Issued by Life Insurers has been used to assess the insurance industry both public and private insurance. This involves plotting the time series data to identify upward, downward, or stationary trends across the study period.

Stationarity Tests

To ensure the reliability of time series data for further analysis, stationarity tests are employed. A stationary time series is one whose properties do not depend on the time at which the series is observed. One common tests is used:

Augmented Dickey-Fuller (ADF) Test:

$$\Delta y_t = \alpha + \beta_t + \gamma y_{(t-1)} + \sum \delta_i \Delta y_{(t-1)} + \varepsilon_t$$

Where Δy_t is the difference in the variable at time *t*, α is a constant, *t* is the trend, $y_{(t-1})$ is the lagged variable, δ*i* are the coefficients of the lagged difference terms, and ε*t* is the error term.

Correlation Metrics

The Correlation Metrics is used shows the factor effectiveness and relations ship among the variables.

Regression Analysis

Regression is basically a statistical technique that predicts the value of dependent variable based on one or more independent variables. The regression model for testing of dependent and independent relationship is given as,

$$Y_t = \alpha + \beta i X t + \varepsilon_t$$

Where Y_t and X_t are the values of the two time series at time *t*, α*i*, and β*i* are coefficients, and ε*t* is the error term.

Granger Causality Test

The Granger Causality Test is applied to examine the cause-and-effect relationship between tax collections and GDP. This test assesses whether past values of one variable can predict the future values of another. The basic model for testing if *X* Granger-causes *Y* is:

$$Y_t = \alpha_0 + \Sigma \alpha_i Y_{(t-i)} + \Sigma \beta_i X_{(t-i)} + \varepsilon_t$$

Where Yt and Xt are the values of the two time series at time t, n is the number of lags, α0, αi, and βi are coefficients, and εt is the error term.

Analysis and Findings

Trend Analysis

Benefit paid by life insurers is the most important parameter to measure the performance of insurance sector. It is the summation of Death Claim, Maturity Benefit, Surrender/ withdrawal money, Annuities/pension and Others benefits, paid by the Life Insurers to their Policy Holders. The benefits paid by LIC had increased from Rs. 17476.64 Crore in 2001–02 to Rs. 285121.81 Crore in 2020–21. The growth rate was highest in the year 2006–07(57.00%). And benefits paid by Private Insurers had increased from Rs. 2.9 Crore in 2001–02 to Rs. 113650.70 Crore in 2020–21, and the growth rate was maximum in the year 2003–04(472%). (Table 1)

Table 1: Benefit Paid by Insurance Company both in Public and Private Insurance

Year	*Public*		*Private*	
	Amount	*Growth (%)*	*Amount*	*Growth (%)*
2001–02	17476.6	–	2.9	–
2002–03	20530.4	17.5	14.3	393.1
2003–04	23930.3	16.6	81.8	472
2004–05	28455.7	18.9	244.9	199.4
2005–06	33956.8	19.3	1306.7	433.6
2006–07	53298.4	57	2470.3	89
2007–08	56550.3	6.1	5136.1	107.9
2008–09	52478.1	–7.2	5865	14.2
2009–10	79162	50.8	16658	184
2010–11	111273	40.6	31251	87.6
2011–12	117497	5.6	35581	13.9
2012–13	134922	14.8	57571	61.8
2013–14	158015.5	17.1	58380.1	1.4
2014–15	144125.8	–8.8	67054.5	14.9
2015–16	142898.1	–0.9	61555.4	–8.2
2016–17	166876.9	16.8	69463	12.8
2017–18	196718	17.9	81235.6	16.9
2018–19	249284.9	26.7	80393.4	–1
2019–20	252760.6	1.4	98706.1	22.8
2020–21	285121.8	12.8	113650.7	15.1

Source: Author's Calculation from Different Annual Report of IRDA

The table 2 shows two part in the first part represent percentage distribution of different types of claim like death claim, maturity, surrender, annuities and others. The percentage distribution of claim in case of public it is higher in case of maturity claim flowingly surrender and death claim. In case of private insurance surrender or withdrawal claim is higher than maturity and death claim. In the second part of the table represent share benefit paid by insurance company both of public and private, in case of public it is higher in every claim but relatively higher in case of maturity claim then surrender and death claim. Table 2.

Table 2: Percentage Distribution of Different Types of Claim Benefits and Share Received by Policy Holder in 2020–21

Claim	*Benefit of Different Claim*				*Benefit Share of Public and Private*		
	Public (LIC)		*Private Insurers*				
	Rs. (Cr)	*Percentage*	*Rs. (Cr)*	*Percentage*	*Public*	*Private*	*Total*
Death Claim	23878.6	8.4	18079.8	15.9	56.91	43.09	100
Maturity	165659.2	58.1	25845.1	22.7	86.50	13.50	100
Surrender/ Withdrawal	80101.0	28.1	49315.9	43.4	61.89	38.11	100
Annuities/ Pensions	14571.4	5.1	1406.3	1.2	91.20	8.80	100
Others	911.6	0.3	17934.5	15.8	4.84	95.16	100
Total	**285121.8**	**100.0**	**113650.7**	**100.0**	71.50	**28.50**	**100**

Source: As in Table 1

Premium Income is the money received by the Insurance Company from the Policy Holders for providing financial preservation. Premium collection is a major source of income of life insurers. The premium income of LIC had increased from Rs. 40725.9 crore in the year 2001–02 to 403286.6 in the year 2020–21. The LIC's growth in Premium Income was highest in the year 2006–07 (40.8%). The premium income of Private Insurers had increased from Rs. 174.5 crore in the year 2001–02 to Rs. 225444.5 crore in the year 2020–21. The growth rate of premium income of private insurers was highest in the year 2002–03 (347.8%).

Commission Expenses is the expenses paid by the Insurance Company to the agent for selling their product. It is the major expenses of the Insurance Company. Commission Expenses of LIC had increased from Rs. 4517.9 crore in the year 2001–02 to Rs. 22170.6 crore in the year 2020–21.And Commission Expenses of Private Insurers had increased from Rs. 49.0 crore in the year 2001–02 to Rs. 10823.4 crore in the year 2020–21. (Table 3)

Table 3: Life Insurance Premium Income and Commission Expenses of both Public and Private Insurance Companies from 2001–02 to 2020–21

Year	*Premium Income*				*Commission Expenses*			
	Public		*Private*		*Public*		*Private*	
	Amount	*Growth (%)*	*Amount*	*Growth (%)*	*Amount*	*Growth (%)*	*Amount*	*Growth (%)*
2001–02	40725.9	–	174.5	–	4517.9	–	49	–
2002–03	49282.5	21	781.4	347.8	4998.6	10.6	152.8	211.8
2003–04	63533.4	28.9	3120.3	299.3	5742.9	14.9	415.4	171.9
2004–05	75127.3	18.2	7727.5	147.7	6203.2	8	854.7	105.8
2005–06	90792.2	20.9	15083.5	95.2	7100.2	14.5	1543.1	80.5
2006–07	127822.8	40.8	28218.8	87.1	9173.6	29.2	3109.7	101.5
2007–08	149790	17.2	51561.4	82.7	9614.7	4.8	5089.6	63.7
2008–09	157288	5	64503.2	25.1	10055.1	4.6	5477.9	7.6
2009–10	186077.3	18.3	79369.9	23	12132.6	20.7	5942.1	8.5
2010–11	203473.4	9.3	88131.6	11	13347.3	10	4982	–16.2
2011–12	202889.3	–0.3	84182.8	–4.5	14063.1	5.4	4470.6	–10.3
2012–13	208803.6	2.9	78398.9	–6.9	14790.3	5.2	4471.2	0
2013–14	236942.3	13.5	77359.4	–1.3	16762.9	13.3	4083.5	–8.7
2014–15	239667.7	1.2	88433.5	14.3	15118.1	–9.8	4342.5	6.3
2015–16	266444.2	11.2	100499	13.6	15500.3	2.5	4766.4	9.8
2016–17	300487.4	12.8	117989.3	17.4	16632	7.3	5485.2	15.1
2017–18	318223.2	5.9	140586.2	19.2	18271.5	9.9	7081.4	29.1
2018–19	337505.1	6.1	170627	21.4	19345.3	5.9	8429.2	19
2019–20	379389.6	12.4	193520.6	13.4	21380.5	10.5	9812.1	16.4
2020–21	403286.6	6.3	225444.5	16.5	22170.6	3.7	10823.4	10.3

Source: As in Table 1

Investment Income is the income earned by the Insurance Company from the investment made by them in different segment. Investment Income is another major source of income of life insurers. LIC's investment income had increased from Rs. 23849.5 crore in the year 2001–02 to Rs. 279378.9 crore in the year 2020–21. On the other hand investment income of Private Sector Insurance had increased from Rs. 5.8 crore in the year 2001–02 to Rs. 186651.5 crore in the year 2020–21.

No. of new life insurance policies issued by life insurers is one another chief indicator for measuring the performance of life insurers. There was a declining trend in no. of new policy issued by LIC from the year 2007–08 to 2014–15, except in the year 2009–10 and 2012–13. From 2015–16 to 2020–21 there was a increasing trend except in 2016–17 and in 2020–21. The growth in no. of new policies issued by LIC was fluctuated during post liberalization period. On the other hand no. of new policies issued by private insurers was increasing consistently from the year 2002–03 to 2008–09. But there was a declining trend in no. of new policies issued by private insurers from 2009–10 to 2014–15. From 2015–16 to 2020–21 no. of new policies issued by private insurers was increasing consistently except in the year 2019–20. (Table 4)

Table 4: Life Insurance Premium Income and Commission Expenses of Life Insurers both Public and Private Insurance from 2001–02 to 2020–21

Year	*Investment Income*				*Number of insurance policies*			
	Public		*Private*		*Public*		*Private*	
	Amount	*Growth (%)*	*Amount*	*Growth (%)*	*Amount*	*Growth (%)*	*Amount*	*Growth (%)*
2001–02	23849.5	–	5.8	–	243.6	–	13.8	–
2002–03	25980.8	8.9	47.6	720.7	245.5	0.8	8.3	–39.9
2003–04	29855.9	14.9	267.6	462.2	269.7	9.9	16.6	100
2004–05	37066.8	24.2	363.4	35.8	239.8	–11.1	22.3	34.3
2005–06	40056.4	8.1	1222.4	236.4	315.9	31.7	38.7	73.5
2006–07	46784.7	16.8	2478.5	102.8	382.3	21	79.2	104.7
2007–08	56595.1	21	6602.6	166.4	376.1	–1.6	132.6	67.4
2008–09	42804	–24.4	10416	57.8	359.1	–4.5	150.1	13.2
2009–10	112425	162.7	42831	311.2	388.6	8.2	143.6	–4.3
2010–11	95949	–14.7	25718	–40	370.4	–4.7	111.1	–22.6
2011–12	84545	–11.9	7083	–72.5	357.5	–3.5	84.4	–24
2012–13	117806	39.3	29534	317	367.8	2.9	74.1	–12.2
2013–14	143244.4	21.6	41819.7	41.6	345.1	–6.2	63.6	–14.2
2014–15	168063.6	17.3	78701.5	88.2	201.7	–41.6	57.4	–9.7
2015–16	158205.2	–5.9	16259.5	–79.3	205.5	1.9	61.9	7.8
2016–17	192478.1	21.7	69184.1	325.5	201.3	–2	63.2	2.1
2017–18	206069.5	7.1	55754.3	–19.4	213.4	6	68.6	8.5
2018–19	223642.3	8.5	61158.1	9.7	214	0.3	72.4	5.5
2019–20	236849.7	5.9	–3106	–105.1	219	2.3	69.5	–4
2020–21	279378.9	18	186651.5	-6109.4	209.8	–4.2	71.5	2.9

Source: As in Table 1

Operating Expenses is the expenses that the insurance company incurs for running smooth of normal business activities. The operating expenses of LIC had increased from Rs. 4260.4 crore in the year 2001–02 to Rs. 34989.5 crore in the year 2020–21. And the operating expenses of Private Insurers had increased from Rs. 413.8 crore in the year 2001–02 to Rs. 26432.8 crore in the year 2020–21.

Profit After Tax of life insurers is another most important parameter to measure the performance of insurance sector. The profit after tax of LIC had increased from Rs. 821.8Crore in 2001–02 to Rs. 2900.6 Crore in 2020–21. On the other hand, initially private insurers were suffering losses from the year 2001–02 to 2020–21. The private insurers earned profit from the year 2009–10 to 2020–21. (Table 5)

Table 5: Operating Expenses and Profit After Tax of Life Insurers both Public and Private Insurance from 2001–02 to 2020–21

Year	*Operating Expenses*				*Profit After Tax*			
	Public		*Private*		*Public*		*Private*	
	Amount	*Growth (%)*	*Amount*	*Growth (%)*	*Amount*	*Growth (%)*	*Amount*	*Growth (%)*
2001–02	4260.4	–	413.8	–	821.8	–	–227.8	–
2002–03	4571.8	7.3	831.7	101	497	–39.5	–386.3	69.6
2003–04	5186.5	13.4	1402.4	68.6	10414.5	1995.5	–1679.5	334.8
2004–05	6241.3	20.3	2229.5	59	15187.7	45.8	–2592.2	54.3
2005–06	6041.6	–3.2	3569.5	60.1	1520	–90	–3637.4	40.3
2006–07	7080.9	17.2	6520	82.7	1133.1	–25.5	–5585.2	53.5
2007–08	8309.3	17.3	11989.3	83.9	844.6	–25.5	–4257.4	–23.8
2008–09	9064.3	9.1	16659.6	39	957.4	13.4	–5835.8	37.1
2009–10	12245.8	35.1	16641.8	–0.1	1061	10.8	1210.3	–120.7
2010–11	16980.3	38.7	15962	–4.1	1172	10.5	1485	22.7
2011–12	14914.4	–12.2	14741.7	–7.6	1313.3	12.1	4660.7	213.9
2012–13	16707.7	12	14854	0.8	1437.6	9.5	5510.4	18.2
2013–14	23760.7	42.2	13704.7	–7.7	1656.7	15.2	5931.3	7.6
2014–15	22395.5	–5.7	14466.1	5.6	1823.8	10.1	5787.2	–2.4
2015–16	22691.8	1.3	16086.1	11.2	2517.9	38.1	4897.6	–15.4
2016–17	28952.1	27.6	17186.8	6.8	2231.7	–11.4	5496.2	12.2
2017–18	30142.4	4.1	18677.3	8.7	2446.4	9.6	6064.3	10.3
2018–19	29182	–3.2	21948.2	17.5	2688.5	9.9	5747.3	–5.2
2019–20	34568	18.5	25553	16.4	2712.7	0.9	5015.6	–12.7
2020–21	34989.5	1.2	26432.8	3.4	2900.6	6.9	5760.1	14.8

Source: As in Table 1

Econometric Insights into Benefit paid by the Insurance Company and others variables

This subsection delves into the intricate relationship between Benefit paid by the Insurance Company and others variables through a rigorous econometric analysis. The analysis is segmented into four critical phases: Stationarity testing, Descriptive statistics, Correlation matrix and Granger Causality testing analysis, providing a comprehensive understanding of the interdependencies Benefit paid by the Insurance Company and investment income of the insurance company.

Stationarity Testing: Foundations for Inference

The investigation begins with stationarity tests, crucial for assessing the time series data's suitability for further analysis. Employing the Augmented Dickey–Fuller (ADF) tests, the study evaluates the stationary properties of the values of Benefit paid by the Insurance Company both public and private insurance company. Results indicate that both series exhibit non-stationarity at their levels but achieve stationarity upon differencing, validating their readiness for subsequent econometric scrutiny. This foundational step ensures the robustness of the analysis by confirming the data's adherence to stationarity prerequisites (Table 6).

Table 6: Stationarity of Augmented Dickey-Fuller Test Result

Public Insurance Company (For the level test t-Statistics (–1.396756) Prob (0.8281) Not Significant*		
(1st Difference Test Result)		
Null Hypothesis: D(BENFP) has a unit root, Exogenous: Constant, Linear Trend	t-Statistic	Prob.*
Augmented Dickey-Fuller test statistic	–4.039144	0.0267
R-squared- 0.521, Prob (F-statistic) - 0.003969, Durbin-Watson statistics - 2.015320		
Private Insurance Company (For the level test t-Statistics - 1.844225) Prob (0.6429) Not Significant*		
(1st Difference Test Result)		
Null Hypothesis: D(BENFP) has a unit root, Exogenous: Constant, Linear Trend	t-Statistic	Prob.*
Augmented Dickey-Fuller test statistic	–4.812300	0.0064
R-squared 0.607, Prob(F-statistic) 0.000904, Durbin-Watson statistics 1.887852		

**MacKinnon-Haug-Michelis (1996 & 1999) p-values,
Source: Author's Calculation

Descriptive Statistics of the variables that determine Benefit paid by the Insurance Company

The variables identified for the determination of Benefits Paid (BENFP) by Insurance Company and their specification are as Premium Income of the Insurance Company (PRIUM), Commission Expanses (COMEXP), Investment Income of the Insurance Company (INVESTI), No of Policies Issues(NPOLIS), Operating Expenses (OPREXP), Profit after tax (PRAT) and time (T). The descriptive statistics of Public and Private Insurance present the summary of all variables used in this analysis.

The following table 7 shows the Mean of Benefits Paid by LIC is Rs. (in crore) 116266.60 and S.D is 83472.80. The mean of Premium Income of LIC is Rs. (in crore) 201877.60 and S.D is 109507. The mean of Commission Expenses is Rs. (in crore) 12846.03 and S.D is 5475.39. The mean of Investment Income is Rs. (in crore) 116082.50 and S.D is 80517.50. The mean of No. of policy issued by LIC is 286.30 lakh and S.D is 74.00. The mean of Operating expenses is Rs. (in crore) 16914.30 and S.D is 10660.80. The mean of Profit After Tax of LIC is Rs. (in crore) 2766.90 and S.D is 3589.60.

Table 7: Descriptive Statistics of Variable taken from Public Sector Insurance (LIC)

	BENFP	*PRIUM*	*COMEXP*	*INVESTI*	*NPOLIS*	*OPREXP*	*PRAT*	*T*
Mean	116266.6	201877.6	12846.03	116082.5	286.3	16914.3	2766.9	10.50
Median	114385	203181.3	13705.18	104187	257.6	15811	1588.3	10.50
Maximum	285121.8	403286.6	22170.64	279378.9	388.6	34989.5	15187.7	20.00
Minimum	17476.64	40725.86	4517.91	23849.5	201.3	4260.4	497	1.00
Std. Dev.	83472.8	109507	5475.394	80517.5	74	10660.8	3589.6	5.92
Skewness	0.542588	0.194324	0.00435	0.5	0.2	0.3	2.7	0.00
Kurtosis	2.20244	2.045865	1.885378	2	1.3	1.7	9.1	1.79
Jarque-Bera	1.5114	0.8845	1.0354	1.6615	2.5828	1.8115	55.3796	1.21
Probability	0.4697	0.6426	0.5959	0.4357	0.2749	0.4042	0	0.55
Observations	20	20	20	20	20	20	20	20

Source: Author's own computation using EViews 8

The table 8 shows the Mean of Benefits Paid by Private Insurers is Rs. (in crore) 39331.08 and S.D is 37839.64. The mean of Premium Income of Private Insurers is Rs. (in crore) 80785.67 and S.D is 64753.18. The mean of Commission Expenses is Rs. (in crore) 4569.09 and S.D is 3029.90. The mean of Investment Income is Rs. (in crore) 31649.64 and S.D is 44859.54. The mean of No. of policy issued by Private Insurers is 70.15 lakh and S.D is 40.49. The mean of Operating expenses is Rs. (in crore) 12993.52 and S.D is 7983.05.

The mean of Profit After Tax of Private Insurers is Rs. (in crore) 1668.21 and S.D is 4337.44.

Table 8: Descriptive Statistics of variable taken from the Private Insurers

	BENFP	*PRIUM*	*COMEXP*	*INVESTI*	*NPOLIS*	*OPREXP*	*PRAT*	*T*
Mean	39331.08	80785.67	4569.093	31649.64	70.15369	12993.52	1668.211	10.50
Median	33416.00	78884.43	4618.780	13337.75	69.04500	14797.87	3072.830	10.50
Maximum	113650.7	225444.5	10823.44	186651.5	150.1100	26432.76	6064.320	20.00
Minimum	2.880000	174.5200	49.00000	–3105.970	8.250000	413.7700	–5835.840	1.00
Std. Dev.	37839.64	64753.18	3029.901	44859.54	40.49297	7983.046	4337.444	5.92
Skewness	0.397380	0.617821	0.260408	2.188966	0.415374	–0.228265	–0.471504	.0001
Kurtosis	1.812712	2.692952	2.581445	8.115619	2.623598	2.099080	1.682034	1.79
Jarque-Bera	1.701081	1.350908	0.372031	37.77987	0.693183	0.850064	2.188583	1.22
Probability	0.427184	0.508925	0.830261	0.000000	0.707094	0.653749	0.334777	0.55
Sum	786621.5	1615713.	91381.86	632992.7	1403.074	259870.4	33364.21	210.0
Sum Sq. Dev.	2.72E+10	7.97E+10	1.74E+08	3.82E+10	31153.94	1.21E+09	3.57E+08	665.0
Observations	20	20	20	20	20	20	20	20

Source: As in Table 6

The following table 9 shows the correlation metrics of different variables in public sector insurance. There exist perfect positive correlation between Benefits paid and Premium collection (.978), between Benefits paid and Investment Income (.978), and between benefits paid and Time (.969) at 1% significant level.

Table 9: Correlation Metrics of the Variables Taken in Public Sector Insurance (LIC)

	BENFP	*PRIUM*	*COMEXP*	*INVESTI*	*NPOLIS*	*OPREXP*	*PRAT*	*T*
BENFP	1							
PRIUM	.978**	1						
COMEXP	.976**	.989**	1					
INVEST	.978**	.973**	.958**	1				
POLIS	–0.437	–0.378	–0.305	–.519*	1			
OPREXP	.976**	.978**	.970**	.983**	–.499*	1		
PRAT	–0.182	–0.227	–0.249	–0.159	–0.286	–0.169	1	
TIME	.969**	.992**	.989**	.967**	–0.39	.977**	–0.214	1

**. Correlation is significant at the 0.01 level (2-tailed).
*. Correlation is significant at the 0.05 level (2-tailed).
Source: As in Table 6

The following table 10 shows the correlation metrics of different variables in private sector insurance. There exist perfect positive correlation between Benefits paid and Premium collection (.934), between Benefits paid and Investment Income (.699), between Benefits paid and Profit after Tax (.861) and between Benefits paid and Time (.964) at 1% significant level.

Table 10: Correlation Metrics of Variables Taken in Private Insurers

	BENFP	*PRIUM*	*COMEXP*	*INVESTI*	*NPOLIS*	*OPREXP*	*PRAT*	*T*
BENFP	1							
PRIUM	.934**	1						
COMEXP	.827**	.963**	1					
INVESTI	.699**	.694**	.629**	1				
NPOLIS	0.066	0.313	.532*	0.117	1			
OPREXP	.850**	.952**	.975**	.605**	.559*	1		
PRAT	.861**	.700**	.536*	.550*	–0.109	.627**	1	
TIME	.964**	.954**	.897**	.655**	0.274	.930**	.789**	1

**. Correlation is significant at the 0.01 level (2-tailed).
*. Correlation is significant at the 0.05 level (2-tailed).
Source: As in Table 6

Regression Analysis

The regression model for this analysis is taken as:

$$BENFP = \alpha + \beta 1PRIUM + \beta 2COMEXP + \beta 3INVEST + \beta 4\ POLIS + \beta 5\ OPREXP + \beta 6PRAT + \beta 7TIME$$

Table 11 shows the Regression Result of Public and Private Insurance Company. In case of public insurance company Benefits Paid not significantly affected by Investment Income but in case of private insurance company Benefits Paid is significantly affected by Investment Income. However, the public and private benefit differently affected by the number factors taken in this model.

Table 11: Regression Result

Variable	*Public Insurance Company*				*Private Insurance Company*			
	Coefficient	*t-Statistic*	*Prob.*	*Result*	*Coefficient*	*t-Statistic*	*Prob.*	*Result*
C	–15798.21	–0.774335	0.4537	R-squared- 0.987 Prob (F-statistic)-	–2385.217	–0.671830	0.5144	R-squared- 0.991 Prob(F-statistic)-
PRIUM	0.280673	1.141297	0.2760		–0.508404	–1.907217	0.0807	
COMEXP	27.51498	4.055848	0.0016		8.700233	2.070656	0.0606	
INVEST	0.193691	0.841939	0.4163		0.090545	2.518635	0.0270	

Variable	*Public Insurance Company*				*Private Insurance Company*			
	Coefficient	*t-Statistic*	*Prob.*	*Result*	*Coefficient*	*t-Statistic*	*Prob.*	*Result*
POLIS	–311.4270	–2.825370	0.0153	(.000)	–515.1064	–3.763655	0.0027	(.000)
OPREXP	–3.654623	–1.599214	0.1358	Durbin-Watson stat-2.17	3.477940	2.139332	0.0537	Durbin-Watson stat-2.58
PRAT	0.154786	0.184578	0.8566		1.592478	2.522533	0.0268	
TIME	–14284.71	–3.039628	0.0103		2710.428	3.244776	0.0070	

Source: As in Table 6

Granger Causality Tests

Table 12 shows that the Pair wise Granger Causality Test between Investment Income and Benefit Paid. There are three types causality bidirectional, uni-directional and no-causal relationship. In causality test both variable are dependent and independent. In granger causality only two variables will be considered at a time. If Ho is X does not granger cause Y, if p value is greater than 0.05, accepted Ho, its means no causality, If p value is less than 0.05, reject Ho, its means causality between the variables. In case of LIC Investment Income does not granger cause Benefit Paid, and Benefit Paid does not granger cause Investment Income as both cases p value is greater than 0.05. In case of Private Insurance Investment Income does not granger cause Benefit Paid, but Benefit Paid does granger cause Investment Income. Its means uni-dimensionality causality run from Benefit Paid to Investment Income in case of private Insurance.

Table 12: Pair wise Granger Causality Tests between Benefit paid by Insurance Company (BENFP) and Investment Income (INVESTI) both in Public (LIC) and Private Insurance

Null Hypothesis	*Obs*	*F-Statistic*	*Prob.*
PUBLIC (LIC)	19		
Investment Income does not Granger Cause Benefit paid by insurance company to Investment Income		2.01303	0.1751
Benefit paid by insurance company to Investment Income does not Granger Cause Investment Income			0.0603
PRIVATE Insurance	19		
Investment Income does not Granger Benefit paid by insurance company to Investment Income		0.57302	0.4601
Benefit paid by insurance company to Investment Income does Granger Cause Investment Income		38.9844	1.E-05

Source: As in Table 6

Summary and Conclusion

After liberalization the benefit amount paid by the public insurance company significantly higher than private company but services of the private company and investment decision are significantly changes after 2010–11. Premium Income, Commission Expenses and new Policy Issue are significantly higher in case of Public than Private Insurance. The Effectiveness of the factors and correlation metrics of the maximum factor significantly determine benefit paid by Insurance Company. Pair wise Granger Causality Tests represent dependent independent relationship between Benefit paid by Insurance Company and Investment Income in case of Public (LIC) is no causality between the variable. In case of Private Insurance Unidirectional causality run from BPIC to Investment Income. In case of public sector, Investment of the insurance company is not significantly determined but in case of private sector it is significantly determined.

References

Journals

[1] Gairola, V. (2016). A Comparative Study of Public and Private Life Insurance Companies in Post Liberalization Era. *International Journal of Management & Business Studies*, *6*(4), 39–43.

[2] Mallick, S., Das, K.K. and Nayak, N. (2017). Financial Performance of Life Insurance Companies and its Impact in Indian Economy. *International Journal of Innovative Research and Advanced Studies (IJIRAS)*, *4*(3), 38–42.

[3] Parida, B.B. (2022). Financial Performance of Public and Private Life Insurance Companies in India. *International journal of Current Science*, *12*(2), 111–120.

[4] Patel, A. and Dwivedi, V.J. (2022). A Comparative Study on Profitability and Long Term Soundness of Selected Private Life Insurance Companies in India. *Gap Gyan, A Global Journal of Social Sciences*, *5*(3), 16–20.

[5] Puri, P. and Gill, H.S. (2017). A Comparative Study of LIC and Private Insurance Companies. *International Journal of Engineering Technology, Management and Applied Sciences*, *5*(5), 321–333.

[6] Shifali and Padmaga, R. (2018). A Study on Investors Perception Towards LIC (With Special Reference to LIC, Machilipatnam). *IOSR Journal of Business and Management (IOSR-JBM)*, *20*(3) 48–53.

[7] Sumathy, M. and Kalyani, V. (2019). Financial Performance of Public and Private Life Insurance Companies in India – A comparative Study. *International journal of Advanced Scientific Research and Management*, *4*(3), 156–164.

[8] Vijay, L. (2019). Financial Performance Analysis: A Study of Life Insurance Companies. *Pramana Research Journal*, *9*(5), 970–974.

Websites

www.irdai.gov.in

Performance Assessment of Selected Public Sector and Private Sector Banks of India: A Comparative Analysis

Tarun Kumar Ray[1] and Abhijit Sinha[2]

ABSTRACT: Indian banking system has experienced tremendous changes during and in the post COVID-19 pandemic period. The use of digital and mobile technology by a large number of people has increased the scope and volume of banking business many times. Both the Public sector and Private sector banks of India are trying to adapt themselves with the new competitive environment. The objective of this study is to analyze the financial performance of some of the selected Public Sector and Private Sector banks in India based on some selected parametrs during this transition period. The study is based on the secondary data collected from annual reports of respective banks, websites and Reserve Bank of India Bulletins. The study covers a period of five years from 2018–19 to 2022–23. A convenient sampling method is used to select six banks, three each from the public and private sector, based on market capitalization. Mean, covariance, graphs and t-tests are used to analyze the data. Though there is an increasing trend in profitability for both sector banks, the rate of growth for the private sector banks is higher. Due to various challenges, the public sector banks are lagging in their financial performances.

Keywords: Financial Performance, Private Sector Banks, Public Sector Banks.

Introduction

Indian Banking system is mainly dominated by two types of banks, viz, Public Sector Banks (PSBs) and Private Sector Banks (PVBs). Public Sector Banks are those in which the union or state governments owns more than 50% of the ownership shares. Private Sector Banks are those in which private firms or individuals own the majority of the shares. Currently, there are 34 nationalised banks in India, with 12 being Public Sector Banks and 22 being Private Sector Banks.The banking industry of India is undergoing a radical shift. Both of them are driven by new competition from Fin-Techs, changing business models, mounting regulation and compliance pressures, and disruptive technologies.The

[1] Associate Professor, Department of Commerce, Kharagpur College, Inda, Kharagpur, India. E-mail: tkraykgp@rediffmail.com

[2] Professor, Department of Commerce, Vidyasagar University, India.
E-mail: abhijitsinha_091279@mail.vidyasagar.ac.in

performance of these two sectors influences the overall economic condition of the country to a great extent. The main objective of the Public Sector Banks is social welfare and reduction of economic disparity within different regions of the country. On the other hand, the Private sector banks are largely driven by the profit motive.

Financial performance indicates the result of the financial transactions of the institution for a given period of time. The financial performance of a bank is reflected by a number of parameters like Return on assets, Return on Capital employed, Return on Equity, Net profit margin, Net Interest Margin etc. The evaluation of financial performance of the banks helps to judge the reason for changes in the overall financial condition during the study period.

Statement of the Problem

In recent years, the banking sector of India has undergone numerous changes in the form of reforms, regulations, and norms. The economic impact of COVID-19 has directly influenced banking performance and activities. In this study, effort has been taken to analyze the financial performance of selected public sector and private sector banks of India before and after the pandemic. The comparative performance measurement and evaluation has been made on the basis of five parameters viz., Return on Assets (ROA), Return on Equity (ROE), Return on Capital Employed (ROCE), Net Interest Margin (NIM) and Net Profit Margin (NP).

Significance of the Study

As, both the public sector and private sector banks operate in almost same economic environment and customer base, their comparative performance analysis can be helpful to identify the individual strengths, weaknesses and overall efficiency. It cannot be denied that the existence of any system should be based on its own strength. So, the financial performance or profitability of public sector banks and private sector banks must be evaluated and analysed on the basis of some common parameters. The comparative analysis may unveil the drivers of the profitability like cost management system, control over the banking assets, pricing strategies etc. The present study also aims to compare the financial performance of public sector banks and private sector banks before and after the Covid 19 pandemic. The outcome of the study will help the government to chalk out various policies with respect to performance of the banks.

Literature Review

The evaluation and analysis of the financial performance of selected Public sector banks and private sector banks of India have been made after several studies on the basic statistical models but in different perspectives and different time periods. The review of literature shows that many researchers analysed the financial performance of commercial banks of India on the basis of various parameters. These studies are different from each other with respect to period of study, sample of banks, parameters and statistical techniques. The present study has been conducted from the year 2018–19 to 2022–23. Hence comparative performance of PSBs and PVBs has been studied to analyse the performance of latest developments till the year 2018 and bridge the gap in existing literature. Shah (2015) discussed about the comparative analysis on performance of new private sector banks and the public sector banks of India during the period 2011–2015 on many key parameters such as the P/E Ratio, Dividend Payout ratio, Return on equity ratio, Capital adequacy ratio, Credit deposit ratio. The above period is chosen since it is very important to know how different banks performed during the recession and inflation duration. Malhotra *et al.* (2011) analyzed the performance of commercial banks in India during the period 2005 to 2009. This period covers the pre-credit crisis and the crisis time period. Specifically, the paper examines the behaviour of profitability, cost of intermediation, efficiency, soundness of the banking system, and industry concentration for public and private sector Indian commercial banks. The empirical results show that competition in the Indian banking industry has intensified. While the net interest margin has improved, cost of intermediation is actually rising and banks are responding to the increased costs with higher efficiency levels. Anand (2015) described banks form a fundamental component of the financial system and they are also active players in financial markets. An efficient banking system capable of mobilizing the savings and channelling them to productive purposes are essential for the development of any economy. Besides providing financial resources for the growth, banks can also influence the direction in which these resources are to be utilized.

Objectives of the Study

1. To generate an idea on the financial performance of top 3 Public Sector Banks (PSB) and Private Sector Banks (PVB) of India.
2. To study the comparative financial performance of selected banks.

Methodology

The study is based on secondary data, which has been collected from various published sources, including websites of different related agencies. Important sources of secondary data were publications of Reserve Bank of India (Reports in Trend and Progress of Banking in India); Research Journals, and websites of different related organisations. Annual reports of the respective banks, Indian Banks Association publications, magazines, documents and other published information. This research covers a period of five years from 2018–2019 to 2022–2023. A sample of six banks i.e. top three from public sector and top three from private sector has been selected and the criterion is based on highest market as of 30th November, 2023. The banks matched under this criterion are State Bank of India, Bank of Baroda, Punjab National Bank from public sector and HDFC Bank Ltd, ICICI bank Ltd, Kotak Mahindra bank, from private sector. The different tools used for the study include t-test, mean, coefficient of variation and graphs which are used to analyze and compare financial performance of public sector and private sector banks.

The following table gives an idea of the comparative structure of three Public Sector Banks and three Private Sector Banks of India.

Table 1: Comparative Size of Top 3 PSBs and PVBs as of November 30, 2023

Banks	*Market Cap (Rs. in Cr)*	*Number of Branches*	*Number of ATMs*	*Number of Employees*
SBI	5,00,179.88	22,405	65,267	2,35,858
BOB	1,00,272.71	9,500	13,400	79,806
PNB	83,518.55	12,609	12,898	1,03,144
HDFC	11,83,434.75	8,344	19,727	1,73,222
ICICI	6,58,452.44	6,074	16,731	1,57,799
KMB	3,49,497.52	1,780	2,963	73,481

Sources: https://en.m.wikipedia.org

Analysis and Findings

The financial performance of three Public Sector Banks and Three Private Sector Banks of India has been measured on the basis of five parameters. They include Return on Assets (ROA), Return on Equity (ROE), Return on Capital Employed (ROCE), Net Interest Margin (NIM) and Net Profit Margin (NP). The selected Public Sector Banks are: State Bank of India, Bank of Baroda and Punjab National Bank. The Private Sector Banks are: HDFC Bank, ICICI Bank and Kotak Mahindra Bank.

Based on Return on Assets (ROA)

It is used to determine whether a company uses its assets efficiently to generate profits. ROA is calculated by dividing the net income of the bank by its total assets.

Table 2: Comparison of Return on Assets of PSBs and PVBs

	ROA of Public Sector Banks			*ROA of Private Sector Banks*		
Year	*SBI*	*BOB*	*PNB*	*HDFC*	*ICICI*	*KMB*
2018–19	0.02	0.05	–1.28	1.69	0.34	1.55
2019–20	0.36	0.04	0.04	1.71	0.72	1.65
2020–21	0.45	0.07	0.16	1.78	1.31	1.81
2021–22	0.63	0.56	0.26	1.78	1.65	1.99
2022–23	0.91	0.96	0.17	1.78	2.01	2.23
Mean ROA	0.474	0.336	–0.13	1.748	1.206	1.846
S.D. of ROA	0.33	0.41	0.65	0.04	0.68	0.27
C.V. of ROA	69.62	122.02	–500	2.29	56.38	14.63

Sources: https://www.moneycontrol.com

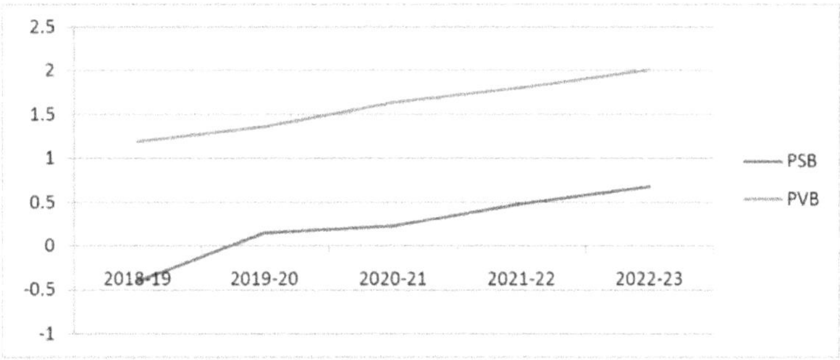

Graph 1: Average Return on Assets (%) of Selected PSBs and PVBs

Testing of hypothesis

t-test: Mean Difference Test for Two Sample

H_o: There is no significant difference between the mean ROA of selected PSBs and PVBs.

H_1: There is significant difference between the mean ROA of selected PSBs and PVBs.

Table 3: Mean Difference Test based on ROA

	PSBs	*PVBs*
Mean	0.2274	1.6006
Variance	0.167568	0.1088213
Degrees of freedom	4	
t-statistic	21.8025***	

Source: Computed by researchers

Comments on ROA

The above table shows that the mean ROA of PVBs is 1.60%, while that of PSBs is only 0.22%. The variance of earnings of the PSBs (0.167) is higher than the corresponding variance of earnings of PVBs (0.108). It reflects that the fluctuation of earnings of the PSBs is also higher than that of the PVBs. As the p value is less than 5%, we reject the null hypothesis. The value of t-statistic is much higher than the critical value both at 5% level of significance and 1% level of significance. Hence, there is no reason to accept the hypothesis that the mean difference of ROA is not significant. In other words, the selected PVBs of India earns significantly higher rate of ROA in comparison to the selected PSBs.

Based on Return on Equity (ROE)

It is a measure of profitability of a business in relation to its equity shareholders' fund. It is calculated by dividing the net income available for equity shareholders by the shareholders' fund.

Table 4: Comparative Statement of Return on Equity of PSBs and PVBs

	Public Sector Banks			*Private Sector Banks*		
Year	*SBI*	*BOB*	*PNB*	*HDFC*	*ICICI*	*KMB*
2018–19	0.39	0.94	–24.20	14.12	3.19	11.47
2019–20	6.95	0.76	0.58	15.35	6.99	12.25
2020–21	8.86	1.07	2.41	15.27	11.21	11.01
2021–22	12.33	8.46	3.90	15.39	13.94	11.90
2022–23	16.75	14.36	2.74	15.74	16.13	13.17
Mean ROE	9.06	5.12	–2.91	15.17	10.29	11.96
S.D. of ROE	6.11	6.11	11.96	0.62	5.23	0.82
C.V. of ROE	67.44	119.33	–410.99	4.09	50.82	6.85

Sources: https://www.moneycontrol.com

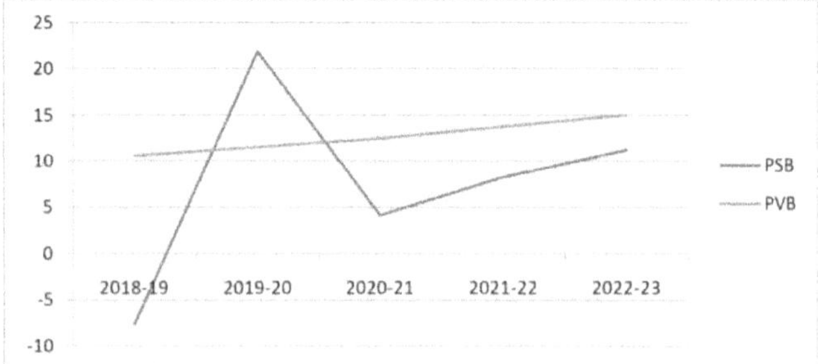

Graph 2: ROE of Selected PSBs and PVBs

t-Test: Two Sample for Means

H_o: There is no significant difference between the mean ROE of selected PSBs and PVBs.

H_1: There is significant difference between the mean ROE of selected PSBs and PVBs.

Table 5: Mean Difference Test based on ROE

	PSBs	*PVBs*
Mean	7.58	12.67
Variance	115.564	3.069
Df	4	
t-stat	–1.10592	
p-value	0.165399	

Source: Computed by authors

Comment on ROE

The above table shows that the mean rate of ROE of all of the PVBs (12.67%) is higher than the comparative figures of PSBs (7.58%). Mean rate of ROE of HDFC Bank is 15.17%, which is a quite good indicator, while the mean rate of ROE for SBI is 9.06% during the study period. The average ROE of PNB is –2.91%. The mean ROE of BOB is far behind the comparative figures of PVBs. The S.D. of earnings of HDFC Bank is only 0.62%. It represents a consistent earning capacity of the bank. The S.D. of earnings of KMB is also very low. But the SD of PNB is very high in comparison to the figures of the corresponding SDs of PVBs. The CV of PSBs also reflects that the fluctuation of earnings of the PSBs is also higher than the PVBs.

Average ROE of both the PSBs and PVBs has been increased significantly after the Pandemic period. Average ROE for PVBs for all the years is more than 11%. It indicates that the Pandemic has not influenced the ROE of PVBs significantly. Average ROE for PSBs in 2020–21 was only 4.11%. It may be due to the negative impact of the pandemic.

Return on Capital Employed (ROCE)

It is a useful measure for comparing the relative profitability of companies after taking into account the amount of capital employed. It is calculated by dividing the operating profit of the company by its capital employed.

Table 6: Comparative Statement of Return on Capital Employed of PSBs and PVBs

	Public Sector Banks			*Private Sector Banks*		
Year	*SBI*	*BOB*	*PNB*	*HDFC*	*ICICI*	*KMB*
2018–19	1.23	1.78	1.70	3.34	2.52	2.77
2019–20	1.79	1.77	1.80	3.33	2.67	2.86
2020–21	1.64	1.85	1.85	3.42	3.10	3.32
2021–22	1.42	1.81	1.61	3.22	2.92	2.93
2022–23	1.59	1.91	1.57	2.97	3.27	3.15
Mean ROCE	1.58	1.82	1.70	3.25	2.89	3.006
S.D. of ROCE	0.082	0.057	0.119	0.175	0.306	0.225
C.V. of ROCE	5.18%	3.13%	7%	5.38%	10.59%	7.48%

Sources: https://www.moneycontrol.com

Table 7: Average Return on Capital Employed of Selected PSBs and PVBs

Year	*PSB*	*PVB*
2018–19	1.163	2.877
2019–20	1.787	2.953
2020–21	1.78	3.28
2021–22	1.613	3.023
2022–23	1.69	3.12

Source: Computed by authors

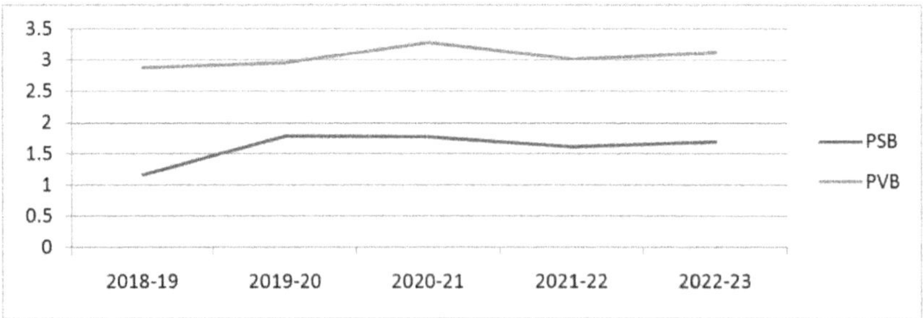

Graph 3: ROCE of Selected PSBs and PVBs

Source: Computed by authors

Mean difference test based on ROCE: t-test analysis

H_o: There is no significant difference between mean ROCE of selected PSBs and PVBs.

H_1: There is significant difference between mean ROCE of selected PSBs and PVBs.

Mean Difference Test based on ROCE

	PSBs	*PVBs*
Mean	1.6066	3.0526
Variance	0.066597	0.024833
t-stat	16.4535***	

Source: Computed by authors
***significant at 1% level

Comment on ROCE

The above table shows that the mean rate of ROCE of all of the PVBs (3.05%) is higher than the comparative figures of PSBs (1.60%). Mean rate of ROE of HDFC Bank is 3.25%, which is a quite good indicator, while the mean rate of ROE for SBI is 1.29% during the study period. The average ROE of all the PSBs is much lower than the comparative figures of the PVBs. The S.D. of earnings of HDFC Bank is only 0.175 with a good average. It is reflected through its C.V. It represents a consistent earning capacity of the bank. The CV of PSBs also reflects that the fluctuation of earnings of the PSBs is also higher than the PVBs. Average ROE of both the PSBs and PVBs has been increased significantly after the Pandemic period. Average ROE for PVBs for all the years is more than 11%. It indicates that the Pandemic has not influenced the ROE of PVBs significantly. Average ROE for PSBs in 2020–21 was only 4.11%. It may be due to the detrimental effect of pandemic.

Net Interest Margin (NIM)

It is a measure of the difference between interest received and paid by the bank. It is calculated by dividing the Net Interest by the average investments.

Table 8: Comparative Statement of Net Interest Margin of PSBs and PVBs

Year	*Public Sector Banks*			*Private Sector Banks*		
	SBI	*BOB*	*PNB*	*HDFC*	*ICICI*	*KMB*
2018–19	2.40	2.36	2.21	3.87	2.80	3.60
2019–20	2.48	2.37	2.09	3.67	3.02	3.74
2020–21	2.44	2.49	2.41	3.71	3.16	4.00
2021–22	2.42	2.55	2.18	3.48	3.36	3.91
2022–23	2.62	2.83	2.35	3.52	3.92	4.39

Year	*Public Sector Banks*			*Private Sector Banks*		
	SBI	*BOB*	*PNB*	*HDFC*	*ICICI*	*KMB*
Mean NIM	2.47	2.52	2.45	3.65	3.25	3.93
S.D. of NIM	0.088	0.191	0.130	0.156	0.426	0.301
C.V. of NIM	3.56%	7.58%	5.31%	4.27%	13.10%	7.66%

Sources: www.moneycontrol.com

Table 9: Average NIM of Selected PSBs and PVBs

Year	*PSB*	*PVB*
2018–19	2.32	3.42
2019–20	2.31	3.48
2020–21	2.45	3.62
2021–22	2.38	3.58
2022–23	2.6	3.94

Source: Computed by researchers

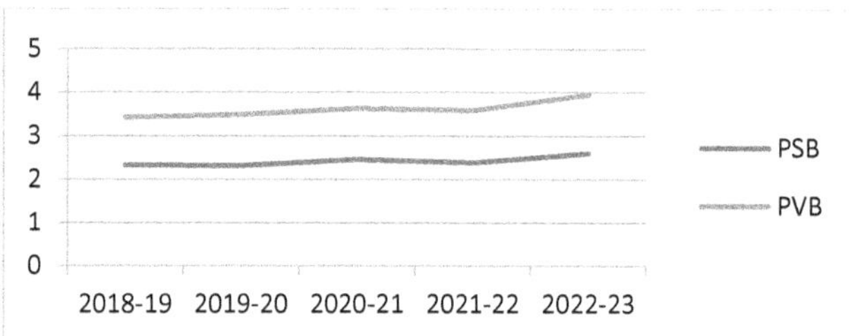

Graph 4: Net Interest Margin of Selected PSBs and PVBs

Source: Computed by researchers

Mean difference test on two sample means

H_o: There is no significant difference between the mean NIM of selected PSBs and PVBs.

H_1: There is significant difference between the mean NIM of selected PSBs and PVBs.

Table 10: Mean difference test based on NIM

	PSBs	*PVBs*
Mean	2.412	3.608
Variance	0.01417	0.04072
t Stat	–30.2228***	

Source: Computed by researchers

Comments on Net Interest Margin

The above table shows that the mean rate of NIM of PVBs is 3.608 %, while the mean rate of ROA for the PSBs is 2.412%. The variance of earnings of the PSBs (0.014) is lower than the corresponding variance of earnings of PVBs (0.040). It reflects that the fluctuation of earnings of the PSBs is lower than the PVBs. As the p value <= 0.05, we reject the Null hypothesis and accept the alternative hypothesis. The absolute value of t-statistic is much higher than the critical value both at 5% level of significance and 1% level of significance; hence, there is no reason to accept the hypothesis that the mean difference of NIM is not significant. In other words, the selected PVBs of India earns significantly higher rate of NIM in comparison to the selected PSBs.

Analysis based on Net Profit Margin

It measures the percentage of profit earned by a company in relation to its revenue. It is calculated by diving the net profit of the company by the net revenue earned by the company.

Table 11: Comparative Statement of Net Profit Margin of PSBs and PVBs

	Public Sector Banks			*Private Sector Banks*		
Year	*SBI*	*BOB*	*PNB*	*HDFC*	*ICICI*	*KMB*
2018–19	0.35	0.87	−19.44	21.29	5.30	20.32
2019–20	5.63	0.71	0.62	22.86	10.60	22.08
2020–21	7.69	1.17	2.50	25.74	20.46	25.94
2021–22	11.49	10.40	4.61	28.93	27.02	31.70
2022–23	15.12	15.74	2.94	27.29	29.20	31.93
Mean NP	8.05	5.78	−1.75	25.22	18.52	26.39
S.D. of NP	5.64	6.92	9.99	3.14	10.34	5.35
C.V.of NP	70.06	119.72	−571.43	12.45	55.83	20.27

Source: Computed by researchers

Table 12: Overall Net Profit Margin (%) of Selected PSBs and PVBs

Year	*PSB*	*PVB*
2018–19	−6.07	15.64
2019–20	2.32	18.51
2020–21	3.78	24.04
2021–22	8.83	29.22
2022–23	11.27	29.47

Source: Computed by researchers

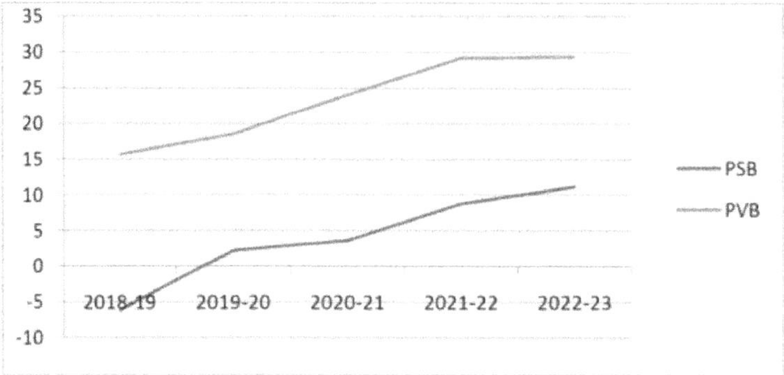

Graph 5: Net Profit Margin of Selected PSBs and PVBs

Source: Computed by researchers

Mean difference test on two samples based on Net Profit Margin

H_o: There is no significant difference between the mean NP Margin of selected PSBs and PVBs.

H_1: There is significant difference between the mean NP Marin of selected PSBs and PVBs

Table 13: Mean Difference Test Based on NPM

	PSBs	*PVBs*
Mean	4.026	23.376
Variance	45.11	38.81
t- Stat	19.9647***	

Source: Computed by researchers

Comment on Net Profit Margin

The above table shows that the mean rate of Net Profit margin of PVBs is 23.376%, while the mean rate of Net Profit for the PSBs is only 4.026%. The variance of earnings of the PSBs (45.11) is higher than the corresponding variance of earnings of PVBs (38.81). It reflects that the fluctuation of earnings of the PSBs is also higher than the PVBs. As the p value <= 0.05, we reject the Null hypothesis and accept the alternative hypothesis. The absolute value of t-statistic is much higher than the critical value both at 5% level of significance and 1% level of significance; hence, there is no reason to accept the hypothesis that the mean difference of Net Profit margin is not significant. In other words, the selected PVBs of India earns significantly higher rate of Net Profit in comparison to the selected PSBs.

Conclusions

The results of all the tests and measures indicate that the banking sector of India has overcome the negative shock of the pandemic to a great extent. But the financial performance of the public sector banks, except SBI is lagging far behind than their private sector counterparts. Again, the performance of HDFC bank is quite satisfactory in respect of all the parameters. The possible reasons for low financial performance of the PSBs may be over-cautious approach in lending, existence of high overhead costs and fulfillment of social obligations. As the existence and sustainability of the PSBs is very much necessary for the well-being of the society and overall economic development of the country, strict government regulations are natural consequences. Such restrictions must have negative impacts on the profitability of the PSBs.

Suggestions

1. PSBs should give more importance on the improvement of their profitability. Operating expenses must be reduced by implementing cost control measures. Employee wise performance should be monitored by the appropriate authorities.
2. Assets must be utilized properly by the PSBs. Underutilized assets must be considered for diversification purposes. New schemes of income generation must be started.
3. The quality of assets must be improved by the PSBs. The process of sanctioning loans and collection of dues should be monitored efficiently.
4. To ensure the adequate performance, branch wise and product wise targets must be fixed by the PSBs.
5. The PVBs should also set targets in respect of Social Welfare Programmes.

References

[1] Almaqtari, F.A., Al-Homaidi, E.A., Tabash, M.I. and Farhan, N.H. (2019). The determinants of profitability of Indian commercial banks: A panel data approach. *International Journal of Finance & Economics, 24*(1), 68–185.

[2] Anand, K. (2015). Financial performance of public sector banks and private sector banks in India. *Research Explorer*, IV(11), July–December.

[3] Athanasoglou, P.P., Brissimis S.N. and Delis, M.D. (2008). Bank-specific, industry-specific and macroeconomic determinants of bank profitability. *J. Int Finan Mark Inst Money, 18*(2), 121–136.

[4] Chaudhary, K. and Sharma, M. (2011). Performance of Indian public sector banks and private sector banks: A comparative study. *International Journal of Innovation, Management and Technology, 2*(3), 249–256.

[5] Malhotra, D.K. (2011). Evaluating the performance of commercial banks in India. *Asia Pacific Journal of Finance and Banking Research, 5*(1), 15–37.

[6] Das and Uppal (2021). NPAs and Profitability in Indian Banks: an empirical analysis. *Future Business Journal, 7*(1), 1–9.

[7] Debnath and Dash (2015). A Study of Non-Performing Assets in the Indian Banking Industry. *Management Today, 5*(1), January–March, 12–22.

[8] Devarajan, S. (2018). The impact of macroeconomic variables on the profitability of public and private sector banks in India: A structural equation modelling approach, *ACADEMICIA, 8*(1), 44–77.

[9] Cooper, D.R. and Schindler, P. (2009). Business Research Methods, Tata McGraw Hill Education Private Ltd., New Delhi.

[10] Jha, D. and Sarangi, D. (2011). Performance of New Generation Banks in India: A Comparative Study. *International Journal of Research in Commerce and Management,* 85–89.

[11] Devanadhen, K. (2013). Performance evaluation of large-size commercial banks in India. *Indian Journal of Finance, 7*(1), 5–16.

[12] Kothari, C.R. (2004). Research Methodology, New Delhi, New Age International Publishers.

[13] Ali, Mohammad Athar, Pervez, Asif, Bansal, R. and Khan, A. (2022). Analyzing Performance of Banks in India: A Robust Regression Analysis Approach. *Discrete Dynamics in Nature and Societ.* DOI: 10.1155/2022/803510, 1, January, 1–9.

[14] Nataraga, N.S., Nagaraja, R.C. and Ganesh, L. (2018). Financial Performance of Private Commercial Banks in India: Multiple Regression Analysis. *Academy of Accounting and Financial Studies Journal, 22*(2), 1–12.

[15] Ongore, V.O. and Kusa, G.B. (2013). Determinants of Financial Performance of Commercial Banks of Kenya. *International Journal of Economics and Financial Issues,* 3(1), 237–252.

[16] Palamalai, S. and Britt, J. (2017). Analysis of financial performance of selected commercial banks in India. *Theoretical Economics Letters, 7*(7), 2134–2151.

[17] Razzak, A. and Gomatheswaran, M. (2019). Comparative Study of Public and Private Sector banks in India—An empirical analysis, *JETIR, 6*(2), 589–593.

[18] Sinha, P. and Sharma, S. (2016). Determinants of Bank Profits and Its Persistence in Indian Banks: A Study in a Dynamic Panel Data Framework. *International Journal of System Assurance Engineering and Management, 7*(1), 35–46.

[19] Shah, V. (2015). An analysis on the performance of private and public sector banks in India; *International Journal For Technological Research In Engineering, 3*(4), 76–89.

Impact of Capital Adequacy on Financial Performance of Indian Public Sector Banks

Gargi[1], Sayan Roy[2] and Saswata Choudhury[3]

ABSTRACT: To ensure resilience, safeguard assets and ability to cope with losses, Capital Adequacy is a critical factor for banking institutions. Maintaining an optimal balance between risk-weighted assets and capital is crucial for the long-term financial stability of these institutions. Regulatory frameworks (such as Basel norms) mandate minimum capital requirements to safeguard depositors and maintain financial stability. NIM measures the difference between interest earned on loans and interest paid on deposits. This study investigates the relationship between capital adequacy and the financial performance of 12 Indian public sector banks over a 15-year period. To analyze the impact of Capital Adequacy on profitability metric Net Interest Margin. The findings will shed light on the risk-return trade-off within the Indian banking industry.

Keywords: Bank, Capital Adequacy, Financial Institution, Net Interest Margin.

JEL Classification: G20, G21,

Introduction

The banking sector is a crucial component of India's financial system, playing a fundamental role in the economy's functioning and development. The Indian banking system consists of 12 public sector banks, 22 private sector banks, 46 foreign banks, 56 regional rural banks, 1485 urban cooperative banks and 96,000 rural cooperative banks in addition to cooperative credit institutions. According to RBI's Scheduled Banks' Statement, deposits of all scheduled banks collectively surged by a whopping Rs.1.98 lakh crore (US$ 24.32 billion) as on May 5, 2023, at a growth rate of 10.2%. Capital Adequacy is a critical measure of a bank's financial health and ability to withstand adverse economic conditions. Since the inception of Basel Committee (1975), the committee has established a

[1] College Whole Time Teacher, The Bhawanipur Education Society College, India. E-mail: gargionly21@gmail.com

[2] College Whole Time Teacher, The Bhawanipur Education Society College, Research Scholar, Adamas University, India. E-mail: subhoroy31@gmail.com

[3] Assistant Professor, Department of Commerce, Balurghat College, West Bengal, India. E-mail: saswata.choudhury@gmail.com

series of international standards for bank regulation, most notably its landmark publications of the accords on capital adequacy which are commonly known as Basel I, Basel II and, most recently, Basel III. There are different forms of capital, including Tier 1 and Tier 2 capital, each with specific characteristics and functions. Common measures of capital adequacy include the capital adequacy ratio (CAR), which compares a bank's capital to its risk-weighted assets. Bank's Net Interest Margin (NIM) is a key indicator on how bank performs its intermediary function and necessary for the financial system stability. This study aims to analyse the impact of capital adequacy on the financial performance.

Literature Review

Kaur and Kapoor (2014) studied the changes in Capital Adequacy Ratio (CAR) public and private sector banks using Compound Annual Growth Rate considering the BASEL Capital Adequacy Requirement. The results of the study concluded that all private and public sector banks crossed the requirements stipulated by RBI, which makes them more resilient towards economic shocks. Silaban (2017) attempted to test and determine the Bank's health level consisting of capital adequacy ratio (CAR), net interest margin (NIM), and non-performing loans (NPL) partially or simultaneously on bank profitability based on data from the Indonesian Stock Exchange. The results of the study indicate that capital adequacy ratio (CAR) does not have a significant effect on bank profitability. Sunaryo (2020) aimed to determine the effect of Capital Adequacy Ratio (CAR), Net Interest Margin (NIM), Non-Performing Loan (NPL), dan Loan to Deposit Ratio (LDR) in the Return on Asset (ROA) on the Commercial Banks in Southeast Asia in 2012-2018. It had been studied using purposive sampling technique, using secondary and quantitative data. Based on the results of the study it can be concluded that 1) Capital Adequacy Ratio (CAR) has a positive and significant effect on Return on Asset (ROA). 2) Net Interest Margin (NIM) has a positive and significant effect on Return on Asset (ROA). 3) Non-Performing Loan (NPL) no has a positive and significant effect on Return on Asset (ROA). 4) Loan to Deposit Ratio (LDR) has a negative and significant effect on Return on Asset (ROA). Rahmi *et al.* (2020) explained the effect of Capital Adequacy Ratio (CAR), Net Interest Margin (NIM), and Loan to Deposits Ratio (LDR) on Return on Assets (ROA). It was concluded ROA, CAR and NIM fluctuated with a tendency to decline whereas LDR fluctuated with a tendency to increase. Saksonova (2014) observed that net interest margin is the most appropriate criterion for evaluating the effectiveness and stability of banks' operations. The author analyzes banking sectors in the Baltic countries, the Euro Area as well as the United States and their management strategies, as well as indicators of their operations to show that net interest margin is one of the most important criteria for asset structure optimization. s. It suggests that net interest margin can be an important complement to an overall profitability indicator such as return on assets. A simple examination of the dynamics of net interest margin and the return on assets shows that net interest margin had a tendency to decline prior to the difficulties in the banking sector, while return on assets remained more stable during that time. Prakash & Sindhasha (2016) explained the linkage between net interest margin of 43 public and private sector banks and bank specific determinants for the period 2002–2003 to 2013–2014. The study aims to find the association between Net Interest Margin (NIM) and bank specific determinants with the help of statistical tools such as descriptive statistics, multiple correlation analysis and multiple regression analysis. The results confirmed the statistically significant relationship between net interest margin of public and private sector banks and bank specific factors such as return on investment, operating profits to total assets, provisions and contingences to total assets and burden to total assets ratios. Goel and Rekhi (2013) attempted to measure the relative performance of Indian public sector banks and private sector banks using different proxy indicators of banking sector. The analysis concluded that new banks are more efficient that old ones. The public sector banks are not as profitable as other sectors are. Efficiency and profitability are interrelated. The key to increase performance depends upon ROA, ROE and NIM. Mahamuni & Jumle (2019) assessed and identified the determinants of NIM in the Indian Banking Industry. The results of the study revealed that cost efficiency, implicit interest payment, competition, and scale efficiency have positive and significant effect on NIM. However, liquidity risk and management efficiency have negative and significant effect on NIM. On the other hand, credit risk, interest rate risk, capital risk, inflation and economic growth do not seem to have significant impact on banks' performance. Mahajan (2018) analyzed determinants of profitability of 26 public and 19 private sector banks of India from 2011–2016. The results indicated that the Indian Banking Sector remained relatively healthy during the economic crisis and the performance of the banks was not impacted negatively and banks paved the way to Service-Led growth in Indian Economic Development. Dudhe (2018) evaluated select private sector banks from each of the important parameter of CAMEL Model Capital Adequacy, Asset Quality, Management capability, Earnings capacity and Liquidity. The study signified there is no significant difference in financial performance of selected private sector banks as assessed by CAMELS model. Jadhav *et al.* (2021) aimed to throw light upon the linkage that capital adequacy has with the bank's profitability. It attempts to establish a relation between the Capital Adequacy Ratio with the Net profits of the bank. The results identified that increase in capital adequacy has resulted in an increase in the overall profitability and the return on assets for private sector banks in India. Torbira (2016) studied impact of capital adequacy indicators (the ratio of shareholders fund to bank total deposit (SHF/BTD) and the ratio of shareholders fund to bank total assets (SHF/BTA)), on bank financial performance measures-net profit margin (NPM), earning per share (EPS) and return on assets (ROA) in Nigeria. The study revealed that capital adequacy strongly and actively stimulates and improve the financial performance of banks in Nigeria.

Objective of the Study

The purpose of this study is to find out the impact of Capital Adequacy Ratio (CAR) on Net Interest Margin (NIM) of each of the 12 Indian public sector banks.

Research Methodology

This study is based on two variables i.e. Capital Adequacy Ratio (CAR), which is an independent variable and the ratio of net interest income to total assets known as Net Interest Margin (NIM), as dependent variable which represents the financial performance. Natural logarithms are taken for both the dependent and independent variables to make the time series stationary as well as to neutralize heteroskedasticity. Data were taken for 12 Public Sector banks for 15 years from 2008 to 2022. Annual Reports and database of Reserve Bank of India (RBI) are considered for collection of data. Descriptive statistics are obtained for each of the variable. Ordinary least square (OLS) regression model is applied in this study. statistical tests are conducted according to the need of the study. Stata 14.0 software has been used for the purpose of analysis.

The hypothesis of this study-

H_0: There is no influence of Capital Adequacy Ratio on financial performance.

H_1: There is an influence of Capital Adequacy Ratio on financial performance.

The regression model of the study is-

$$\text{Log(NIM)} = \alpha + \beta_1 \text{Log(CAR)} + \epsilon$$

Data Analysis and Findings

Table 1: Descriptive Statistics

Variables	*Obs.*	*Mean*	*SD*	*Max.*	*Min.*
NIM	180	2.376	0.407	3.62	1.40
CAR	180	12.617	1.614	18.54	9.04

Source: Calculated by authors

Table 1 shows the descriptive statistics of the variables used in this study. Average NIM and Average CAR are 2.376 and 12.617 respectively during the study period. The highest value of NIM is observed as 3.62 and lowest is 1.40. Similarly for CAR the maximum value is 18.54 and minimum is 9.04. The standard deviation for NIM is 0.407 and for CAR is 1.614.

Table 2: Regression Analysis (Dependent Variable: NIM)

Bank	*F*	*Prob(F)*	R^2	*Coeff.*	*Prob (Coeff.)*
SBI	0.43	0.52	3.19	0.65	0.52
BOB*	17.28	0.00*	57.07	1.20	0.00*
BOI	0.04	0.84	0.03	–0.05	0.84
BOM	1.66	0.21	11.35	0.37	0.21
CANB*	8.55	0.01*	39.68	0.62	0.01*
CBI	0.07	0.79	0.05	0.07	0.79
INB	0.18	0.68	1.33	–0.22	0.68
IOB*	10.94	0.00*	45.69	0.46	0.00*
PSB	0.93	0.35	6.65	0.22	0.35
PNB	1.83	0.19	12.35	0.47	0.19
UCO*	7.95	0.01*	37.96	1.05	0.01*
UNION	2.40	0.14	15.56	0.47	0.14

Source: Calculated by authors
*Significant at 5% level.

Table 2 estimates the influence of independent variable CAR on dependent variable NIM. Simple regression model (Ordinary least square method) is conducted for all the twelve public sector banks individually. F values indicated the goodness of fit of the model. The probability of F statistics is observed 0.00 for Bank of Baroda, 0.01 for Canara bank, 0.00 for Indian Overseas Bank and 0.01 for UCO Bank. That means for these four banks the model is a good fit. Probability of coefficients are found as 0.00 for Bank of Baroda and Indian Overseas Bank and 0.01 for Canara Bank and UCO Bank, which is significant at 5% level of significance.

Table 3: Test for Cointegration
(Engle-Granger Augmented Dickey-Fuller test)

Bank	*Existence of Cointegration*
SBI	Not Cointegrated
BOB	Not Cointegrated
BOI	Not Cointegrated
BOM	Not Cointegrated
CANB	Cointegrated
CBI	Not Cointegrated
INB	Not Cointegrated
IOB	Not Cointegrated
PSB	Cointegrated
PNB	Not Cointegrated
UCO	Not Cointegrated
UNION	Not Cointegrated

Source: Calculated by authors

To find out the stochastic trend between two or more series test of cointegration is required. Table 3 established the nature of stochasticity of all the series of all the banks. After conducting the test, it has been found that variables are cointegrated for two banks i.e. Canara Bank and Punjab and Sind Bank. The series of other banks are not cointegrated.

Conclusion

The objective of the study is to find out the impact of the Capital Adequacy Ratio (CAR) on the financial performance in terms of Net Interest Margin (NIM). After analysing the results it has been found that for Bank of Baroda, Canara bank, Indian Overseas Bank and UCO Bank CAR is affecting the financial performance positively. For all the other banks it cannot be concluded similarly as the models are failed to pass the test for goodness of fit. The value of R^2signifies that CAR is explaining the movement of NIM by 57.07% for Bank of Baroda and 39.68%, for Canara bank, 45.69% for Indian Overseas Bank and 37.96% for UCO Bank

Scope for Further Study

The entire study is based only on the public sector banks. More exhaustive study can be done taking private sector banks into consideration. Study can also be conducted on of Bank of Baroda and Indian Overseas Bank, where no cointegration is found though there is an influence of CAR on NIM. On the other hand, further study can be done on Punjab and Sind Bank, where cointegration is detected but still there is no influence of CAR on NIM.

References

[1] Kaur, M. and Kapoor, S. (2014). Capital Adequacy and Growth in Banks: An Indian Scenario. *Amity Business Review,* Vol. 15, No. 1, June 2014, 31–38.

[2] Silaban, P. (2017). The Effect of Capital Adequacy Ratio, Net Interest Margin and Non-Performing Loans on Bank Profitability: The Case of Indonesia. *International Journal of Economics and Business Administration,* Volume V. Issue 3, 58–69.

[3] Sunaryo, D. (2020). The Effect of Capital Adequacy Ratio (CAR), Net Interest Margin (NIM), Non-Performing Loan (NPL), and Loan to Deposit Ratio (LDR) Against Return on Asset (ROA) In General Banks in Southeast Asia 2012–2018. *Ilomata International Journal of Management,* 1(4), 149–158.

[4] Rahmi, P., Herlina, L. and Novitasary, S. (2022). The Effect of Capital Adequacy Ratio (Car), Net Interest Margin (Nim), And Loan To Deposits Ratio (LDR) On Return On Asset (ROA) In Pt Bank Negara Indonesia Persero TBK Period Of 2011–2021, *Journal of Business and Management Inaba, 1*(1), 45–63.

[5] Saksonova, S. (2014) The Role of Net Interest Margin in Improving Banks' Asset Structure and Assessing the Stability and Efficiency of their Operations. *Procedia – Social and Behavioral Sciences,* 150 (2014), 132 –141.

[6] Prakash, A.P. and Sindhasha, A.M. (2016). Impact of Bank Specific Determinants on Net Interest Margin: Empirical Evidence from Public and Private Sector Commercial Banks in India. *ICTACT Journal on Management Studies,* 2(4), 389–393.

[7] Goel, C. and Rekhi, C.B. (2013). A Comparative Study on the Performance of Selected Public Sector and Private Sector Banks in India. *Journal of Business Management & Social Sciences Research, 2*(7), July, 46–56.

[8] Mahamuni, P.N. and Jumle, A.G. (2019). Comparative Study of Net Interest Margin (Nim) of Selected Indian Public and Private Sector Banks. *International Journal of Management, IT & Engineering,* 9(6), June, 388–405.

[9] Mahajan, P. (2019). A Panel Data Analysis of Profitability Determinants: Empirical Study of Indian Public and Private Sector Banks. *Business Analyst,* 39 (1), 46–63.

[10] Dudhe, C. (2018). A Selective Study: Camels Analysis of Indian Private Sector Banks. *International Journal of Engineering and Management Sciences, 3*(5), DOI: 10.21791/IJEMS.2018.5.28. 277–283.

[11] Jadhav, J.J., Kathale, A. and Rajpurohit, S. (2021). An Impact of Capital Adequacy Ratio on the Profitability of Private Sector Banks in India—A Study. *International Journal of Engineering and Management Research, 11*(5), October, 37–45.

[12] Torbira, L., Lenee, A. and Sulaiman, Z.A. (2016). Capital Adequacy Measures and Bank Financial Performance in Nigeria: A Cointegration Analysis. *Journal of Finance & Economic Research, 3*, 15–33.

Does Digital Transaction Influence Consumer Confidence In India? An Inquest

Priyajit Kumar Ghosh[1] and Biswajit Paul[2]

ABSTRACT: One of India's digital payment innovations that has grabbed global attentions in recent years is UPI transaction mechanism. This digital transaction mechanism presents numerous benefits in front of its users such as faster, safer and hassle-free transactions. But whether the use of digital transactions influence on consumer confidence is a subject that needs to be examined. This paper investigates the influence of digital transactions on consumer confidence in India using ARDL model during April, 2021 to November, 2023. Results of ARDL model showed that digital transactions increase the consumer confidence in long run in India. Whereas, in short run positive but insignificant influence of digital transactions on consumer confidence is documented. The study recommends policymakers to promote digital transactions to boost consumer confidence and improve household consumption levels in India through framing and implementing array of policy initiatives along with awareness and educational programs.

Keywords: ARDL, Consumer Confidence, Digital Transaction, Household Consumption.

JEL Classification: D12, E21, G5, O33.

Introduction

For Indians, using physical currency is one of the most common methods for executing transactions. Indians are deeply accustomed to accepting physical currency in most of their activities (Shree *et al.*, 2021). However, it's not always as easy and efficient to use physical currency as it seems. Making transaction in physical currency has several drawbacks. Carrying large amount of physical currency to make transactions is risky as well as inconvenient. It is also difficult to tack the origine and trail of transactions (McAndrews, J.J., 2020). Further, it involves printing costs. In order to address these issues and to transform India into a digitally empowered and cash less economy, Government of India as well as RBI put so much thrust on digital transactions by introducing several digitally

[1] Assistant Professor, Department of Commerce (Morning), St. Xavier's College (Autonomous), Kolkata, India. E-mail: priyajitkumarghosh97@gmail.com

[2] Assistant Professor, Department of Commerce, University of Gour Banga, Malda, India. E-mail: ugb.biswajitpaul@gmail.com

enabled transactions mode such as UPI, Internet Banking, mobile banking, banking cards, NEFT, IMPS, RTGS, point of sales, Aadhaar Enabled Payment System (AEPS) etc. (Ramya *et al.*, 2017). This digitally enabled transactions mode presents numerous benefits in front of its users including faster, safer and hassle-free transactions. India witnessed a sharp increase in the volume and value of digital transactions following the launch of UPI and the outbreak of Covid-19 pandemic (Jain *et al.*, 2020, Chaudhari & Kumar, 2021). Specifically, a significant portion of the population began utilising the digital transaction system during this pandemic to avoid the risk of transmission through physical payment methods (Achutamba & Hymavathi, 2022). In the year 2011–12, only 50.20 crores of transaction were made through digital mode in India. But in 2017–18 it raised to 2,071 crores and in 2022–23 it reached to 13,462 crores (figure 1).

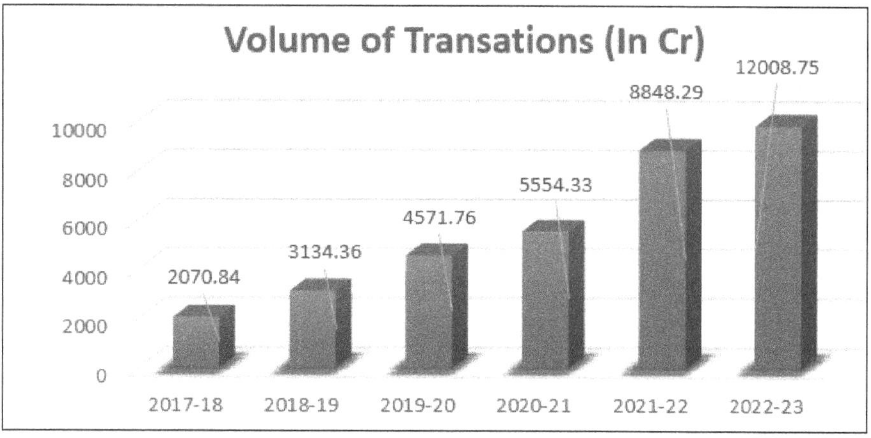

Figure 1: Trends of Digital Transactions in India

Source: National Informatics Centre (https://www.nic.in/blogs/digital-payments-driving-the-growth-of-digital-economy/)

While digital transactions started gaining popularity among Indians another thing i.e., consumption expenditure of Indian also raised gradually in India during the past few years. In the year 2021–22, the proportion of private Final Consumption Expenditure (PFCE) to GDP (at constant price) reached to 58.30 percent. This indicates that one of the main forces which fuels India's economic expansion is consumption (Mishra, P.K., 2011). In the same vein, several researchers tried to examine whether the consumption expenditure drive economic growth in various countries or not. The study of Mishra, P.K. (2011) found a one-way causal relationship from private consumption expenditure to economic growth in India. The study of Dey & Tareque (2018) also documented the similar results in Bangladesh. They reported a uni-directional causality from private consumption expenditure to GDP in Bangladesh.

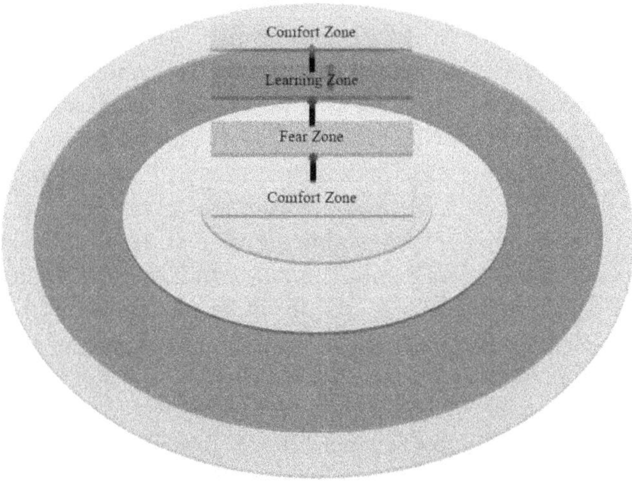

Figure 2: Use of Digital Transaction and Consumer Behavior - Conceptual Framework

Source: Researchers' own presentation

Based on the above-mentioned discussion, it can be observed that Indians are deeply habituated to using physical currency in the majority of their transactions (Shree *et al.*, 2021). Since people are accustomed to using cash or physical transactions, this stage could be considered a comfort zone. Initially, people in India are reluctant to move from their comfortable zone to digital mode of transactions (UPI, Internet Banking, mobile banking, banking cards, NEFT, IMPS, RTGS, point of sales, Aadhaar Enabled Payment System (AEPS) etc.) because of various fear factors, such as phone hacking, transaction leaks, transaction declines, network outages during transactions, and tampering with information (Patra & Gupta, 2022). This zone cam be regarded as fear zone. However, when more people gained access to mobile phones and the internet and became aware of the benefits of using digital transactions, they began to learn how to use digital mode of transactions effectively and got over different fear factors. Most notably, during the Covid-19 pandemic, there was a notable surge in the use of digital transactions as people reconsidered earlier ways of transaction owing to concerns about contamination from using physical currency (Achutamba & Hymavathi, 2022). As a result, after the Covid-19, digital transactions have rapidly increased in India (Gupta & Singhal, 2021). Similar to cash transactions, digital transactions are now entering the comfort zone of Indians, as evidenced by the growing trend of digital transactions and the growing confidence of Indians towards them.

It is important to mention that the study of Shree *et al.* (2021) highlighted that when people make transactions through digital payment mechanism, they feel less the pain of paying than in paying through physical currency. Hence, they save less and consume more when they follow digital transactions. In this regard, several researchers such as Sumathy & Vipin (2017), Ranjith *et al.* (2021), Shree *et al.* (2021) and others examined whether or not digital payment influence consumer perception and buying behavior. The study of Kusnawan *et al.* (2020) reported digital payments have a positive influence on consumer purchase decisions. Oyelami *et al.* (2020) also found the similar results in case of Nigeria. The study of Hou *et al.* (2021) argues that the use of digital payments increases impulsive spending while facilitating smooth consumption. Zhou, R. (2022) revealed that digital payments significantly increase customer demand. Similar results were also obtained by Zhang *et al.* (2022), i.e., digital payments facilitate consumption of rural households in China. On the other hand, this increase level of consumption ultimately leads to economic development of a country Mishra, P.K. (2011), Dey & Tareque (2018). Therefore, it can be said that digital payment mechanism influence consumption behavior of people which further influence on economic development of a country. Thus, at this crucial time, when India transiting into digital economy, it is pertinent to check whether or not the digital transaction has any significant effect on Indian consumers' confidence? It is noteworthy to mention that no comprehensive study has done yet on this matter. In this regard present study aims to examine the influence of digital transactions on consumer confidence in India using ARDL estimation techniques.

Research Methodology

Data Source and Variables Selection

In this paper uses monthly data of consumer confidence index that are collected from OECD database during April 2021 to November 2023. Data on digital transactions are obtained from National Payments Corporation of India (NPCI). Whereas, data on consumer price index and economic growth are obtained from FRED and OECD database respectively.

In this study Consumer Confidence Index developed by OECD is used as dependent variable. This index is one of the most promising indicators that capable to captures consumer sentiment regarding their consumption expenditure. Studies of Kwan & Cotsomitis (2006), Dees & Brinca (2013), Lahiri *et al.* (2016). and others highlighted the predictive power of consumer confidence regarding consumption expenditure. Whereas, UPI Transaction Volume is used as independent variable. UPI Transaction Volume is used as an indicator of digital transactions in India. The studies of Mahapatra, S. (2018), Sharma *et al.* (2022) also used Unified Payments Interfaces (UPI) as indicators of digital transactions in India. Further present study uses inflation and economic development as

Control Variables. Because several studies identified the nexus between inflation and economic development with consumer confidence. Studies of Sum, V. (2012), Aberu, F. (2022) identified that inflation impacts consumer confidence. Similarly, studies of Islam & Mumtaz (2016), Borisov, L. (2022) and others found the link between economic development and consumer confidence in different countries. Here, Consumer Price Index (CPI) and Gross Domestic Product (GDP) is used as proxy variable of inflation and economic development respectively.

Model Specification

Present study uses the following basic regression model to satisfy the research objective.

Consumer Confidence = *f* (Digital transactions, Inflation, Economic Development)

The below stated econometric model is used in this study:

$$L\_CCI_t = \beta_0 + \beta_1 L\_UPI_t + \beta_2 L\_CPI_t + \beta_3 L\_GDP_t + \varepsilon_t$$

Where,

$\beta_0, \beta_1, \beta_2, \beta_3 \ldots\ldots \beta n$ = the model parameters

L_CCI_t = Log of Consumer Confidence Index

L_UPI_t = Log of UPI Transactions

L_CPI_t = Log of Consumer Price Index

L_GDP_t = Log of GDP

ε_t = Disturbance term exist in the model.

Econometric Tools Employed

The present study's econometric estimating process is presented below:

Unit Root Test

A unit root test helps to track whether the select variables are non-stationary and carry unit root within data series or not. To examine this, at first, the researchers adopted the ADF and PP approaches, which were put forth by Dickey & Fuller (1979) and Phillips & Perron (1988), respectively, to perform the unit root test. If variables are stationary or don't possess unit root within them, further time series econometrics estimation procedures can be performed. Prior research by Sana *et al.* (2020), Nyoni *et al.* (2021), Ghosh & Paul (2023), Ghosh *et al.* (2023), and others also evaluated the stationarity status of variables considering the ADF and PP techniques.

Autoregressive Distributed Lag (ARDL) Bounds Test

Based on the outcomes of unit root test, ARDL estimation technique can be performed. This ARDL estimation technique can be utilized if outcomes of unit root test showed mixed order of integration. This mixed order of integration implies variables are integrated at level and at fist difference i.e., I (1) and I (0). Numerous authors of previous studies, including Sana *et al.* (2020), Reda & Nourhan (2020), Ghosh *et al.* (2023), Ghosh *et al.* (2024) and others, suggest applying the ARDL bound test approach of cointegration then using the long run estimation model and Error Correction (ECM) – ARDL model to evaluate the degree of long-run association among the selected variables and their dynamics.

Estimated Long Run and Short Run Coefficients

It is now necessary to go through the outcomes of the ARDL Bounds test. If the F Stat. value exceeds than the probability value, it indicates that there is a long-term linkage between the chosen variables. Both short-term and long-term estimating tests are carried out at this point. Long-run coefficients are produced from long-run estimate, whereas short-run coefficients and the value of the error correction term are derived from short-run estimation.

This ECM coefficient defines how swiftly variables return to their equilibrium point, it should have a negative sign and appears statistically significant. Present study also followed the procedures used by Sana *et al.* (2020), Reda & Nourhan (2020), Ghosh & Paul (2023), Ghosh *et al.* (2023).

The following is the ECM-ARDL model's empirical form:

$$\Delta L\_CCIt = \alpha + \sum_{i=0}^{n} \beta i \, \Delta L\_CCI\, t - i + \sum_{i=0}^{n} \lambda i \, \Delta L\_UPI\, t - i + \sum_{i=0}^{n} \theta i \, \Delta L\_CPI\, t - i + \sum_{i=0}^{n} \alpha i \, \Delta L\_GDP\, t - i + \mu_1 L\_CCIt + \mu_2 L\_UPIt + \mu_3 L\_CPIt + \mu_4 L\_GDPt + \lambda\, ECM\, t{-}1 + \varepsilon t$$

Where the λ implies error correction term which talks about the rate of adjustment at which variables restore equilibrium point, and 'n' implies ideal lag-length(s) select for the present study's estimation. Short-run multiplier is denoted by the symbols of β, γ, θ and α, whereas long-run multiplier represented by symbols of μ_1, μ_2, μ_3 and μ_4.

Diagnostic Test

Now, researchers conducted the Breusch-Pagan-Godfrey heteroscedasticity test and the Histogram Normality test, accordingly, to evaluate the presence of heteroscedasticity of the residual value of the regression model and to get idea on overall distribution of the data.

Stability Tests

Lastly, the stability of the regression model's parameter is examined and any systematic shifts in the regression coefficients are detected applying the two major tests for determining model stability: the cumulative sum (CUSUM) and cumulative sum of squares (CUSUM).

Results and Discussion

Table 1 presents descriptive statistics of select variables in this study. It demonstrates that every variable has a positive mean value. The mean and median values of model variables indicate their normal distribution, with differences between average and median not exceeding 10% (Yitzhaki, S., 2003, Busu, M., 2020), as shown in the table. Whereas, L_UPI_t and L_GDP_t variable have negative value of skewness, indicating that the distribution is left-skewed, with remaining observations i.e., L_CCI_t and L_CPI_t on the right tail.

Table 1: Summary of Descriptive Statistics of Selected Variables

Variables	*L_CCI_t*	*L_UPI_t*	*L_CPI_t*	*L_GDP_t*
Mean	4.5883	8.7055	5.1544	4.5955
Median	4.5873	8.7693	5.1579	4.5972
Maximum	4.6096	9.3421	5.2668	4.6202
Minimum	4.5705	7.8975	5.0524	4.5359
Std. Dev.	0.0125	0.4428	0.0568	0.0185
Skewness	0.2237	–0.3845	0.4070	–1.5120
Kurtosis	1.9109	2.0940	2.5218	5.3460
Observations	32	32	32	32

Source: Researchers' own estimation

Table 2 displays the outcomes of unit root tests. Here, two different types of unit root tests are utilized to check the existence of unit root in the selected

Table 2: Results of Unit Root Tests

Variable	*ADF*	*PP*
L_CCI_t	–4.4893* at I (0)	–1.8088*** at I (1)
L_UPI_t	–8.1057* at I (1)	–4.0364* at I (0)
L_CPI_t	–4.9886* at I (1)	–5.1043* at I (1)
L_GDP_t	–7.2210* at I (1)	–2.8885*** at I (1)

*, **, *** denotes significance at 1%, 5% and 10% level respectively.
Source: Researchers' own estimation

series. Under the ADF unit root test, only one variable i.e., L_CCI_t is found stationary at level. In contrast, the ADF unit root test indicates that the remaining three variables are stationary at first difference. On the other hand, under the PP unit root test only one variable i.e., L_UPI_t, is found stationary at level. Whereas the other variables are shown stationary at first difference.

Table 3: Results of ARDL Bound Test

Statistics	*Value*	*K*
F-stat	11.89482	2
Significance	I (0)	I (1)
10%	2.37	3.20
5%	2.79	3.67
2.50%	3.15	4.08
1%	3.65	4.66

Source: Researchers' own estimation

Table 3 displays the results of ARDL Bounds test. Since the calculated F statistics value (i.e., 11.89) exceeds than the crucial value at I (1) (i.e., 4.66), a cointegrating link between L_CCI_t, L_UPI_t, L_CPI_t, and L_GDP_t is found to exist over the long term. Now, long run estimations can be performed.

Table 4: Results of Long-run Estimations

ARDL (4,1,1,4) Model - select based on Akaike Information Criterion (AIC)			
Variable	*Coefficient*	*t-Statistic*	*Prob.*
L_UPI_t	0.067101	2.666512	0.0184
L_CPI_t	–0.093255	–1.569269	0.1389
L_GDP_t	1.519080	4.01192	0.0013
C	11.45594	6.464688	0.0000

Source: Researchers' own estimation

Results of long run estimations are reported in table 4. Results indicates L_UPI_t has a positive influence on L_CCI_t. 1 unit increase in L_UPI_t will lead to increase L_CCI_t by 0.0671 unit. This means digital transactions enhance consumer confidence significantly in long run. Here, India's increasing working population and digital financial literacy rate play a vital role. Here, India's huge working population, rising income trends, and young people's aspirational outlook contribute to the country's robust growth in consumption and consumer optimistic perception regarding economic development (Report of HSBC Mutual Fund). As per table 4, economic expansion also imposes a favorable effect on consumer confidence. On the other hand, inflation does not provide significant effect on consumer confidence index.

Table 5: Results of Short-run Estimations

Variable	*Coefficient*	*t-Statistic*	*Prob.*
D (L_CCI$_t$(–1))	0.500561	3.452381	0.0039
D (L_UPI$_t$)	0.002224	1.696972	0.1118
D (L_CPI$_t$)	0.006236	1.264649	0.2266
D (L_GDP$_t$)	0.058287	3.328369	0.0050
ECT(–1)	–0.141289	–8.744524	0.0000
R-squared	0.983946		
Adjusted R-squared	0.975920		

Source: Researchers' own estimation

Results of short run estimations are reported in table 5. Results indicates digital transactions have a positive but insignificant influence on consumer confidence index. The Error Correction Term (ECT), which is statistically significant and negative, shows that, after a short-term shock, a deviation from the long-run equilibrium is corrected by approximately 14 percent in less than a month. However, economic growth reports a significant positive influence on the consumer confidence index in the short term as well, which is consistent with long run estimation results.

Table 6: Results of Heteroscedasticity Test and Normality Test

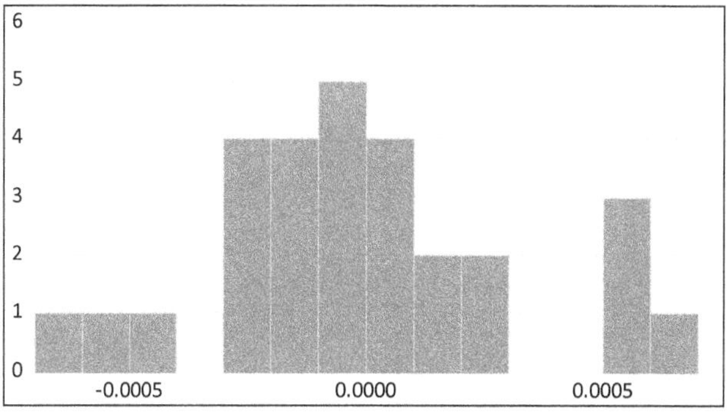

Heteroskedasticity Test (Breusch Pagan Godfrey)		*Normality Test (Jarque Bera)*	
F- Stat.	1.2880	Jarque Bera Value	0.2526
Prob. F (13,14)	0.3216	Prob. Value	0.8814

Source: Researchers' own estimation

Results of different residual diagnostic tests are displayed in table 6. As the probability value of Godfrey Pagan Godfrey heteroscedasticity test is greater than 0.05, it implies error variance are homoscedastic. Similarly, probability value of Histogram Normality test is greater than 0.05, it implies select model is normal.

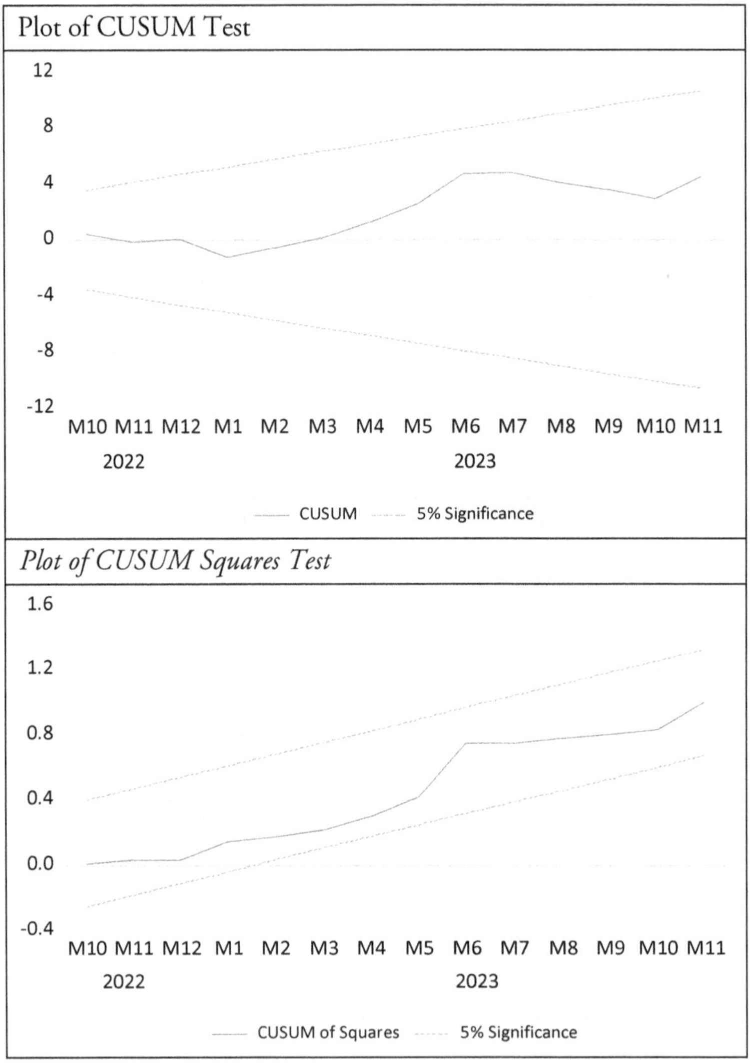

Figure 2: Plots of CUSUM Test and CUSUM Squares Test

Source: Researchers' own estimation

The CUSUM and CUSUM Squares tests are used to validate the model's stability. Since the blue lines are stay inside the red lines in both the figures, it denotes the select model is structurally stable.

Concluding Remarks

India is now passing through a transformative stage from physical currency to cashless economy. Government took several initiatives to address several fear factors of Indians relating to digital transactions and ensure digital ecosystem in India. As a result, during the past few years various digital transactions mechanism are invented in India and a large number of Indians started using digital payment system. Further, increase in internet and smartphone penetration, and the rise of e-commerce also drive to more use of digital transactions. In this regard present paper aims to investigate the influence of digital transaction on consumer confidence in India using ARDL model during April, 2021 to November, 2023. Results of ARDL model showed that digital transaction increases the consumer confidence in long run in India. This may be due to the fact that when people make transactions through digital payment mechanism, they feel less the pain of paying than in paying through physical currency (Shree *et al.*, 2021). Further, past economic development track record and several initiatives of Indian Government regarding digital payment mechanism make Indian consumer to be more optimistic about their future economic situation and digital payment mechanism. Hence, they save less and consume more by making digital transactions. Results of this study suggests policy makers to promote digital transactions mechanism in every region of India by conducting awareness programs and establishing prominent digital infrastructures. These digital transactions mechanism will influence over the perception of consumer, enhance their confidence and level of consumption. Ultimately this higher level of consumption will ensure the path of economic development of India and ensure the goal of 5 trillion economy very soon.

Limitations of the Study

This study has certain drawbacks even though it offers novel insights regarding the relationship between digital transactions and customer confidence. The monthly data used in this study spans the months of April 2021 through November 2023. Further, this study only uses secondary data. Present study could demonstrate more accurate image regarding the relationship between digital transactions and customer confidence if it covered more time periods and included the direct responses of consumers of digital payments.

References

[1] Aberu, F. (2022). Headline inflation and consumers' confidence in Nigeria. *Jurnal Ekonomi dan Bisnis Airlangga, 33*(1).

[2] Achutamba, V. and Hymavathi, C. H. (2022). Impact of Covid-19 on Digital Payments in India. *Journal of Positive School Psychology, 6*(3), 4394–4400.

[3] Achutamba, V. and Hymavathi, C.H. (2022). Impact of Covid-19 on Digital Payments in India. *Journal of Positive School Psychology, 6*(3), 4394–4400.

[4] Banerjee, A., Dolado, J. and Mestre, R. (1998). Error-correction mechanism tests for cointegration in a single-equation framework. *Journal of time series analysis, 19*(3), 267–283.

[5] Borisov, L. (2022). Consumer confidence and real economic growth in the eurozone. Baltic *Journal of Economic Studies, 8*(3), 7–13.

[6] Busu, M. (2020). Analyzing the impact of the renewable energy sources on economic growth at the EU level using an ARDL model. *Mathematics, 8*(8), 1367.

[7] Chaudhari, C. and Kumar, A. (2021). Study of Impact of the covid-19 outbreak on digital payment in India. *Vidyabharati International Interdisciplinary Research Journal, 12*(02), 99–102.

[8] Dees, S. and Brinca, P.S. (2013). Consumer confidence as a predictor of consumption spending: Evidence for the United States and the Euro area. *International Economics, 134,* 1–14.

[9] Dey, S.R. and Tareque, M. (2018). Aggregate consumption expenditure and economic growth: Evidence from Bangladesh. *Global Journal of Management and Business Research, 18*(5B).

[10] Ghatak, S. and Siddiki, J.U. (2001). The use of the ARDL approach in estimating virtual exchange rates in India. *Journal of Applied statistics, 28*(5), 573–584.

[11] Ghosh, B.C., Eyasmin, F. and Adeleye, B.N. (2023). Climate change and agriculture nexus in Bangladesh: Evidence from ARDL and ECM techniques. *PLOS Climate, 2*(7), e0000244.

[12] Ghosh, P.K. and Paul, B. The Effects of Education on Poverty Reduction in India: Striving Towards Sustainable Development. In B. Bagchi & B. Paul (Eds.), *Sustainable Roadmap Development Strategies in India: Paving the Way for a Better Future* (1st ed., pp. 162–174). Lincoln University College, Malaysia. https://doi.org/10.31674/book.2023srdsi013

[13] Ghosh, R., Ghosh, P.K., Bagchi, B. and Paul, B. (2024). Measuring the Impact of Technology Innovations and Renewable Energy Consumption for Enhancing Environmental Sustainability in India: Empirical Evidence from ARDL Approach. *International Journal on Recent Trends in Business and Tourism (IJRTBT), 8*(1), 14–28. https://doi.org/10.31674/ijrtbt.2024.v08i01.002

[14] Gupta, A. and Singhal, R. (2021). Impact of COVID-19 on digital payment services at towns and villages. IJCRT2106045 International Journal of Creative Research Thoughts (IJCRT).

[15] Hou, L., Hsueh, S.C. and Zhang, S. (2021). Digital payments and households' consumption: A mental accounting interpretation. *Emerging Markets Finance and Trade, 57*(7), 2079–2093.

[16] Islam, T.U. and Mumtaz, M.N. (2016). Consumer Confidence Index and Economic Growth: An Empirical Analysis of EU Countries. *Euro Economica, 35*(2).

[17] Jain, A., Sarupria, A. and Kothari, A. (2020). The Impact of COVID-19 on E-wallet's Payments in Indian Economy. *International Journal of Creative Research Thoughts, 8*(6), 2447–2454.

[18] Johansen, S. (1991). Estimation and hypothesis testing of cointegration vectors in Gaussian vector autoregressive models. *Econometrica: journal of the Econometric Society*, 1551–1580.

[19] Kusnawan, A., Andy, A., Silaswara, D. and Sefung, T. (2020). The Effect of Digital Payment to Millennial Consumer Purchase Decisions. 82, 5116–5129.

[20] Kwan, A.C. and Cotsomitis, J.A. (2006). The usefulness of consumer confidence in forecasting household spending in Canada: A national and regional analysis. *Economic Inquiry, 44*(1), 185–197.

[21] Lahiri, K., Monokroussos, G. and Zhao, Y. (2016). Forecasting consumption: The role of consumer confidence in real time with many predictors. *Journal of Applied Econometrics, 31*(7), 1254–1275.

[22] Mahapatra, S. (2018). Cashless financial transaction behaviour of urban middle class in Bhubaneswar. *Parikalpana: KIIT Journal of Management, 14*(1), 91–104.

[23] McAndrews, J.J. (2020). The case for cash. *Latin American Journal of Central Banking, 1*(1–4), 100004.

[24] Mishra, P.K. (2011). Dynamics of the relationship between real consumption expenditure and economic growth in India. *Indian Journal of economics & Business, 10*(4), 553–563.

[25] Nyoni, T., Mose, N. and Thomi, J. (2021). International tourism and economic growth in Zimbabwe: An ARDL–Bounds testing approach. *Asian Journal of Economics, Business and Accounting, 21*(6), 61–81.

[26] Oyelami, L.O., Adebiyi, S.O. and Adekunle, B.S. (2020). Electronic payment adoption and consumers' spending growth: empirical evidence from Nigeria. *Future Business Journal, 6,* 1–14.

[27] Pesaran, M.H. and Shin, Y. (1996). Cointegration and speed of convergence to equilibrium. *Journal of econometrics, 71*(1–2), 117–143.

[28] Pesaran, M.H., Shin, Y. and Smith, R.J. (2001). Bounds testing approaches to the analysis of level relationships. *Journal of applied econometrics, 16*(3), 289–326.

[29] Pesaran, M.H. and Pesaran, B. (1997). Working with Microfit 4.0: Interactive Econometric Analysis. *Oxford University Press.* UK.

[30] Phillips, P.C. and Perron, P. (1988). Testing for a unit root in time series regression. *Biometrika, 75*(2), 335–346.

[31] Press Release issued by PIB Delhi, titled "Second Advance Estimates of National Income, 2022–23, Quarterly Estimates of Gross Domestic Product for the Third Quarter (October-December), 2022–23 and First Revised Estimates of National Income, Consumption Expenditure, Saving and Capital Formation, 2021–22" (on 28th February 2023). https://pib.gov.in/PressReleseDetail.aspx?PRID=1903091

[32] Press Release issued by PIB Delhi, titled "Total digital payment transactions volume increases from 2,071 crore in FY 2017–18 to 13,462 crore in FY 2022–23 at a CAGR of 45 per cent: MoS Finance" (on 19th December 2023). https://pib.gov.in/PressReleaseIframePage.aspx?PRID=1988370

[33] Ramya, N., Sivasakthi, D. and Nandhini, M. (2017). Cashless transaction: Modes, advantages and disadvantages. *International Journal of Applied Research, 3*(1), 122–125.

[34] Ranjith, P.V., Kulkarni, S. and Varma, A. J. (2021). A literature study of consumer perception towards digital payment mode in India. *Psychology and Education, 58*(1), 3304–3319.

[35] Reda, A.M. and Nourhan, E. (2020). Using the ARDL bound testing approach to study the inflation rate in Egypt. *Economic consultant, 3*(31), 24–41.

[36] Samreth, S. (2008). Estimating Money Demand Function in Cambodia: ARDL Approach. Munich Personal RePEc Archive, July. Retrieved From: https://mpra.ub.uni-muenchen.de/16274/1/ Money-Demand-in-Cambodia.pdf

[37] Sana, A.K., Poddar, S. and Paul, B. (2020). Contribution of small and medium enterprises (SMES) towards Malaysian economic growth: an empirical study. *International Journal on Recent Trends in Business and Tourism (IJRTBT)*, 4(2), 18–27.

[38] Sharma, A., Bhimavarapu, V.M., Kanoujiya, J., Barge, P. and Rastogi, S. (2022). Financial Inclusion–An Impetus to the Digitalization of Payment Services (UPI) in India. *The Journal of Asian Finance, Economics and Business, 9*(9), 191–203.

[39] Shree, S., Pratap, B., Saroy, R. and Dhal, S. (2021). Digital payments and consumer experience in India: a survey based empirical study. *Journal of Banking and Financial Technology, 5*, 1–20.

[40] Sum, V. (2012). Unemployment, consumer confidence, business confidence, inflation and monetary policy. Inflation and Monetary Policy (September 14, 2012).

[41] Sumathy, M. and Vipin, K.P. (2017). Digital payment systems: Perception and concerns among urban consumers. *IJAR, 3*(6), 1118–1122.

[42] Yitzhaki, S. (2003). Gini's mean difference: A superior measure of variability for non-normal distributions. *Metron, 61*(2), 285–316.

[43] Zhang, J., Zhang, H. and Gong, X. (2022). Mobile payment and rural household consumption: Evidence from China. *Telecommunications Policy, 46*(3), 102276.

[44] Zhou, R. (2022). Sustainable Economic Development, Digital Payment, and Consumer Demand: Evidence from China. *International Journal of Environmental Research and Public Health, 19*(14), 8819.

Websites

1. https://www.assetmanagement.hsbc.co.in/assets/documents/mutual-funds/en/8333d7d3-fc29-4d26-b84c-a99a4728224f/take-adv-india-consumption-wave.pdf
2. https://data.oecd.org/leadind/consumer-confidence-index-cci.htm
3. https://fred.stlouisfed.org/series/INDCPIALLMINMEI
4. https://www.npci.org.in/statistics

Does Awareness Serve as Key Determinant in Making Crop Insurance Decision? A Study in the Context of Hooghly District

Palash Naskar[1] and Sk. Naushad[2]

ABSTRACT: India is an agrarian country where agriculture is heavily influenced by unpredictable nature of the environment. Crop insurance serves as a protective measure for agricultural production, playing a crucial role in stabilizing farmers' incomes. By mitigating risks, it enables farmers to allocate more investments to their agricultural endeavors. The efficacy of crop insurance is closely tied to the number of participants in the program. In developing countries like India, where a significant portion of farmers falls into the marginal category, the crop insurance penetration remains low. This study aims to investigate the relationship between the uptake of crop insurance and awareness levels among farmers. This study is based on primary data collected from Hooghly district of West Bengal in 2023. The logit regression model was employed as the methodology for analysis. The results shows positive relationship between awareness and the likelihood of farmers opting for crop insurance.

Keywords: Awareness, Crop Insurance, Logistic Regression.

Introduction

Agriculture has played a very crucial role in the Indian economy, generating a significant number of employment opportunities and contributing to the country's economic and social development (Borah *et al.*, 2021). However, the agricultural sector is inherently associated with various risks, including governmental regulations and policies, volatile price fluctuations, and unpredictable weather patterns. To mitigate these risks, farmers employ strategies such as marketing strategies and hedging. Hedging, in particular, involves shifting the risk to a risk-taker through future contracts (Boehlje & Trede, 1977). But, among the diverse risk management strategies, crop insurance stands out as a popular technique that not only reduces risks but also stabilizes farmers' income (Chambers & Quiggin, 2004). Crop insurance covers various risks, including

[1] Assistant Professor, Department of Commerce, Purash Kanpur Haridas Nnandi Mahavidyalaya, India. E-mail: palashnaskar59@gmail.com

[2] Research Scholar, Department of Commerce, Vidyasagar University, India. E-mail: thesknaushad@gmail.com

hailstorms, weather-related perils, fire and lightning, and production losses due to other reasons (Wright & Hewitt, 1994). Despite these benefits, only about 5 percent of Indian farmers participate in crop insurance programs, and of those, 87 percent do not receive any compensation (Cariappa *et al.*, 2020). This low participation rate and the high rate of uncompensated claims underscore the need to understand the determinants of farmers' decisions to engage in crop insurance programs.

This study focuses on awareness as potential determinants influencing the crop insurance decisions of farmers in the state of West Bengal. The interplay between these factors and their impact on the adoption and efficacy of crop insurance programs in the region necessitates thorough examination. The state of West Bengal, known for its diverse agricultural practices and varied climatic conditions, provides a compelling backdrop for this investigation. As the agricultural landscape continues to evolve, it becomes essential to dissect the nuanced relationship between farmers' awareness levels regarding available crop insurance schemes and the decision of participating in these programs.

Against this backdrop, this study seeks to unravel the extent to which awareness serve as decisive factor in shaping the crop insurance decisions of farmers in West Bengal. By delving into the motivations and perceptions that underlie these decisions, the research aims to contribute valuable insights that can inform policy interventions and strategies to enhance the effectiveness of crop insurance programs in the region. Through a comprehensive examination of this factor, this study aspires to shed light on the intricate dynamics of crop insurance decision-making and pave the way for a more resilient and sustainable agricultural sector in West Bengal.

Survey of Literature

The participation in crop insurance programs is basically influenced by its popularity and the level of awareness among farmers. Trivedi and Soni (2013) identified awareness as a key factor in the decision-making process for farmers considering crop insurance. They suggested that higher levels of awareness about crop insurance schemes and their benefits significantly motivate farmers to adopt these programs. This assertion is supported by Kumari *et al.* (2017), who found that well-informed farmers are more likely to purchase crop insurance because they understand the advantages it offers. Moreover, the level of satisfaction with crop insurance services also plays a vital role in farmers' decisions to continue or re-enroll in insurance programs. Jamanal, Natikar, and Halakatti (2019) emphasized that satisfied farmers are more inclined to buy crop insurance for the subsequent crop seasons. This indicates that both the initial awareness and the subsequent satisfaction with the insurance services are integral to the continued participation of farmers in these schemes.

Additionally, the perceived satisfaction of non-insured farmers and their overall awareness of crop insurance options are critical factors influencing participation rates. Sadati *et al.* (2010), Kumari *et al.* (2010), and Anisa (2021) all highlighted the importance of these elements in their studies. They found that farmers who are aware of crop insurance schemes but are not satisfied with the available options or the benefits they provide are less likely to participate. Conversely, enhancing both awareness and satisfaction could lead to higher adoption rates and more effective risk management in the agricultural sector. Makki and Somwaru (2016) proposed several strategies to increase farmer participation in crop insurance programs. They suggested that expanding the range of available insurance products and improving risk assessment methods could significantly boost farmer participation. Their study concluded that offering a diverse range of products tailored to the specific needs of different regions and farmers, setting premiums that accurately reflect risk levels, and judicious use of premium subsidies could sustain interest and participation in crop insurance programs. Historically, the Indian government has introduced various crop insurance schemes to protect farmers against potential losses. However, these schemes often suffered from inefficiencies and operational flaws, making them ineffective in providing adequate protection (Chatterjee *et al.*, 2005). To address these issues, the government has periodically implemented new and improved policies aimed at overcoming previous inconsistencies and enhancing the overall effectiveness of crop insurance programs.

Despite the significant role that awareness plays in a farmer's crop insurance decision, there exists a notable gap in the current research landscape regarding this relationship. While few literatures exist on global perspectives, there is little study in Indian context and even lesser in the context of West Bengal. This calls for an in-depth exploration and analysis of the relationship of crop insurance decision with farmer's awareness level.

Conceptual Framework

Cultivation is one of the riskiest occupations in the world because it depends on different uncontrollable factors like adverse weather events and output price volatility (Das & Gangopadhyay, 2021). According to Haile, Wossen, Tesfaye, and Braun's study, global agriculture production fluctuates by 1-3% due to climate. In the case of price, it also negatively influences crop productivity. At present, different types of risk mitigation techniques are there: crop insurance, futures hedging, and forward contracting (Velandia, Rejesus, Knight and Herrick, 2009). The study of Kumari, Singh, Mishra, Sinha & Ahmad showed that awareness and satisfaction positively influence crop insurance. These two factors motivate farmers to insure their crops.

Conceptual Framework

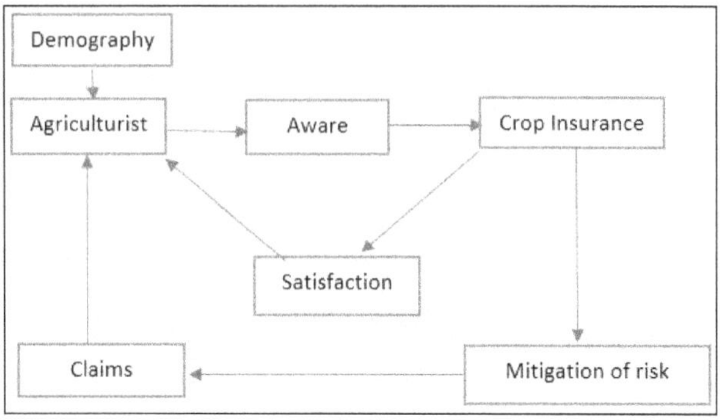

Source: Authors

Research Gap

Despite the extensive literature on the factors influencing the adoption of crop insurance, there are still noteworthy gaps that warrant further investigation. Previous studies have highlighted the crucial roles of awareness and satisfaction in driving farmers' decisions to participate in crop insurance programs (Trivedi & Soni, 2013; Kumari *et al.*, 2017; Jamanal, Natikar, & Halakatti, 2019). However, these studies often take a broad national perspective or focus on diverse regions without delving deeply into specific local contexts where agricultural practices and challenges can vary significantly.

Most research to date has been concerned with identifying general trends and factors influencing crop insurance adoption, often overlooking the intricate dynamics within specific districts or regions. For instance, while Makki and Somwaru (2016) have suggested the importance of diversifying insurance products and improving risk assessment methods, there is a lack of empirical studies examining how these strategies impact farmer participation at a more localized level.

The current body of research also lacks a thorough investigation into the interplay between awareness, satisfaction, and the subsequent decision-making processes of farmers within the specific context of Hooghly district. While Sadati *et al.* (2010), Kumari *et al.* (2010), and Anisa (2021) have highlighted the importance of awareness and satisfaction, their studies do not focus on the detailed regional dynamics that might influence these factors.

Given these gaps, there is a pressing need for a focused study that examines how awareness influence crop insurance decisions in Hooghly district. Such a study would provide valuable insights into the local factors affecting farmers' adoption of crop insurance and could inform more tailored and effective policy interventions.

Objectives of the Study

The Government of India has consistently rolled out diverse crop insurance programs over time with the principal goal of safeguarding the interests of farmers. When shortcomings are identified in existing schemes, the government actively works towards resolving them, often introducing new types of crop insurance in the process. The effectiveness of these initiatives is complicatedly tied to their popularity among farmers and the perceived quality of service provided. The success of crop insurance is contingent upon both widespread participation and the perceived satisfaction of the services. The government's objectives in this realm can be achieved when a substantial number of farmers actively engage in crop insurance programs.

Against this backdrop, the present study endeavors to explore and understand the relationship between the adoption of crop insurance and levels of awareness among farmers. By examining these factors, the study aims to provide insights that contribute to the improvement and effectiveness of crop insurance initiatives in the agricultural landscape of India.

Hypothesis of the Study

In order to achieve the objective of finding the relationship between the farmer's participation in crop insurance and awareness of farmers, the following null hypothesis is set:

- **Null Hypothesis (H_0):** There is no significant relationship between the farmer's participation in crop insurance and awareness of the farmer.

Data Set and Sample Design

The research is conducted using primary data gathered through a field survey conducted in selected villages of Hooghly. The villages were chosen using a simple random sampling method, and the study encompasses a sample size of 59 respondents. The structured questionnaire, designed for data collection, focused on potatoes as the primary crop of interest. The data collection occurred in December 2023. To study the objective, we used the participation of crop insurance schemes as a dependent variable. The independent variables used in the study were awareness (Trivedi and Soni, 2013). Also, some control variables like experience in farming, satisfaction (Jamanal, Natikar and Halakatti, 2019), age and education were incorporated into the study's framework.

Methodology

To analyze the objectives of our study, we employed logistic regression. Logistic regression offers various types of analyses, including logistic regression for coefficients, logistic regression for odds ratios, and logistic regression for marginal effects. Through the marginal effect analysis, independent variables can explain the behavior of the dependent variable while holding all other variables constant. Odds ratios, on the other hand, provide insights into the likelihood of the occurrence or non-occurrence of a specific event. For the study, we used all the three types of logistic regression. But, before applying logistic regression, several pre-estimation tests, like the normality test, multicollinearity test, and heteroscedasticity test, were also done.

The model employed to investigate the relationship between crop insurance decisions and awareness is as follows:

$$Y = a + b_1X_1 + b_2X_2 + b_3X_3 + b_4X_4 + b_5X_5 + u_i$$

where,

Y = Insured or Not

X_1 = Awareness

X_2 = Satisfaction

X_3 = Experience in Farming

X_4 = Education

X_5 = Age

a = Constant

u_i = Error Term

This model allows us to explore the impact of awareness on the likelihood of farmers participating in crop insurance, providing valuable insights into the dynamics of decision-making in this context.

Research Results and Discussions

The presence of multicollinearity among independent variables can potentially distort the accuracy of model results. To address this concern, the Variance Inflation Factor (VIF) test is employed. A commonly accepted threshold to identify multicollinearity issues is a maximum VIF value of 10. In our case, both individual VIF values and the mean VIF are below 2 (as shown in table 1).

Table 1: VIF Test Results

Variable	*VIF*
Awareness	1.22
Satisfaction	1.15
Age	1.74
Experience	1.76
Education	1.04
Mean VIF	1.38

Source: Computed by Authors

Consequently, we can assert that multicollinearity is not a significant concern for this model.

In this study, the Breusch-Pagan test was employed to assess the presence of heteroscedasticity issues in the variables. This method relies on the assumption that the error terms follow a normal distribution and are utilized in the linear regression model. Within the table, if the p-value associated with the test exceeds the predetermined significance level ($\alpha = 0.05$), we retain the null hypothesis. Table 2 shows the results of the Breusch-Pagan test.

Table 2: Breusch-Pagan Test Results

Chi2(1)	1.80
Prob> Chi2	0.1792

Source: Computed by Authors

Consequently, based on the results, we conclude that there are no significant heteroscedasticity concerns in the model.

Now, to assess normality, the Shapiro-Wilk Test (as indicated in Table 3) was employed in this study. The null hypothesis postulates that the population follows a normal distribution. For all independent variable and control variables—namely, awareness, satisfaction, age, experience and education, p-values exceed the threshold of 0.05, we fail to reject the null hypothesis. In conclusion, based on these results, we can affirm that the population exhibits a normal distribution.

Table 3: Shapiro-Wilk Test

Variable	*Obs*	*W*	*V*	*Z*	*Prob>z*
Awareness	59	0.99567	0.232	–3.142	0.99916
Satisfaction	59	0.96349	1.958	1.447	0.07397
Age	59	0.98722	0.686	–0.813	0.79182
Experience	59	0.98075	1.033	0.069	0.47252
Education	59	0.99378	0.334	–2.364	0.99097

Source: Computed by Authors

Following the pre-testing phase, we proceeded with logistic regression analysis. In the case of our model, the obtained p-value is less than 0.05, indicating a good fit for the data in the model. It is a standard practice for the p-value of the model to be below 0.05 for a 5% significance level or 0.01 for a 1% level of significance.

Table 4: Logit Model of Insured

6	*Number of Obs = 59* *LR chi2(5) = 46.83*	*Prob>chi2 = 0.0000* *Pseudo R2 = 0.5785*
Insured	Coef	P>IZI
Awareness	1.8841	0.022
Satisfaction	3.2900	0.001
Age	.1190	0.111
Experience	–.0883	0.070
Education	.1795	0.173
Cons	–8.5041	0.029

Source: Computed by Authors

Examining the results presented in Table 4, the logistic regression model indicates that the awareness level is statistically significant at the 5% level. The respective coefficient for awareness is 1.8841. These findings underscore the significance of awareness in influencing the likelihood of participating in crop insurance, providing valuable insights into the determinants of farmers' decisions in this context. The interpretation of odds ratios pivots on whether the value of the independent variable is greater or less than 1. In our context, if the value exceeds 1 then it suggests that a farmer is more inclined to purchase a crop insurance scheme. As outlined in Table 6, the independent variable awareness, exhibit odds ratios greater than 1. This implies that higher levels of awareness are associated with an increased likelihood of farmers opting for crop insurance.

Table 5: Odds Ratio for Insured or not Insured

Log likelihood =–17.062849	*Number of Obs = 59* *LR chi2(5) = 46.83*	*Prob>chi2 = 0.0000* *Pseudo R2 = 0.5785*
Insured	Odds Ratio	P>IZI
Awareness	6.5805	0.022
Satisfaction	26.8443	0.001
Age	1.1263	0.111
Experience	0.9154	0.070
Education	1.1966	0.173
Cons	.00020	0.029

Source: Computed by Authors

The marginal effect measures the impact of a one-unit change in the independent variable on the dependent variable. Examining Table 6, we observe that the p-values associated with awareness are less than 0.05, indicating their statistical significance. Specifically, one unit change in awareness positively influences the likelihood of being insured by 0.1685. These results underscore the statistically significant and positive relationships between awareness, satisfaction, and the likelihood of farmers opting for crop insurance.

Table 6: Marginal Effect of Logit Model

Log likelihood=–17.062849	*Number of Obs=59* *LR chi2(5) = 46.83*	*Prob>chi2=0.0000* *Pseudo R2=0.5785*
	Delta-method	
	dy/dx	*P>IZI*
Awareness	.1685	0.005
Satisfaction	.2942	0.000
Age	.0106	0.081
Experience	–.0079	0.038
Education	.0160	0.146

Source: Computed by Authors

Conclusion

This study investigates the interplay between crop insurance participation and awareness. The findings indicate a positive relationship, suggesting that awareness favorably influences crop insurance participation. Another significant finding is the impact of satisfaction on farmers' decisions regarding crop insurance. The results show that farmers' satisfaction also positively affects their crop insurance decisions. Here, satisfaction refers to the perceived satisfaction that a farmer anticipates from taking a particular crop insurance. This perceived satisfaction is based on the word-of-mouth from farmers who have already taken crop insurance. We conclude that the success of any crop insurance scheme hinges on its popularity and perceived quality

In the broader context of India, the penetration of crop insurance remains low. However, within our study area some participants expressed grievances, noting the absence of organized awareness programs by competent authorities or having received information only after the completion of such programs. Additionally, the satisfaction of individuals plays a pivotal role in the success of the scheme. When people invest in a crop insurance scheme, they harbor certain expectations. The extent to which these expectations are met directly influences their satisfaction. Satisfied individuals are more inclined to make repeat purchases. In our study, we observed that farmers who reported high levels of satisfaction were more likely to purchase crop insurance.

In conclusion, the government's efforts should be directed toward organizing effective awareness programs accessible to all. During such awareness programs, it is to be ensured by the competent authority that perceived satisfaction is created and also, when a farmer undertakes a crop insurance, they need to feel satisfied. Furthermore, enhancing the service quality of crop insurance will contribute to broader acceptance. The service quality can be improved by adopting a more scientific method of accessing the crop loss and by increasing the crop loss compensation. Through these initiatives, the government can bridge the gap and achieve broader reach, ultimately fostering the success of crop insurance schemes. As this study focused on the loanee farmers so there remains a scope for further research on crop insurance of non-loanee farmers.

References

[1] Boehlje, M.D. and Trede, L.D. (1977). Risk management in agriculture. *Journal of ASFMRA*. 41(1). 20–29.

[2] Borah, M., Borah, D. and Gogoi, D. (2021). Unearthing India's Economic Backbone: The Vital Role of Agriculture and Its Impact on GDP Growth. *The Seybold report.* 18(107). DOI 10.17605/OSF.IO/Y29X8

[3] Cariappa, A.A., Mahida, D.P., Lal, P. and Chandel, B.S. (2020). Correlates and impact of crop insurance in India: evidence from a nationally representative survey. *Agricultural Finance Review.* Vol. 81 No. 2, pp. 204–221. doi.org/10.1108/AFR-03-2020-0034

[4] Chambers, R.G. and Quiggin, J. (2004). Technological and financial approaches to risk management in agriculture: An integrated approach. *Australian Journal of Agricultural and Resource Economics*. 48(2). 199–223.

[5] Chatterjee, K., Chatterjee, A. and Das, S. (2005). Community Adaptation to Drought in Rajasthan. *Institute of Development Studies*. 36 (4). 33–52.

[6] Dandekar, V.M. (1985). Crop Insurance in India: A review 1976–1977 to 1984–85. *Economic and Political Weekly*. 20(25–26). 1–15.

[7] Das, B. and Gangopadhyay, S. (2021). Occupational agricultural injuries among the preadolescent workers of West Bengal, India. *International journal of adolescent medicine and health*. 33(4). 20180178.

[8] Goodwin, B.K., Vandeveer, M.L. and Deal, J.L. (2004). An empirical analysis of acreage effects of participation in the federal crop insurance program. *American Journal of Agricultural Economics*. 86(4). 1058–1077.

[9] Haile, M.G., Wossen, T., Tesfaye, K. and Von Braun, J. (2017). Impact of climate change, weather extremes, and price risk on global food supply. *Economics of Disasters and Climate Change*. 1. 55–75.

[10] Jain, R.C.A. (2014). Challenges in Implementing Agriculture Insurance and Re-insurance in Developing Countries. The Journal. 5(1). 14–23.

[11] Kumar, D. and Phougat, S. (2021). Performance evaluation of crop insurance schemes in Haryana. *Journal of Economics and Trade*. 6(1). 34–39.

[12] Kumari, M., Singh, K.M., Mishra, R. R., Sinha, D. K. and Ahmad, N. (2017). Role of socio-economic variables in adoption of crop insurance: A Discriminant Function Approach. *Economic Affairs*. 62(3). 361–365.

[13] Makki, S.S. and Somwaru, A. (2001). Farmers' participation in crop insurance markets: creating the right incentives. *American Journal of Agricultural Economics*. 83(3). 662–667.

[14] Nair, R. (2010). Crop insurance in India: changes and challenges. *Economic and Political weekly*. 45(6). 19–22.

[15] Quiggin, J. and Chambers, R.G. (2004). Drought policy: a graphical analysis. *Australian Journal of Agricultural and Resource Economics*. 48(2). 225–251.

[16] Quiggin, J. and Chambers, R. G. (2004). Invariant risk attitudes. *Journal of Economic Theory*. 117(1). 96–118.

[17] Quiggin, J. and Chambers, R.G. (2006). The state-contingent approach to production under uncertainty. *Australian Journal of Agricultural and Resource Economics*. 50(2). 153–169.

[18] Raju, S.S. (2014). Studies on ageing in India: A review. *Population Ageing in India*. 180–213.

[19] Sadati, S.A., Ghobadi, F.R., Saduti, S.A. Mohamudi, Y. Sharifi, O. and Asakereh, A. (2010). Survey of Effective Factors on Adoption of Crop Insurance among Farmers: A Case Study of Behbahan Country. *African Journal of Agricultural Research*. 5(16). 2237–2242.

[20] Sarangi, S.K. and Panigrahi, D. (2016). Crop Insurance, the Backbone of Indian farming community-Issues and challenges. *International Journal of Engineering Research and Applications*. 6(1). 39–47.

[21] Shivaswamy, G.P., Singh, K.N., Anuja, A.R., Rajesh, T. and HarishKumar, H.V. Logit, Probit and Tobit Models. Training Manual-I. 143.

[22] Sindhu, C. and Ariff, U.T. (2017). A study on farmers preference towards crop insurance. *International Journal of Interdisciplinary Research in Arts and Humanities*. 2(2). 2456–3145.

[23] Singh, P. and Agrawal, G. (2020). Development, present status and performance analysis of agriculture insurance schemes in India: Review of evidence. *International Journal of Social Economics*. 47(4). 461–481.

[24] Tiwari, R., Chand, K. and Anjum, B. (2020). Crop insurance in India: A review of pradhan mantri fasal bima yojana (PMFBY). *FIIB Business Review*. 9(4). 249–255.

[25] Velandia, M., Rejesus, R.M., Knight, T.O. and Sherrick, B.J. (2009). Factors affecting farmers' utilization of agricultural risk management tools: the case of crop insurance, forward contracting, and spreading sales. *Journal of agricultural and applied economics*. 41(1). 107–123.

[26] Vyas, V.S. and Singh, S. (2006). Crop insurance in India: Scope for improvement. *Economic and Political Weekly*. 4585–4594.

[27] Sahib, W., Luan, J., Xiao, S. and Sanaullah, N. (2016). Significance of Agricultural Finance in Agricultural and Rural Development of Pakinstan: A Case Study of

Qamba Shahadadkot District. *Research Journal of Finance and Accounting.* 7(9). 89–94.

[28] Wright, B.D. and Hewitt, J.A. (1994). All-risk crop insurance: lessons from theory and experience. In Economics of agricultural crop insurance: theory and evidence (pp. 73–112). Dordrecht: Springer Netherlands.

Performance Analysis of Select Open-Ended Equity Linked Savings Schemes in India

Manoj Kumar Singh[1]

ABSTRACT: A unique type of mutual fund scheme known as equity linked savings plans has the advantage of both tax savings under section 80C of the Income Tax Act of 1961 and investment growth similar to that of regular mutual fund schemes. As widely understood, a mutual fund is a type of financial vehicle that invests money in equity rather than other more conventional investing channels by pooling the funds of several investors who share similar financial objectives. Although ELSS and other similar instruments have similar financial benefits, they differ in terms of the lock-in duration. An ELSS has a three-year lock-in period, whereas an ordinary mutual fund has none. The mutual fund industry has undergone ups and downs since it was first launched in India in 1964, but it is currently expanding very quickly. As of November 2023, the Asset Under Management (AUM) has grown at a pace of 19.23% annually. The number of persons investing in mutual funds expanded significantly as a result of this robust expansion. The purpose of this essay is to 1) ascertain the reader's comprehension of the idea of equity-linked savings plans; 2) to evaluate the chosen ELSS's performance using risk-return criteria; 3) to contrast its results with those of the selected benchmark; and 4) to determine if the chosen ELSS is successful in reaching diversification. The top 10 AUM as of December 31, 2019, is used to select the ELSS. Compound Annual Growth Rate (CAGR), Standard Deviation (SD), Sharpe Ratio, Beta, Jensen alpha, R-squared (R2), or the coefficient of determination are among the performance analysis tools used.

Keywords: Asset Under Management, Equity Linked Savings Schemes.

Introduction

An economy's capacity for capital production and sustainable development go hand in hand. In the sustainably developed economy, capital generation is portrayed as a given. The creation of capital is a requirement for a country's economy to experience "Sustainable Development." Individuals' patterns and behaviors when it comes to investing and saving are very important for capital accumulation. Governments everywhere announce tax breaks and rebates for specific financial products in an effort to entice people to save and invest

[1] Assistant Professor, Department of Commerce, Joypur Panchanan Roy College, Howrah, India. E-mail: memanojsingh72@gmail.com

responsibly. Section 80C of the Income Tax Act, 1961 in India contains a list of financial instruments that offer tax benefits up to Rs. 1,50,000 per financial year, provided the individual chooses to pay taxes under the old regime instead of the new one, which does not allow for tax deductions. Fixed-interest instruments such as Public Provident Fund (PPF), Fixed Deposit, National Saving Certificate (NSC), Traditional Insurance Plan, and so on are popular among them. Under section 80C, the equity option is restricted. One such alternative is Equity Linked Savings Schemes (ELSS), which offer tax advantages in addition to the ability to yield respectable profits over time. The ELSS funds' assets under management (AUM) as of December 31, 2019, was Rs. 99,817.35 crores, while the similar amounts for December 31, 2018, and December 31, 2017 were Rs. 88,152 crores and Rs. 80,981 crores, respectively. It is evident from the numbers that ELSS membership has been steadily rising over time. The SEBI announced the categorization and rationalization of mutual fund schemes in its Circular dated October 6, 2017. This Circular states that mutual fund schemes fall under five general categories: debt schemes, hybrid schemes, equity schemes, solution-oriented schemes, and other schemes. Additionally, there are 10 other categories into which equity schemes can be categorized: Equity Linked Savings Scheme (ELSS), Focused Fund, Sectoral/Thematic Fund, Value Fund, Contra Fund, Small Cap Fund, Large Cap Fund, Large & Mid Cap Fund, and Mid Cap Fund. In India, tax-saving mutual funds are frequently referred to as "Equity Linked Saving Schemes (ELSS)". Mutual funds that have at least 80% of their investments in equity or equity-related products are known as ELSS. Unlike PPF (15 years) and Tax-saving Fixed Deposit (5 years), both plans have a statutory lock-in term of only three years. Furthermore, even after the three-year lock-in term has ended, redemption is not required. To benefit from long-term profits, investors can keep their money in ELSS for as long as they like. According to Vidhyadharan (2018), there were two positive developments for the Indian mutual fund industry, and ELSS in particular: (1) a rise in penetration outside of the top 15 cities and metro areas; and (2) the effectiveness of systematic investment programs. The implementation of the Long Term Capital Gains (LTCG) tax on mutual fund returns could potentially deter regular investors from choosing ELSS.

Review of Literature

A brief review of select literature dealing with ELSS is presented below.

In the analysis of a few ELSS from 1994–1995 to 2001–2002, Tripathy (2005) discovered that the fund managers' abilities to time the market were insufficient. Bondyopadhyay (2008) observed that assured return schemes did not yield as high of returns as equity-linked saving schemes. According to Chandrakumarmangalam and Govindasamy (2011), the chosen ELSS performed better than the market. According to Santhi and Gurunathan's (2011) research, investors in Tamil

Nadu have relatively little involvement in ELSS and prefer assets like fixed deposits, insurance, and postal deposits. According to Roy and Ghosh (2012), the selected ELSS did not perform better when it came to risk-adjusted returns in the 2008–2009 financial crisis. Moreover, the fund managers were unable to demonstrate their stock selection and market timing abilities. According to Garg and Gupta (2014), between 2008 and 2013, the chosen equity-linked savings plans outperformed the market in terms of absolute gains. According to Das (2014), the selected ELSS are defensive, sufficiently diversified, have produced superior risk-adjusted returns, have shown superior stock selection abilities from the fund managers, and have produced satisfactory returns from the "Systematic Investment Plan (SIP)". According to Ghosh's (2014) observations, three of the nine ELSSs that were chosen outperformed the benchmark index. Sharma (2015) discovered that openness, after-sales support, and grievance redressal procedures significantly influence customer satisfaction and positively influence investors' perceptions of ELSS. According to Kadambat *et al.* (2015), the selected ELSS outperformed benchmark indexes and diversified equity funds when considering risk-adjusted returns. On the other hand, variations in ELSS performance were noted over time. According to Srivastava (2017), because ELSS offers both tax savings and a strong return, it may be a viable choice for investors who are unfamiliar with the stock market. According to Pathak (2018), investors have to consider investing in Axis Long Term Equity Fund due to its reasonable return generation and low expense ratio. Additionally, the researcher mentioned that investors have the option to invest in IDFC Tax Advantage Fund and Franklin India Tax Shield. Pareek (2018) recommended including ELSS in a portfolio that is optimally diversified throughout the whole range of tax-saving options. Chisti and Rahman (2018) discovered that every selected ELSS produced average returns significantly higher than the market return and exceeded the market index. According to Panigrahi *et al.* (2020), the chosen ELSS had strong performance in terms of risk-adjusted return. According to Research Desk (2022), given that fixed-return products like PPF underperformed ELSS by a significant margin, investors could be prudent to venture outside of their comfort zone and invest a portion of their corpus in ELSS. According to Prakash and Biswanath (2023), certain ELSS beat benchmarks (the Nifty 500 and BSE 500) on metrics such as Treynor Ratio, Sharpe Ratio, and Jensen Alpha. Using the Nifty 50 as the benchmark index, Naik *et al.* (2023) examined 15 equity mutual fund schemes from April 2015 to March 2018 and discovered that, over the previous three years, all of the schemes had superior and satisfactory performance compared to the benchmark.

Research Gap

The literature on mutual funds is plentiful. However, there has been very little in-depth study on ELSS. In light of this, the current study makes an effort to thoroughly analyze the performance of a chosen ELSS while accounting for a number of factors, including risk and return. Aside from that, the study divided the duration into four intervals: three, five, seven, and ten years, in order to assess performance consistency. Another novel aspect of this study is the selection of the benchmark, which is Nifty 500 TRI. Most previous research had taken into account benchmark indexes such as Sensex, Nifty, BSE 200, NSE 500, etc. Because the Price Return Indices, such as Sensex, Nifty, BSE 200, etc., can only capture the capital appreciation portion and neglect the dividend payout element, the study will provide a holistic view as a consequence. However, the Total Return Index (TRI) accounts for both the dividend and capital appreciation components. The goal of this study is to draw attention to the crucial elements that investors should consider before selecting a specific ELSS.

Research Questions

The present study attempts to address the following research questions:

1. Do the chosen ELSS provide a superior return in comparison to the benchmark?
2. Do the selected schemes outperform the benchmark in terms of total risk?
3. Whether the chosen ELSS generate a better risk-adjusted return than the benchmark index?
4. Are the selected schemes aggressive or defensive?
5. How is the ability of the fund managers of the chosen ELSS in picking quality stocks?
6. Whether the objective of 'diversification' has been achieved by the selected schemes?
7. How is the overall performance of the chosen schemes?

Objectives of the Study

The objectives of the study include:

1. To have an understanding of the concept of equity-linked saving schemes;
2. To analyse the performance of the chosen ELSS on the basis of risk-return parameters;
3. To compare the performance of the selected ELSS with that of the chosen benchmark; and
4. To judge whether the chosen ELSS succeed in achieving diversification.

Data and Methodology

The research is empirical as well as exploratory. Current literature in the form of articles from journals, daily, periodicals, reports, and online resources forms the basis of the study's exploratory phase. Secondary data are used in the research.

December 2009 through December 2019 are the study's covered years. The effects of "brokerage," "entry load," and "exit load" have not been considered. The benchmark index for the research is the Nifty 500 TRI. It is assumed that the average annualized risk-free rate of return is 8.2675%. It represents the Public Provident Fund (PPF) scheme's average rate from December 2009 to December 2019. Instead of the "Direct Plan," the study takes into account the "Regular Plan" of open-ended ELSS. Three ELSS from three asset management companies (AMCs), namely HDFC, ICICI Prudential, and SBI, are considered in this study. The prominent investor schemes that have been around for more than ten (10) years and have more than Rs. 6500 crores in assets under management (AUM) as of December 31, 2019, are taken into consideration for the study. All of the schemes that meet these standards are selected. The ICICI Prudential Long Term Equity (ICICIPLTE), SBI Magnum Taxgain (SBIMTG) (now SBI Long Term Equity), and HDFC Tax Saver (HDFCTS) are these programs. As of December 31, 2019, the select schemes with the biggest AUM are ICICIPLTE (Rs. 6,707 crore), SBIMTG (Rs. 7,370 crore), and HDFCTS (Rs. 7,454 crore). Instead of the "Dividend" option, the "Growth" option is taken into consideration in this study. In order to investigate the specifics of performance consistency, the study period was divided into four distinct time periods: three, five, seven, and ten years. There were numerous bull and bear markets within the chosen period. The official websites of the AMCs have provided the month-end Net Asset Values (NAVs) of the ELSS. The benchmark index's month-end closing values were retrieved from the National Stock Exchange's (NSE) official website. The monthly returns of the chosen ELSS (Rp) and that of the benchmark (Rb) have been computed as follows:

$$R_p = [(NAV_t - NAV_{t-1})/NAV_{t-1}] \times 100$$

$$R_b = [(Value_t - Value_{t-1})/Value_{t-1}] \times 100$$

Where, NAV_t = Closing NAV of the ELSS for month t, NAV_{t-1} = Closing NAV of the ELSS for the preceding month (t-1), $Value_t$ = Closing Value of the Benchmark Index for month t, $Value_{t-1}$ = Closing Value of the Benchmark Index for the preceding month (t–1). Likewise, annualised Standard Deviation of the chosen ELSS (SD_p) and benchmark (SD_b) have been computed for measuring the total risk. Measures like Compound Annual Growth Rate (CAGR), Standard Deviation (SD), Sharpe Ratio, Beta, Jensen alpha and R-squared (R^2) or the coefficient of determination have been employed. When it comes to ranking, scheme 1 is the one with the highest value under a particular parameter. In contrast, the scheme with the lowest value is ranked 1 in the case of standard deviation. To determine the total rank score of the selected ELSS, rankings of the ELSS under 5 different measures or parameters (CAGR, SD, Sharpe Ratio, Alpha, and RSQ) for 4 different periods (3-year, 5-year, 7-year, and 10-year) are added. The total rank score is then divided by 20 (5 different measures or parameters X 4 different periods) to determine averages. The scheme that has the lowest average rank score is rated 1 in the end, and so on.

Results and Discussion

Table 1 presents the Compound Annual Growth Rate of the chosen ELSS and Benchmark.

Table 1: Compound Annual Growth Rate (CAGR) of the ELSS and Benchmark Index

ELSS	*CAGR (%)*				*RANK*			
	3Y	*5Y*	*7Y*	*10Y*	*3Y*	*5Y*	*7Y*	*10Y*
HDFCTS	8.60	5.26	11.35	10.15	3	4	4	2
ICICIPLTE	11.28	8.36	13.87	12.42	2	2	1	1
SBIMTG	8.24	5.97	11.43	9.49	4	3	3	4
BENCHMARK	13.65	9.11	12.34	9.85	1	1	2	3

Source: Computed by Researcher

It is evident from Table 1 that ICICIPLTE was the only ELSS which outperformed the benchmark throughout the study period. At the same time, ICICIPLTE remained the best performing ELSS on all occasions. No ELSS outperformed the benchmark in 3-year and 5-year periods. However, ICICIPLTE outperformed the benchmark in 7-year and 10-year periods. In the 10-year, ICICIPLTE and HDFCTS funds outperformed the benchmark. On the other hand, SBIMTG was the worst performer in 3-year and 5-year; whereas HDFCTS remained the worst performing ELSS in 5-year and 7-year. Further, SBIMTG underperformed the benchmark during the entire study period except in 10-year. In terms of consistency (taken the rank of 3-year, 5-year, 7-year and 10-year together), ICICIPLTE was only the best performer outperforming the benchmark.No other funds outperformed the benchmark index consistently.

Table 2: Annualised Standard Deviation (SD) of the ELSS and Benchmark Index

ELSS	*SD*				*RANK*			
	3Y	*5Y*	*7Y*	*10Y*	*3Y*	*5Y*	*7Y*	*10Y*
HDFCTS	13.71	15.04	16.41	16.19	4	4	4	4
ICICIPLTE	11.41	12.70	13.85	13.66	1	1	1	1
SBIMTG	12.94	13.72	14.19	14.03	2	2	3	2
BENCHMARK	12.97	13.71	14.18	15.65	3	3	2	3

Source: Computed by Researcher

Table 2 depicts the total risk of the chosen ELSS and Benchmark Index. Standard Deviation (SD) is used to measure the total risk. The lower value of SD denotes lower risk and vice versa.

Table 2 shows that ICICIPLTE ELSS underperformed the benchmark in all the study periods in terms of the total risk and remained the best performer. However, SBIMTG outperformed the benchmark in 3 out of 4 periods. In 7-year, SBIMTG underperformed the benchmark. On the other hand, HDFCTS remained the worst performer since it occupied the last position throughout the study period. From the viewpoint of consistency, ICICIPLTE remained the least risky ELSS followed by SBIMTG (2nd). These two funds outperformed the benchmark index consistently. From the above, it can be said that, among the chosen funds ICICIPLTE is the least risky and HDFCTS is the most risky funds in terms of total risk.

Table 3 presents risk-adjusted return of the chosen ELSS and Benchmark Index. Sharpe Ratio measures the risk-adjusted return. Sharpe Ratio of an ELSS and the benchmark index are expressed as follows:

$$SR_p = (R_p - R_f)/SD_p$$

Where
SR_p = Sharpe Ratio of the ELSS,
R_p = CAGR of the ELSS,
R_f = Average Risk-free Return,
SD_p = Annualised Standard Deviation of the ELSS

$$SR_b = (R_b - R_f)/SD_b$$

Where
SR_b = Sharpe Ratio of the benchmark,
R_b = CAGR of the benchmark,
R_f = Average Risk-free Return,
SD_b = Annualised Standard Deviation of the benchmark

Sharpe Ratio of the benchmark is expressed as:

Table 3: Risk-adjusted Return (RAR) of the ELSS and Benchmark Index

ELSS	*Sharpe Ratio*				*Rank*			
	3Y	*5Y*	*7Y*	*10Y*	*3Y*	*5Y*	*7Y*	*10Y*
HDFCTS	0.024	–0.200	0.188	0.116	3	4	4	2
ICICIPLTE	0.264	0.007	0.404	0.304	2	2	1	1
SBIMTG	–0.002	–0.168	0.223	0.087	4	3	3	4
BENCHMARK	0.415	0.062	0.287	0.101	1	1	2	3

Source: Computed by Researcher

A look at Table 3 reveals that ICICIPLTE was the only ELSS which outperformed the benchmark index 7-year and 10-year and HDFCTS outperformed the benchmark index in 10-year.No ELSS could outperform the benchmark in 3-year and 5-year. SBIMTG was the only ELSS which underperformed the benchmark index during the entire study period. In terms of consistency, ICICIPLTE stood first followed by HDFCTS (2nd) and SBIMTG (3rd). In terms of risk-adjusted return, it is evident that funds underperform benchmark only in 7-year or more.

Table 4 shows the aggressiveness or defensiveness/conservativeness of the selected ELSS with respect to the benchmark index. Beta measures the aggressiveness or defensiveness of the chosen ELSS. Beta value > 1 denotes aggressiveness and beta value < 1 indicates defensiveness. The value of beta for the benchmark index is one (1).

Table 4: Aggressiveness/Defensiveness of the ELSS and Benchmark Index

ELSS	*Beta*				*Aggressive/Defensive*			
	3Y	*5Y*	*7Y*	*10Y*	*3Y*	*5Y*	*7Y*	*10Y*
HDFCTS	0.99	1.03	1.09	0.98	D	A	A	D
ICICIPLTE	0.82	0.87	0.91	0.91	D	D	D	D
SBIMTG	0.97	0.97	0.97	0.92	D	D	D	D
Benchmark	1.00	1.00	1.00	1.00	XXXXXXXXXXXXXXXX			

Source: Computed by Researcher

It is observed from Table 4 that ICICIPLTE and SBIMTG were the defensive ELSS throughout the study period. On the other hand, HDFCTS remained the aggressive ELSS during 5-year and 7-year periods.

Table 5 depicts the stock-picking ability of the fund managers of the selected ELSS. Alpha is used to measure the skill of the fund managers in picking quality stocks. Alpha is expressed as:

$$\text{Alpha} = R_p - [R_f + \text{Beta}^*(R_b - R_f)]$$

where,

Alpha = Differential return earned by the ELSS out of the ability of the fund manager in selecting correct stocks,

R_p = ELSS Return,

R_f = Average Risk-free Return,

R_b = Benchmark Return,

Beta = Systematic risk of the ELSS.

Table 5: Stock-picking Ability of the Fund Managers of the Chosen ELSS

ELSS	*ALPHA*				*RANK*			
	3Y	*5Y*	*7Y*	*10Y*	*3Y*	*5Y*	*7Y*	*10Y*
HDFCTS	–0.362	–0.309	–0.145	0.049	2	3	3	3
ICICIPLTE	0.007	0.037	0.207	0.267	1	1	1	1
SBIMTG	–0.376	–0.224	–0.039	0.031	3	2	2	2

Source: Computed by Researcher

Table 5 shows that ICICIPLTE was the best ELSS throughout the study period and it generated positive alpha during the entire study period. On the other hand, HDFCTS and SBIMTG generated negative alpha on 3 out of 4 occasions. However, all the select funds generated positive Alpha in 10-year period. From the point of view of consistency, ICICIPLTE stood first followed by SBIMTG (2nd) and HDFCTS (3rd).

Table 6 indicates the extent or degree of diversification of the chosen ELSS. RSQ or coefficient of determination is used to measure diversification. The value of RSQ lies between 0 and 1. The nearer the value to 1 the better diversified the fund is.

Table 6: Diversification of the Chosen ELSS

ELSS	*RSQ*				*Rank*			
	3Y	*5Y*	*7Y*	*10Y*	*3Y*	*5Y*	*7Y*	*10Y*
HDFCTS	0.876	0.878	0.89	0.887	2	3	3	3
ICICIPLTE	0.879	0.88	0.863	0.901	3	2	2	2
SBIMTG	0.945	0.948	0.943	0.946	1	1	1	1

Source: Computed by Researcher

It is evident from Table 6 that chosen ELSS are well diversified. SBIMTG remained the best performerduring the entire study period; whereas HDFCTS was the worst performer in 5-year, 7-year and10-year. In terms of consistency, SBIMTG performed the best followed by ICICIPLTE and HDFCTS. It is evident that SBIMTG is prudently diversified.

Table 7 presents the overall ranking of the selected ELSS.

It is observed from Table 7 that ICICIPLTE was the best performing ELSS followed by SBIMTG. On the other hand, HDFCTS remained the worst performing ELSS.

Table 7: Overall Rank of the Chosen ELSS

ELSS	*Sum of Rank Point of 3, 5, 7 and 10 Year*					*Total (6) [(1)+(2)+(3)+(4)+(5)]*	*Avg. (7) [(6)/20]*	*Rank (8)*
	CAGR (1)	*SD (2)*	*Sharpe Ratio (3)*	*Alpha (4)*	*RSQ (5)*			
HDFCTS	13	16	13	11	11	64	3.2	3
ICICIPLTE	6	4	6	4	9	29	1.45	1
SBIMTG	14	9	14	9	4	50	2.5	2

Source: Computed by the Researchers, AVG: Average

Conclusion

Based on the research questions, the findings are as follows:

1. The ELSS (ICICIPLTE) performed better than the benchmark index in the long term (7-year and 10-year) in terms of return (CAGR) (Table 1).
2. Majority of the chosen ELSS outperformed the benchmark index in 3-year, 5-year and 10-year in terms of total risk. In terms of consistency, the ELSS (ICICIPLTE and SBIMTG) performed better than the benchmark index (Table 2).
3. Majority of the chosen ELSS performed better than the benchmark index in the long term (7-year and 10-year) in terms of risk-adjusted return (Sharpe Ratio) (Table 3).
4. Beta values exhibit a mixed result. ICICIPLTE and SBIMTG were the defensive ELSS throughout the study period. On the other hand, HDFCTS remained the aggressive ELSS during the 5-year and 7-year period of study (Table 4).
5. Alpha values exhibit a mixed result as well. ICICIPLTE was the only ELSS which generated positive alpha during the entire study period. On the other hand, HDFCTS and SBIMTG generated negative alpha on 3 out of 4 occasions. However, all the select funds generated positive Alpha in 10-year period. From the point of view of consistency, ICICIPLTE stood first followed by SBIMTG (2nd) and HDFCTS (3rd) (Table 5).
6. The value of RSQ ranges between 0.863 and 0.964. SBIMTG remained the best performer in entire period of study. ICICIPLTE remained the worst performing ELSS in 3-year; whereas HDFCTS was the worst performer in 5-year, 7-year and 10-year. On the whole, the chosen ELSS succeeded in minimising the unsystematic risk satisfactorily. As such, the chosen ELSS were well diversified.
7. Overall ranking reveals that ICICIPLTE remained the best performing ELSS and HDFCTS was the worst performer.

It requires collaborative efforts from the regulators, AMCs, distributors and others. Investors should keep in mind that investing in ELSS can be a very good option for tax saving, wealth creation and beating inflation. However, choosing the right ELSS is very important. The task of identifying the right ELSS is not simple because of the existence of many such schemes and selecting only on the basis of recent past returns will not be a wise one. Factors like risk, return, diversification, aggressiveness, risk-adjusted return and the track record of the fund managers should be considered together before taking a call in this regard. At the same time, the national political environment, global economic outlook, the role of regulators and the performance of the industry concerned are significant factors as well. To attract retail investors and to ensure that they remain invested, the chosen ELSS must provide decent returns consistently without taking unnecessary risks.

Suggestions

Some of the policy suggestions are given below:

1. Investors wishing for earning more should be encouraged to invest in open-ended ELSS.
2. Regulator (SEBI) should seek an explanation from the Fund Houses for the continuous underperformance of ELSS.
3. It is necessary to prevent corporate frauds and scams to build the confidence of the investors.
4. Speedy grievance redressal should be ensured.
5. AMCs should focus on expanding their geographical reach to broaden their investor base.
6. Training and educating mutual fund distributors should be the important agendum for preventing mis-selling of ELSS.
7. Awaring investors regularly by organizing seminars, conferences, workshops etc. should be on the priority list of the regulator.

Limitations of the Study

1. The study considers only three ELSS while the Indian mutual fund industry has more such schemes managed by different AMCs.
2. The study has taken into consideration a few measures to analyse the performance of the chosen ELSS. However, there are other measures as well with their specific interpretations to assess the performance.
3. Mergers and Acquisitions (M&A) between the chosen ELSS and the same between the Fund Houses are not considered.
4. The outcome of change in fund managers is not taken into account.
5. The impact of brokerages, entry load, exit load, taxes, and inflation are not taken into consideration.

Scope for Further Research

Similar or different research may be carried out in the following areas:

- Research may be conducted to compare the performance of actively managed equity funds with that of passively managed equity funds.
- An in-depth study may be made on the impact of the expense ratio and other costs on fund performance.
- Comparative study between ELSS and "Flexi Cap Funds" may be carried out.
- Research may be conducted to analyse the performance of sector-specific and thematic funds in India.
- Research can be conducted on the investors' perception of investment in ELSS.
- Examining the performance of different tax-saving instruments in India may be an area of research.

References

[1] Bondyopadhyay, S. (December 8, 2008). No Place ELSS. The Telegraph. Retrieved from http://www.telegraphindia.com/1081208/jsp/business/story_10221313.jsp on 08.09.2014.

[2] Chandrakumarmangalam, S. and Govindasamy, P. (2011). Study on ELSS Fund & Its Performance Analysis with reference to Karvy Stock Broking Ltd. *International Journal of Human Resource Management and Research*, 1(2), 43–61.

[3] Chisti, K.A. and Rahman, A. (2018). Performance Evaluation of Equity Linked Saving Schemes: An Evidence from India. *Global Journal of Management and Business Research*, 18(6), 45–51.

[4] Das, S. (December, 2014). Performance of Indian Mutual Funds: An Empirical Study of Select Equity Linked Saving Schemes. *Research Bulletin*, 40, 175–186.

[5] Garg, M. and Gupta, S.L. (2014). An Empirical Study of Performance Evaluation of Selected Equity Linked Saving Schemes (ELSS) Of India. *International Journal of Research in IT & Management (IJRIM)*, 4(1), 32–48.

[6] Ghosh, R. (2014). Performance Evaluation of Mutual Funds in India. *The Indian Journal of Commerce*, 67(3), 66–73.

[7] Kadambat, K.K., Raghavendra, T.S. and Singh, B.M. (2015). Investment Performance of Equity Linked Savings Schemes (ELSS) of Indian Mutual Funds. *International Journal of Recent Scientific Research*, 6(5), 4076–4083.

[8] Panigrahi, A., Mistry, M., Shukla, R., and Gupta, A. (January, 2020). A Study on Performance Evaluation of Equity Linked Saving Schemes (ELSS) of Mutual Funds. *NMIMS Journal of Economics and Public Policy*, 5(1), 48–68.

[9] Pareek, M.S. (2018). Equity Linked Saving Schemes– A Smart Way for Tax Planning. *IJETSR*, 5(1), 1371–1376.

[10] Pathak, R. (2018). A Study on Performance Evaluation of ELSS Mutual Funds with Special Reference to Growth Funds. *Journal of Emerging Technologies and Innovative Research (JETIR)*, 5(5), 312–320.

[11] Research Desk. (February 8, 2022).PPF Has Grossly Underperformed ELSS. Retrieved on 22.08.2022 from https://www.valueresearchonline.com/stories/32274/ppf-has-grossly-underperformed-elss/.

[12] Roy, S. and Ghosh, S.K. (2012). Performance Evaluation of Open-Ended ELSS Mutual Fund Schemes In India during Recession. *KCA Journal of Business Management (KJBM),* 4(1).

[13] Santhi, N.S. and Gurunathan, K. B. (2011). An Analysis of Investors' Attitude towards Tax Saving Mutual Funds in India. *European Journal of Economics, Finance & Administrative Sciences*, 41, 54. Retrieved on 08.09.2014 from http://connection.ebscohost.com/c/articles/67703512/analysis-investors-attitude-towards-tax-saving-mutual-funds-india.

[14] Sharma, S. (2015). ELSS Mutual Funds in India: Investor Perception and Satisfaction. *International Journal of Finance and Accounting*, 4(2), 131–139.

[15] Srivastava, S. (2017). Equity Linked Saving Schemes (ELSS) Vis-A-Vis Fixed Income Schemesunder the Income Tax Act 1961. *Journal of Business & Financial Affairs*, 6(1), 1–6.

[16] Tripathy, N.P. (2005). An Empirical Evaluation of Market Timing Abilities of Indian Fund Managers on Equity Linked Savings Scheme. *Delhi Business Review,* X, 6(2).

[17] Vidhyadharan, J. (November, 2018). Retail Investors Take a Shine to Mutual Funds. Retrieved from https://www.thehindubusinessline.com/opinion/retail-investors-take-a-shine-to-mutual-funds/article25469309.ece on 23.08.2022.

[18] Prakash, M.S. and Viswanath, P. (August, 2023). A Study on Performance of Selected Tax Saving Mutual Funds at Angelone, Ananthapur. *JuniKhyat,* 13(8), 25–30.

[19] Naik, G.R., Gaude, V.P. and Kapdi, G. (Jan.–March, 2023). Performance Evaluation of select Equity Mutual Fund Schemes in India, *Education and Society,* 47(17), 83–90.

The Effect of Dividend Payment Decision on Firm's Financial Performance: A Study of BSE 100 Companies

Sourav Hansda[1]

ABSTRACT: This study investigates the relationship between dividend payment decisions and the financial performance of companies listed on the Bombay Stock Exchange (BSE). The research gap is examined in the study, after which a research model is constructed with rate of dividend and dividend payment decision as independent variables and ROA, and Tobin's Q as dependent variables. Dividend policy is a crucial aspect of corporate finance, influencing both investors and firms alike. The objective of this research is to analyze how dividend payment decisions impact the financial health and overall performance of companies within the BSE 100 index. The analysis is based on secondary data from 100 companies whose shares are traded on the Bombay Stock Exchange The findings of the analysis show that, although the dividend payout ratio has a negative effect on BSE 100 companies as determined by accounting-based performance, it also raises market expectations for these firms. The study also discovers that moderate dividend rates are offered by BSE 100 companies, which has a favorable influence on accounting-based performance but a detrimental effect on market expectations. Based on the findings, this article makes some insightful recommendations, such as a more suitable dividend policy model, a lower dividend rate, and a clear dividend payment choice.

Keywords: Dividend Payment Decision, Financial Performance, Financial Performance, Tobin's Q.

Introduction

The goal of all studies is to uncover the mysteries that lie inside the corpus of information within a certain field. In scientific study, it is frequently noted that researchers reach a definitive result that is subsequently accepted by all. However, studies in social science have realized that various research conducted at different times on different samples with different techniques has produced diverse results. Thus, the discussion does not end. That kind of field of study is finance. Academic literature on financial management has made it widely known that any company's current goal is to maximize the wealth of its shareholders

[1] Assistant Professor, Department of Commerce (UG & PG), Pingla Thana Mahavidyalaya, Pingla, India. E-mail: souravmid1986@gmail.com

(Ward, 1993). Put differently, the policymakers' decisions ought to result in an increase in the firm's valuation. It is critical in this setting for directors to understand the many policies that maximize value.

An examination of history reveals that researchers have been fascinated by this field for a considerable amount of time. As a result, models have been tested and their validity has been empirically verified. Black (1976) made the following observation about the intricacy of the effects of dividend decisions: "The more closely we examine the dividend picture, the more it resembles a puzzle with pieces that just don't fit together." It is still unclear why shareholders value dividends and why they commend management that consistently raises their payouts. Similarly, dividend policy was listed as one of the ten financial puzzles by Bearly and Myers (2002). Consequently, this has left corporations perplexed about the dividend declaration and payment procedure to implement. Therefore, the goal of the current study is to unravel the mysteries surrounding the impact of dividend decision payment on the Financial performance of the firm.

Literature Review

Managers of businesses are always debating whether to distribute dividends to shareholders or save them for potential future reinvestment, as well as what proportion should be used in the event that dividends are distributed. It is vital to study the existing literature in order to comprehend the problem area and the previously discussed features before venturing into the unknown.

Aderian and Alade (2013): This study looked at the relationship between dividend policy and corporate performance in Nigeria using data from 25 companies that were listed on the Nigeria Stock Exchange in 2010. Iterative regression and the multiple regression technique were used. The study's findings indicated that there was a positive correlation between the dividend policy and investment, profitability, and earnings per share.

Aggarwal and Pasricha (2012): The goal of the study was to determine how dividend policy and firm value are related. The empirical data was gathered between 2001 and 2010 through a survey of 20 Indian IT and pharmaceutical enterprises. The use of statistics revealed a significant correlation for both industries between the worth of the companies and their dividend payout.

Ahmed (2008): To determine the effect of corporate ownership, dividend policy, and financing policy on business performance, the researchers conducted an in-depth investigation. The study was made on 100 companies taken from the KSE in Malaysia for the period 1999 to 2002.

The "t" test was employed in conjunction with the suitable regression model. The analysis revealed the presence of a positive relationship between dividends and performance in the absence of growth opportunities. On the other hand, a negative correlation was discovered between the leverage and performance ratio. The dividend trend study showed no discernible pattern in the presence or lack of growth prospects. It was discovered that each company's overall dividend policy was stable.

Litzenberger and Ramaswamy (1982): As demonstrated by the author difference in taxes between dividends and capital gains is the reason why dividend policy affects investor behavior. According to the writers, investors choose low-dividend companies since there are fewer taxes to be paid.

Al Haddad *et al.* (2011): The study's foundation was an investigation conducted from 2000 to 2006 on 17 banks that were listed on the Amman Stock Exchange in Jordan. The study's goals were to look at dividend payout ratios and the stability of the corresponding dividend policy. Using the dividend per share as a dependent and earning per share as an independent inconstant, the panel data methodology was used. They also used regression models and pooled EGLS and least squares. According to the report, the banking industry has erratic cash dividend practices.

Bawa and Kaur (2013): The study looked at the relationship between the wealth of shareholders and dividend payouts for 308 Indian IT businesses listed on the BSE and NSE between 2006 and 2010. The study also examined the effect of dividend policy on the wealth of shareholders in companies that pay dividends and those that don't. With market price per share as the dependent variable and dividends per share, retained earnings per share, lagged price-earnings ratio, and lagged market price per share as the independent variables, they used fixed and random effects of panel data regression methods. They also utilized the "t" test, which produced varied results for dividend-paying corporations but demonstrated that the market value of dividend-paying companies was higher than the book value.

Das and Samanta (2013): The study looked at the correlation between dividend policy and stock price in 69 Indian stock exchange-listed information technology companies from 2002–03 to 2011–12. Using the current monthly adjusted market price per share as the dependent variable and the equity dividend percentage and retained profits to total assets ratio as the independent variables, they conducted a cross-sectional analysis. The retained earnings to total assets ratio and the equity dividend percentage were additional explanatory variables included in these investigations. The Dividend Irrelevance Theory was validated by their results.

Geng and Liu (2011): The research was based on an analysis of cash dividend-paying shares listed on the Shenzhen and Shanghai Shares Exchange to ascertain the correlation between cash dividends and business valuation. The years of study were 2005–2009. A positive association between the enterprise value and a steady cash dividend policy was found in the cross-sectional analysis. On the other hand, a negative correlation was noted in other instances of rising or falling cash dividends.

Gul *et al.* (2012): The goal of the 75 KSE-listed companies' study was to determine how shareholders' wealth was affected by dividend policies. Additionally, it looked into the differences in wealth brought about by changes in the dividend policy as well as the effects of retained earnings and previous performance on the wealth of shareholders. Regression models and the "t" and "F" tests were used to determine whether there was a significant difference between the average market value and book value of companies that paid dividends and those that did not. The dividend-paying companies experienced a notable impact from the dividend policy. In contrast to the large influence of the lagged value of the stock, the wealth was not affected by the lag in the price-earnings ratio.

Amidu (2007): investigated the possibility that dividend policy affects Ghanaian corporate performance. Data from the financial statements of companies listed on the Ghana Stock Exchange (GSE) for the last eight years is used for the studies.

The findings indicated that growth in sales, dividend policy, and return on assets were all positively correlated. Remarkably, the analysis shows that larger GSE companies do worse in terms of return on assets. The findings also showed a negative correlation between dividend payout ratio and return on assets.

Murekefu and Ouma (2012): From 2002 to 2010, 41 companies registered on the Nairobi Stock Exchange in Kenya were the subject of an extensive investigation by the researchers to determine the correlation between dividend payout and firm performance. With net profit margin as the dependent variable and dividends paid, total assets, and revenue as the independent variables, the study used correlation and regression analysis. Positive relationships were found in the study between total assets, revenue, net profit after tax, dividends, and total assets as well as between total assets, revenue, and firm performance (a) and (b). Additionally, the study demonstrated a significant positive correlation between firm success and dividend payout.

Onanjiri and Korankye (2014): Investigated the effect of dividend policy on the financial performance of manufacturing companies that trade on the Ghana Stock Exchange, also utilizing the dividend payout variable. The findings of the regression show that dividend payout has a major detrimental effect on businesses' financial success. Size and leverage, the control variables, showed a negative relationship with performance, whereas sales growth showed a positive correlation. Every control variable was determined to be statistically significant, with the exception of size. It stands to reason that Ghanaian quoted industrial companies looking to highlight their return on assets would need to justify the size of their dividend payments. This will enable them to build up substantial retained earnings to support investments in projects with positive net present values, which will spur sales growth and subsequently lower their

Parua and Gupta (2009): The researchers sought to ascertain the trends and factors that influence dividends in 607 BSE-listed companies. They discovered that there was an overall increase in the trend, with variations according to the firm. Companies paying little or no dividends were becoming more numerous. Additionally, businesses with greater sales paid out more dividends.

Zakaria *et al.* (2012): From 2005 to 2010, 77 Malaysian construction and material companies listed on the Kuala Lumpur Stock Exchange had their share prices volatile. The study examined the effect of dividend policy on these fluctuations. The effect of dividend policy and dividend pay-out ratio on share price was also examined in the study. With share price volatility as the dependent variable and dividend payout ratio, dividend yield, growth, size, leverage, and earning volatility as the independent variables, the researchers used the least squares regression technique and descriptive statistics. The research discovered that the share price volatility was 94.41%, indicating a significant positive correlation between the dividend payout ratio and share price volatility. In contrast, the dividend yield was found to have a negative correlation with stock price volatility. Only firm size and leverage, two of the control variables, significantly correlated with changes in firm price.

Tran *et al.* (2015), used the dividend payout ratio and the choice to pay a dividend (binary value) as independent variables and ROE, ROA, and Tobin's Q as dependent variables. The information was gathered from listed companies of the Vietnam Stock Exchange for the period from 2009–2013 audited financial statements. According to the author, the firm's performance metrics are significantly impacted by the cash dividend distribution. Nonetheless, the financial success of businesses is negatively impacted by the dividend payout ratio.

A similar study was carried out by **Khan *et al.* (2016)** for a few companies that were listed between 2010 and 2015 on the Pakistan Stock Exchange. Applying the OLS technique, the study's findings show a positive relationship between sale growth, dividend policy, and return on assets. The study's findings mostly concur with those of Ali *et al.* (2015).

More specifically, the findings indicate a substantial negative relationship between the return on equity and leverage and the dividend payout ratio.

Research Gap

As we can see from the above, numerous academicians from developed as well as developing countries have studied the effect of dividend policy on a firm's performance. Furthermore, the outcomes are inconsistent. Certain authors contend that a dividend has a substantial and favorable impact on a company's performance; others, however, present the opposite picture, and yet others suggest that these two variables have no connection at all. Furthermore, depending on the study, different elements affect or have an effect on the variables, which allows this research to spread farther. As a result, the debate is still ongoing, and if a correct response to the query is found via empirical research, the study would be groundbreaking.

Objective of the Study

The objective of the study is to examine how dividend payment decisions affect on firm's financial performance.

Hypotheses of the Study

Two research hypotheses are put out as follows:

- **Hypothesis 1 (H1):** Decision on dividend payment has a positive impact on a firm's financial performance.
- **Hypothesis 2 (H2):** The dividend payout ratio has a negative impact on a firm's financial performance.

Research Design

The following important points—which come under the category of "research design"—are kept in mind while conducting the research. The core of the research is secondary data on BSE 100 companies in India that was gathered from the AceEquity database between 2009 to 2022. The study's foundation is panel data, which is an accumulation of multiple cross-sectional units collected over a number of years. The finance businesses were removed from the study, while companies for which data is missing or incomplete data were also excluded from the study. Overall, the panel has been strongly balanced. The objective of the research is to examine the effect of dividend policy on a firm's financial performance on BSE 100 companies. For the panel regressions explained variables included are Tobin's Q, ROA (Return on Assets), and ROE (Return on Equity) which measures the firm's financial performance. On the other hand dividend payout ratio and decision of dividend payments proxies for dividend policy. These variables were also taken by Nguyen et. al.(2021). The other control variables are taken for the study the other control variables are the debt-equity ratio which represents leverage, the current ratio proxy for liquidity, the

Ln of total assets represents as size of the firm and growth in sales representatives for business growth.

Tabachnick and Fidell (1996) state that n = 50 + 8*m, where m is the number of variables, should be the sample size. This suggests that the research sample is suitable for performing a statistical test or regression, and the findings of the study can be generalized to the entire population.

Research Model

It is seen that majority of the studies have examined the effect of dividend policy on the financial performance of the company through a review of prior research models' literature.

Tobin's Q, ROA, and ROE are used as a representation of the companies' financial performance, while six other variables serve as independent variables in the study model. This measurement agrees with the research of other researchers including Nguyen *et al.* (2021), Khan *et al.* (2016), Velnampy *et al.* (2014), Murekefu and Ouma (2012), and Amidu (2007).

Based on the explained variables three separate models were developed which are as follows:

1. $TOBIN'SQit = \alpha + \beta_1\ DPRit + \beta_2\ DDPit + \beta_3\ SIZEit + \beta_4\ LEVit + \beta_5 LIQit + \beta_6\ GROWTHit + \varepsilon_{i,t}$
2. $ROAit = \alpha + \beta_1\ DPRit + \beta_2\ DDPit + \beta_3\ SIZEit + \beta_4\ LEVit + \beta_5 LIQit + \beta_6\ GROWTHit + \varepsilon_{i,t}$
3. $ROEit = \alpha + \beta_1\ DPRit + \beta_2\ DDPit + \beta_3\ SIZEit + \beta_4\ LEVit + \beta_5 LIQit + \beta_6\ GROWTHit + \varepsilon_{i,t}$

Here, 't' is used for the time series element, 'i' for the cross-sectional unit, 'α' is a constant term that represents the intercept, and 'β' is the coefficient. The decision of dividend payment (DDP) is depicted using a dummy variable 1 or 0. It takes the value 1 if the dividend is given otherwise 0. The description of the notation of the other variable is given in table 2.

Analysis and Findings

We must employ the proper data processing technique because panel data is being used. Step by step, the following statistical and economic methodologies and procedures are used:

Data descriptions by mean, mode, standard deviation, median, max, and min are presented first. This will give some broad information about the company, like its size, growth, leverage, liquidity, and dividend payout ratio. The variance between firms for each variable in the study model is also reported in the statistical description. After that the researcher tests whether there is any correlation amomg the independent variables. To get a sense of the bivariate correlation between the variables, the correlation matrix is displayed. An idea of their relationship is provided by the sign and the coefficient. In fact, the strength as observed from the value gives an idea about the multicollinearity problem. Generally, it is accepted that any value exceeding a value of 0.70 raises an alarm about the possible problem of multicollinearity in the data. For testing whether the issue of multicollinearity exists in the given case, we calculate the values of the variance inflation factor (VIF) for each of the variablesIt is suggested that one compute the VIF predictor. According to Hoang and Chu (2013), there is a multicollinearity problem if the VIF is more than 5. The problem of multicollinearity arises because of the following reasons:

(a) Inclusion of independent variables that are very closely related.
(b) Creation of a new variable that is in close relation with the existing variables.
(c) Inclusion of identical variables in the dataset.

Inappropriate use of dummy variables can also lead to a multicollinearity problem. It is popularly called a 'dummy trap' that can result in redundant information.

The sample firms had an average ROE of 25%, an average ROA of roughly 13%, and an average Tobin's Q of approximately 20.37, according to the statistical description in Table 1; listed firms have a lower market value than their book value. According to the dividend variables, over 94% of the sample enterprises (as determined by DDP) paid dividends to their shareholders.

Table 1: Summary Statistics

Variable	*Obs*	*Mean*	*Std.Dev.*	*Min*	*Max*
tobinsq	840	20.37274	262.4821	.0004226	6956.501
dividendpa~o	840	37.83985	38.3904	0	715.7172
DDP	840	.9452381	.2276505	01	
roa	840	13.09676	9.807031	-42.71393	76.51508
roe	840	25.20643	25.78455	-198.0291	317.7106
debtequity~o	840	1.019308	13.01766	7.009172	375.8249
currentratio	840	1.682356	1.322292	.2617755	16.06512
lntotalass~s	840	9.358053	1.841127	.1570236	14.53241
growthinsa~s	840	-32.22823	796.8667	-23035.39	.9865532

Source: Computation by author

As seen from the depicted table, the correlation coefficient between the variables is quite low, thereby giving an indication of multicollinearity which is tested after this.

Table 2: Correlation Matrix

	divide~o	*ddp*	*debteq~o*	*curren~o*	*lntota~s*	*growth~s*
dividendpa~o	1.0000					
DDP	0.2374	1.0000				
debtequity~o	0.0366	0.0074	1.0000			
currentratio	-0.0391	-0.0177	-0.0243	1.0000		
lntotalass~s	-0.0315	0.0087	0.0234	-0.2061	1.0000	
growthinsa~s	0.0079	-0.0097	0.0023	-0.0639	0.0135	1.0000

Source: Computation by author

Table 3: Results of VIF

Variable	*VIF*	*1/VIF*
dividendpa~o	1.06	0.939425
ddp	1.06	0.943209
currentratio	1.05	0.951410
lntotalass~s	1.05	0.955347
growthinsa~s	1.00	0.995735
debtequity~o	1.00	0.997722
Mean VIF	1.04	

Source: Computation by author

VIF detects the problem of multicollinearity in multivariate analysis. The problem exists when there is a correlation between predictors (i.e. independent variables) within a model which affects the results of the regression. The above table results show that the average VIF value is much below the threshold level. Since the VIF value for each variable is less than 10, there is no problem with multicollinearity.

Following multicollinearity and correlation checks, we proceed with the assessment of the regression model's suitability for panel data. In order to accomplish this, we first run the Fixed effect model (FEM) and Pooled OLS. The F-test findings indicate that FEM is a better fit than OLS. As a result, the Hausman test is used to compare the Random effect model (REM) and the FEM. The results show that the FEM is the better option.

The regression results of the three models are depicted as follows:

Table 4: Results of Regression at a Glance

Independent & Control Variables	*Indicators*	*Tobin's Q*	*ROA*	*ROE*
DPR	Coefficient	.1347705	–.0169786	–.0235573
	t-value	0.53	–2.79	–1.12
	Sig. level	0.595	0.005	0.265
DDP	Coefficient	4.842466	2.878262	31.46532
	t-value	0.08	1.97	6.22
	Sig. level	0.937	0.049	0.000
LEV	Coefficient	–.0357033	.0205185	.2545672
	t-value	–0.05	1.29	4.62
	Sig. level	0.957	0.197	0.000
LIQ	Coefficient	–31.91974	–.1889675	–.5800272
	t-value	–4.10	–1.01	–0.89
	Sig. level	0.000	0.313	0.371
SIZE	Coefficient	–21.55962	.0295421	–.6573656
	t-value	–3.66	0.21	–1.34
	Sig. level	0.000	0.835	0.181
GROWTH	Coefficient	–.0003285	–.0000714	–.0007322
	t-value	–0.03	–0.28	–0.82
	Sig. level	0.976	0.783	0.414
Cons	Coefficient	266.178	11.03683	3.200013
	t-value	3.37	5.82	0.49
	Sig. level	0.001	0.000	0.005
Model	F Statistics	84.46	125.57	111.46
	p-value (F-statistic)	0.000	0.000	0.000
	R-squared	0.3160	0.3940	0.3393

Model 1

No explanatory variables are statistically significant but have a positive impact on the firm financial performance. For controlling variables, Liquidity and firm size have a negative impact on Tobin's Q and they are all statistically significant.

Regarding the model's appropriateness, the regression results also demonstrate that the independent variables of the model could account for 31.60% of the variation in Tobin's Q, with an R-square value of 0.3160.

Model 2

Firstly, there was a statistically significant impact of the dividend payout ratio (DPR) on ROA at the 1% level. This finding suggests that, although the effect level is quite low, a higher dividend rate decreases the return on total assets. The ROA only decreases by 0.0169% when the dividend rate increases by 1%. This result is in line with the findings of the Khan *et al.* (2016) study, however, it differs from the findings of the study, Amidu (2007) which showed a negative correlation between ROA and dividend payout ratio. This pattern could be explained by the fact that shareholders want more capital gain than dividends. Second, at a statistical significance level of 5%, the dividend payment decision (DDP) positively impacts ROA. It suggests that a dividend declaration has a favorable impact on a company's success. When the company pays dividends it indicates a positive increase in ROA.

In the case of control variables leverage and firm size have a positive impact on the firm's financial performance. On the other hand liquidity and Growth of the firms have a negative impact on the firm's financial performance.

Regarding the model's appropriateness, the regression results also demonstrate that the explanatory variables of the model could account for 39.40% of the variation in ROA, with an R-square value of 0.3940.

Model 3

The dividend payout ratio has a negative but insignificant impact on the financial performance of the firm.

The Decision of Dividend Payment (DDP) has a 1% statistically significant positive effect on ROE. Similar to ROA, a company's declaration of dividends has a positive relationship with its financial performance.

Thirdly, with regard to the controlling variables, the findings indicate that just one variable—leverage has a statistically significant effect on ROE in distinct ways. However, all other control variables have a negative impact on the financial performance of the firm.

Additionally, the regression results display an R-square value of 0.3393, meaning that 33.93% of the change in the explained variable can be explained by the model's explanatory variables. The return on equity is influenced by numerous different factors.

Conclusions and Recommendations

It is evident from the aforementioned research findings that Indian companies pay relatively moderate dividend rates—an average of about 37%. On the one hand, this moderate dividend rate shows that businesses are saving money for operations and capital improvements. Because of this, some investors continue to put money into the companies because they are optimistic about the future. On the other side, the market's expectations for the firms' future growth decline when they yield a moderate to low dividend. The large variance range of dividend rate (0 to 715%), along with the high deviation value (38.39%), could be interpreted as evidence of the absence of a rational and consistent dividend policy in Indian listed companies. Businesses may arbitrarily offer a high cash dividend or high dividend rate for the year they wish to raise funds, without considering how these policies would affect the firm's financial performance, either at the accounting-based value or the market-based value. Investment and finance policies for every phase of the company life cycle should be integrated into dividend programs. For example, companies should have a modest dividend rate throughout the introduction and growth stages, but a high dividend during the maturity era when there is substantial profit and cash available.

Evidence exists that a variety of factors also influence dividend policy. Consequently, companies ought to consider variables such as the nature of the nation, the stage of development, and the agency cost of debt. Numerous academics have supported these ideas (Brockman and Unlu, 2009, for example), as has national culture (Zheng and Ashraf, 2014). Businesses should select and implement an economic model for their dividend policies, taking into account the dividend rate and dividend payment decision. A dividend policy model ought to be strategic, long-term, stable, and immune to the short-term whims of company managers. By doing that, the businesses can maintain control over the necessary capital structure and cash flow to produce the greatest possible financial results. Studies examining the influence of dividend policies on the financial performance of Indian listed companies show that the choice to pay a dividend and the dividend rate have distinct effects on a company's financial success as determined by ROA, and ROE. Based on the results, we also offer some insightful advice for businesses, such as adopting a more suitable dividend policy model, maintaining a low dividend rate, and making a clear announcement about dividend payments. When making investment decisions for businesses, listed companies, regulators, investors, and others may find these valuable. However, the research model might still have certain restrictions. One of these has to do with the model's low R-square. This suggests that not all the other dividend policy-related elements that might have an impact on the firm's performance, either directly or indirectly, have been fully explored in the article. Furthermore, the effects of time, industry, firm age, etc. have not been considered in this research. We think that these possible downsides could be the area that needs more investigation in the future.

References

[1] Aderian, S.A. and Alade, S.O. (2013). Dividend Policy and Corporate Performance in Nigeria. American Journal of Social and Management Sciences, 4(2), 71–77.

[2] Aggarwal, D. and Pasricha, J.S. (2012). Relationship between dividend policy and value of Firm—A study of Information Technology Industry and Pharmaceuticals Industry in Indian context. www.ccfr.org.cn/cicf2012/papers/20120104143625.pdf

[3] Ahmed, A.J.H. (2008). The impact of Financing decision, Dividend policy, Corporate ownership on firm performance at presence or absence of growth opportunity: A Panel data Approach, Evidence from Kuala Lumpur Stock Exchange. http:// ssrn.com/ abstract = 1246563, 1–21.

[4] Amidu, M. (2007). How does dividend policy affect Performance of the Firm on Ghana Stock Exchange? Investment Management and Financial Innovations, 4(2), 103–112.

[5] Brockman, Paul, and Emre Unlu (2009). Dividend policy, creditor rights, and the agency costs of debt. *Journal of Financial Economics* 92: 276–99.

[6] Bawa, S.K. and Kaur, P. (2013). Impact of dividend policy on shareholders' wealth : An Empirical Analysis of Indian Information Technology Sector. *Asia-Pacific Finance and Accounting Review,* 1(3), 17–24.

[7] Das, A. and Samanta, A. (2013). Stock Price Behaviour and Dividend Policy—An Empirical Investigation in Information Technology Sector of Corporate India in Liberalized Era. *International Journal of Marketing, Financial Services & Management Research,* 2(9), 146–153.

[8] Frankfurter, George M. and Bob, G. Wood. (2002). Dividend policy theories and their empirical test. *International Review of Financial Analysis,* 11: 111–38.

[9] Ghosh, S. and Ghosh, A. (2008). Do Leverage, Dividend Policy and Profitability influence the Future Value of Firm? Evidence from India. http://ssrn.com/ abstract=1158251.

[10] Gill, Amarjit, Nahum Biger and Rajendra, Tibrewala (2010). Determinants of Dividend Payout Ratios: Evidence from United States. *The Open Business Journal,* 3: 8–14.

[11] Gordon, Myron, J. (1963). Optimal investment and financing policy. *The Journal of Finance,* 18: 264–72.

[12] Gul, S., Sajid, M., Razzaq, N. and Iqbal, M.F. (2012). The Relationship between Dividend Policy and Shareholder's Wealth—Evidence from Pakistan. *Economics and Finance Review,* 2(2), 55–59.

[13] Haddad, A.W., Zorqan, A.S., Musa, S., Noor, M. (2011). The Effect of Dividend Policy Stability on the Performance of Banking sectors listed on Amman Stock Exchange. *International Journal of Humanities and Social Science,* 1(5), 201–205.

[14] Murekefu, T.M. and Ouma, O.P. (2012). The Relationship between Dividend Payout and Performance: A Study of Listed Companies in Kenya. *European Scientific Journal,* 8(9), 199–215.

[15] Hoang, T. and Chu., N.M.N. (2013). Applied Statistics in Socio-Economic Research. Hanoi: Statistical Publisher.

[16] Jensen, Michael C. and William, H. Meckling (1976). Theory of the firm: Managerial behavior, agency costs, and ownership structure. *The Journal of Financial Economics* 3: 305–60.

[17] Khan, Mula Nazar, Babar Nadeem, Fahad Islam, Muhammad Salman and Hafiz Muhammad Ikram Sarwar Gill (2016). Impact of dividend policy on firm performance: An Empirical Evidence from Pakistan Stock Exchange. *American Journal of Economics,* Finance and Management 2: 16–25.

[18] Onanjiri, Richard and Thomas, Korankye (2014). Dividend payout and performance of quoted manufacturing firms in Ghana. *Research Journal of Finance and Accounting,* 5: 37–42.

[19] Parua, A. and Gupta, A. (2009). Dividend history and determinants in selected Indian companies: A study during 1993–94 to 2004–05. Australasian Accounting, *Business and Finance Journal,* 3(4), 45–83.

[20] Shefrin, Hersh, M. and Meir, Statman (1984). Explaining investor preference for cash dividends. *Journal of Financial Economics,* 13: 253–82.

[21] Tran, P.L., Le, D.H. and Tran, M.T. (2015). Effects of dividend policies on the financial performance of listed manufacturing firms in the Vietnam stock market (Vietnamese version). *Journal of Economics and Development,* 218: 34–41.

[22] Velnampy, T., Nimalthasan, P. and Kalaiarasi, K. (2014). Dividend policy and firm performance: Evidence from the manufacturing companies listed on the Colombo Stock Exchange. *Global Journal of Management and Business Research,* 14: 1–7.

[23] Zheng, Changjun and Ashraf, Badar Nadeem (2014). National culture and dividend policy: International evidence from banking. *Journal of Behavioral and Experimental Finance,* 3: 22–40.

[24] Zakaria, Z., Muhammad, J. and Zulkifli, H.A. (2012). *International Journal of Economics and Management Sciences,* 2(5), 01–08.

Factors Affecting Profitability of Insurance Companies: An Empirical Study in India

Chaitali Ghosh[1] and Luxmi Jha[2]

ABSTRACT: Economic growth requires a robust insurance industry since it not only boosts the nation's capacity to take on risk but also offers long-term funding for infrastructure development. Examining the factors impacting the profitability of Indian insurance businesses is the primary goal of the research. A well-balanced panel dataset of top 15 sample Indian insurance companies taken from Insurance Regulatory and Development Authority of India for the period of 2013–14 to 2022–23 (10 years). As profitability indicator Return on Equity (ROE) has been taken as dependent variable. The study also measured Expenses ratio (ER), Financial leverage (FL) and Size of company (LnTA) factors as independent variables. Descriptive statistics, Correlation analysis and Regression analysis have been carried out for empirical analysis. To analysis the data MS EXCEL and SPSS software has been utilized. According to the results, one of independent variable Expenses ratio have positive relationship with return on equity. Based on the study's findings, Indian insurance businesses' profitability is mostly determined by their size and financial leverage.

Keywords: Financial Risk, Infrastructure, Insurance Companies, Profitability.

JEL CODE: G22, P2, G32, H54.

Introduction

Any nation's financial system is made up of the two main financial sectors, the banking and insurance industries, which transmit risk from one economic unit to another, mobilize savings, and effectively channel money to support commerce and resource mobilization. The insurance industry, which falls under the financial system's purview, is crucial in controlling the flow of money to various businesses and, as a result, provides the bulk of cash inflows that support the country's financial and economic development. The foundation of a nation's risk management system is its insurance providers, who provide a range of products to both individuals and companies to protect them against risk and

[1] State Aided College Teacher, Surendranath Evening College, Kolkata, India.
E-mail: ghoshchaitali1503@gmail.com

[2] State Aided College Teacher, Surendranath Evening College, Kolkata, India.
E-mail: luxmijha10@gmail.com

guarantee their financial stability. It is a major player in the service-based economy, and the financial industry is starting to include its services (Malik 2011). In addition to enhancing the solvency of insurers, profit is crucial in convincing policyholders and investors to contribute capital to insurance companies. Without revenues, no insurer can draw in outside funding to accomplish its goals in this dynamic, cutthroat global marketplace. As a result, achieving profit is a primary goal of insurance company management and is a must for carrying out any insurance operation. It is also possible to evaluate the insurance industry's profitability at the macro and local levels of the economy. The impact of firm-specific variables on profitability, including size, capital, efficiency, age, and ownership structure, is referred to as the micro level. The effect of support institutions and macroeconomic forces, respectively, are referred to as the macro level. Profit is the least expensive source of funding and a necessary condition for the survival, expansion, and competitiveness of insurance companies on a micro level (Buyinza *et al.,* 2010). Researchers from both established and emerging nations expressed interest in examining the profitability of businesses, with a focus on the banking compared to the insurance industries.

To oversee and advance the insurance sector, the Insurance Regulatory and Development Authority (IRDA) was established as an independent organization in 1999. In case of life insurance sector, net premium revenue climbed from Rs. 236942 crore in 2013–14 to Rs 474668 crore in 2022–23, i.e., 100.33% approximately. Research on the profitability situation of life insurance is desperately needed to determine whether they are maintaining a fair level of earnings and demonstrating a sustainable rise in profits. Return on assets (ROA) and operating ratio were the two types of profitability indicators utilized by Chen-Ying Lee (2014) to assess the profitability of insurance companies; other researchers have used the combination of ROA and ROE as a profitability indicator. Accordingly, this study was made to analyze the profitability of life insurance companies in India at the same time what factors influencing their performance.

Literature Review

Bawa & Bhagat (2015) conducted a study to ascertain the elements influencing the financial performance of Indian private life insurance companies. The study employed return on asset as the dependent variable and leverage, liquidity, size, age, underwriting risk, and capital volume as the independent variables, an attempt has been made to simulate the factors influencing the profitability of life insurers operating in India. The twelve Indian life insurers for the years 2006–07 through 2012–13 comprise the study's sample. It has been discovered that age, size (as shown by the logarithm of Total Assets), volume of capital, and leverage all have a positive and significant impact on life insurers' profitability. The study's data does not support the hypothesis that liquidity and profitability are related. Ullah *et al.* (2016) presented a study on factors determining the profitability of the Insurance Industry of Bangladesh. This study aims to examine the factors that significantly predict the profitability of non-life insurance companies in Bangladesh. It analyzed panel data of eight different insurance companies—selected using convenience sampling method from the years 2004–2014 to assess whether any significant relationship exists between Profitability (ROA), and certain independent variables Underwriting Risk, Expense Ratio, Solvency Margin, Premium Growth, Asset Growth, and Company Size using an Ordinary least squares (OLS) regression model. It analyses panel data of eight different insurance companies—selected using convenience sampling method from the years 2004–2014 to assess whether any significant relationship exists between Profitability (ROA), and certain independent variables Underwriting Risk, Expense Ratio, Solvency Margin, Premium Growth, Asset Growth, and Company Size using an Ordinary least squares (OLS) regression model. This study discovered a strong negative correlation between size and profitability (ROA) and underwriting risk. Expense Ratio, Solvency Margin, and Growth all significantly positively correlate with profitability (ROA). Financial managers will benefit from this study's understanding of which internal aspects to prioritize to increase profitability.

Daare (2016) tried to look at the variables that affect general insurance profitability in India. The study took ten general insurance companies—six of which were private and the other six were public—provided financial accounts of their non-life insurance from 2006 to 2016. Panel data are evaluated using the Fixed Effect Model (FEM) once the Random Effect and Pooled Regression models have been used to assess the model's suitability. The regression model offers a comprehensive view of the profitability of insurance companies by accounting for their growth rate, net operating expenditures, and liquidity—the three key value drivers. Omundu and Muturi (2013) discovered that liquidity played a significant role in determining the performance of insurers. The regression analysis shows that GDP and capital adequacy have a positive impact on profit, whereas inflation and liquidity harm general insurance profitability in India. To keep the industry's profitability position, managers might place more focus on current liability management and capital adequacy. Boyjoo & Ramesh (2017) studied a paper to comprehend how and what factors influence performance under the statutory preview of the Financial Service Commission Mauritius (FSC Mauritius) and Integrated Regulatory Framework, this study aims to understand the factors influencing the performance of general insurance companies in Mauritius. Employing return on assets (ROA) as the dependent variable, this study has identified key factors and examined their connection and predictive power to create a model that could be used to track their performance to achieve growth and success. The regression model offers a comprehensive view of the profitability of insurance companies by accounting for their growth rate, net operating expenditures, and liquidity—the three key value drivers. Bodla (2017) presented a study to evaluate and contrast the profitability performance of both public and private life insurance businesses in India. Out of a total of 24 life insurance firms, the authors selected a sample consisting of 13 private-sector life insurance and one public-sector company (LICI). The study's ten-year reference period stretched from 2007 to 2016. Seven criteria were taken into consideration for the analysis of the profitability and financial performance: Net Premium, Income from Investments, Underwriting Income, Return on Assets, Combined Ratio, Solvency Ratio, and Profit after Tax. The importance of variance in the profitability of different insurers was tested using ANOVA. According to the survey, of the private sector life insurers, ICICI Prudential had the greatest average net premium over the previous five years, followed by HDFC Standard and SBI Life; on the other hand, IDBI Federal mobilized the lowest premium, followed, by the upside, by Exide Life. Over the last five years, from 2012 to 2016, ICICI Prudential had the highest compound annual growth rate (CAGR) of investment income, followed by Birla Sunlife (63.79%) and Tata AIA (57.9%). For practically all private sector companies, the CAGR of underwriting income has decreased throughout the last five years.

Tesfaye (2016) analyzed a paper having the primary goal of looking at the variables influencing Ethiopian insurance companies' financial performance. These factors are categorized into firm-specific, industry, and macroeconomic variables using Return on Asset used for measuring financial performance. The researcher applied a quantitative approach explanatory research design and purposive sampling. Secondary data was collected from 12 insurance companies out of 17 and the National Bank of Ethiopia (NBE) from 2011 to 2016. Descriptive statistics and Random Effect econometric model applied for data analysis. These variables were grouped using Return on Asset, which is a financial performance metric, into firm-specific, industry-specific, and macroeconomic variables. The researcher used purposive sampling, an explanatory research design, and a quantitative technique. Secondary data was gathered between 2011 and 2016 from the National Bank of Ethiopia (NBE) and 12 out of the 17 insurance companies. For data analysis, descriptive statistics and the Random Effect econometric model were used. The study used Ethiopian Bank (NBE) between 2011 and 2016. For data analysis, descriptive statistics and the Random Effect econometric model were used. The study's conclusions showed that while solvency margin and loss ratio have a negative correlation and a considerable impact on financial performance, prior profit performance and capital volume have a positive and large impact. In contrast to the lag inflation and exchange rate, which had a negative and large impact on ROA, the lag GDP rate and current inflation have a positive and considerable impact. Consequently, businesses ought to increase their solvency margin, and the government ought to keep the currency exchange rate stable. Rashid & Kemal (2018) conducted a study to examine the effects of both external and internal factors on the insurance industry's profitability by examining three key indicators of insurer profitability: investment income (INI), underwriting profit (UP), and overall profit (ROA). Regression using panel data is employed to analyze life insurance businesses operating in Pakistan between 2006 and 2016. According to the study's findings, the profitability of insurance firms is significantly impacted by gross written premium, management expenses, size, and interest rate. The results show the underwriting losses that have been incurred by life insurance companies, emphasizing the need of separate actuary departments for proper validation of the policies. The paper facilitates the risk managers and regulatory authorities by depicting the factors affecting the performance of the insurance sector. The research helps the management and policymakers in expediting the growth and performance of the insurance sector. NazishIshtiaq & Siddiqui (2019) wrote a paper to look into what influences the life insurance industry's financial performance in Pakistan. While sector ROA was used to access performance, other potential internal and external factors, such as liquidity, net premium, premium growth, underwriting risk, debt to equity, insurance leverage, tangibility, equity capital, capital surplus, GDP, inflation, and market share, were used to assess their impact. Data was collected from 2008 to 2017 from nine life insurance firms, eight of which were private and one of which was public. Two of the observations in this study exclusively focused on takaful life insurance, whilst the remaining three either relied primarily on conventional methods or on both. Panel regression was utilized to examine the data. The generalized method of the moment is used to estimate the outcomes in the panel ordinary least square regression model. The study's findings indicate that the financial performance of Pakistani Life Insurance Company is not considerably impacted by tangibility, market share, net premium, insurance leverage, or GDP. Other independent variables that are positively and strongly correlated with Pakistani life insurance businesses include liquidity, underwriting risk, debt to equity, equity capital, capital surplus, and inflation. Bhattarai (2020) conducted a study on factors influencing the profitability of insurance companies in Nepal. The study's primary goal is to investigate the factors affecting Nepalese insurance companies' profitability. Based on panel data from ten insurance firms spanning five years, from 2012–2013 to 2017–18, the study produced fifty observations. Return on Equity (ROE) has been used in the study as a dependent variable and as a measure of profitability. Employee Expense Ratio (ER), Financial Leverage (FL), and Size of Company (LnTA) factors are also included in the study as independent variables. SPSS 25 software has been used to process the data. The findings show that there is a positive association between the cost's ratio and other independent variables. The study's findings indicated that size and financial leverage were the two main factors influencing Nepalese insurance businesses' profitability. Tsvetkova (2021) tried to examine the factors affecting insurance businesses' financial performance in the Russian Federation, despite a dearth of research on these factors in other nations. The study used descriptive analysis, correlation analysis, multiple linear regression, and factor analysis to examine the financial secondary data of 45 insurance businesses and groups that were continuously operating in the Russian Federation between 2012 and 2018. The study found a favourable correlation between the company's size, claim ratio, liquidity ratio, and return on equity (ROE) and return on assets (ROA). The premium growth rate and inflation have a negative correlation with ROA. The study discovered that 45.1% of the variance in insurance firms' performance may be attributed to the variables that were examined, including size of the business, ROE, liquidity ratio, premium growth rate, claims ratio, and inflation. Other factors affect 54.9% but are not covered in this study. Scientists and insurance experts can use the study's findings for more research in the Russian Federation and abroad, including industry-based studies aimed at defining factors and creating guidelines and policies for the insurance sector. Professionals and upper management in insurance can define and adjust the strategies and tactics of insurance companies based on the findings of this study. Ramji & Das (2021) conducted a study with the purpose of this study is to identify the financial variables that influence the market stock price fluctuations of insurance businesses that are listed on the Dhaka Stock Exchange. Ten years of panel data from 2010 to 2019 from 15 insurance firms have been examined for this purpose. Economic modelling methods like Pooled OLS regression and the Random-effect and Fixed-effect models have been used to construct and test hypotheses. Return on Assets (ROA), Price-Earnings ratio (P/E), Book Value Per Share (BVPS), Earnings Per Share (EPS), and Firm Size (SZ) are the independent variables in this study. The results of pooled OLS indicate that the market stock price is significantly positively impacted by ROA, BVPS, EPS, and P/E ratio. The Fixed-effect model demonstrates that while company size harms market stock price, ROA and P/E ratio have large beneficial impacts. Sah & Magar (2021) presented a paper to investigate the variables influencing profitability in the context of insurance firms in Nepal. The dependent variables chosen for the study are return on equity and return on assets. The independent variables that have been chosen include firm age, firm size, premium growth, tangibility, and liquidity. The study's foundation is secondary data from 21 insurance firms, totalling 168 observations during 2011–12–2018–19. The information is gathered from selected insurance firms' annual reports as well as those released by Beema Samiti. The factors influencing the profitability of insurance businesses in Nepal are tested through the estimation of regression models. The study demonstrated that return on equity and return on assets are positively impacted by firm size. It suggests that higher returns on equity and assets are correlated with greater firm sizes. Similarly, return on equity and return on assets both benefit from premium growth. It suggests that the return on equity and the return on assets would increase with the premium increases. Liquidity ratios also have a detrimental effect on return on equity and return on assets. It implies that a rise in the liquidity ratio causes the return on equity and assets to decline. Abdeljawad *et al.* (2022) presented a study to investigate the elements influencing Palestine's insurance businesses' profitability. Seven insurance businesses that operated in Palestine between 2006 and 2018 provided unbalanced panel data that was used to develop a linear model between factors that are theoretically predicted to have an impact on performance and insurance firms' profitability. The results showed that, while automobile claims have a major negative impact on the insurance company's profitability, size, growth, and liquidity greatly positively affect the insurance firm's profitability. The claims ratio and leverage ratio, among other variables, have little bearing on how profitable insurance companies are. These findings primarily suggest that to increase profitability, Palestinian insurance companies should diversify their insurance portfolios away from auto insurance and maintain higher levels of liquidity. Thirupathi & Subhashini (2022) conducted an empirical examination of the principal factors influencing HDFC Life Insurance Company's financial performance to evaluate several important factors that aid in the analysis of the financial performance of particular life insurance providers. Secondary data from India's HDFC Life Insurance Company was used in the current investigation. The necessary information was gathered from the company's website, IRDA publications, periodicals, public disclosures, and annual reports over 12 years, from 2009–10. The findings of the study indicated the success of the company was measured using key performance indicators such as the ratios of liquidity, profitability, solvency, claims management, operating expenses, etc. One of the best private life insurance providers in India, HDFC Life Insurance Company, is a financially successful insurance provider after investigation.

Research Gap

The stability of every organization has been determined by its superior performance. Even with excellent public relations, organizational performance is essential for sustainable success. This state is not distant from the insurance industry. A few indicators have been utilized to assess the organization's profitability. There is interest in both theory and practice around the factors that determine an insurance company's profitability. Very few studies have looked at the traditional factors that affect insurance businesses' profitability. The findings of earlier research are contradictory. The elements that previous research has shown to be most significant will be examined in this study. The majority of research have emphasized the management-controlled internal factors that determine profitability. From the review of literature, it is clear that most of the studies confined to a smaller period of three to five years only. To the best of our knowledge, no other study has been carried out recently to determine the factors influencing the profitability of insurance companies using the data available on the insurance sector from 2013–14 to 2022–23.

Objectives of the Study

(a) To calculate and analyze the profitability of selected life insurance companies,
(b) To investigate the factors that affect the profitability of Indian life insurance companies.

Research Methodology

Selection of sample: The study is based on secondary data. Our study is confined to top 15 Indian insurance companies listed in Insurance Regulatory and Development Authority of India (IRDAI). By this criterion our sample consisted of 3 Government insurance companies and 12 private insurance companies. The list of the companies displayed in appendix.

Collection of data: The annual reports of the respective insurance companies as main source of data which were collected through their respective web page. Also, www. moneycontrol.com has been followed to gather the information.

Study period: The study conducted over a period of 10 years from 2013–14 to 2022–23 and leading to 150 observations.

Tools and techniques applied: The present study analyses the factors affecting profitability of Indian insurance companies. The profitability has been measured by Return on Equity (ROE) as dependent variable. On the other hand, Expenses ratio (ER), Financial leverage (FL) and Size of the company (LnTA) as independent variables.

For analyzing the data Descriptive statistics, Correlation analysis and Regression analysis has been carried out to check the impact of factors on profitability of insurance companies. To analyse the data MS EXCEL and SPSS has been used.

Research Hypotheses

To attain the objectives of the study, the following hypotheses (H_0) have been tested:

H_{01}: There is no significant variance in the profitability of selected life insurance companies;

H_{11}: There is significant variance in the profitability of selected life insurance companies;

H_{02}: There is no significant impact of factors on the profitability of various life insurance companies;

H_{12}: There is significant impact of factors on the profitability of various life insurance companies.

Performance Variables

1. **Return on Equity:** A firm's profitability is gauged by its return on equity (ROE), which shows how much profit the company makes on the capital that shareholders have contributed. Any corporation that has both positive net income and equity may compute return on equity (ROE), which is represented as a percentage. Net income is determined after interest to lenders and before payouts to preferred shareholders but before dividends paid to common shareholders.

   ROE= (Net income after tax/ Total shareholders' equity)

2. **Expenses Ratio:** The amount of a fund's assets that go toward operational and administrative costs is determined by the expense ratio. The expense ratio is paid to the fund management and subtracted from the fund's gross return for investors. By dividing a fund's operational costs by the average dollar amount of its assets under management (AUM), one may get an expense ratio. The fund's assets are diminished by operating expenditures, which lowers the return to investors.

   ER= (Management expenses/Gross premium)

3. **Financial Leverage:** The whole amount of the company's debt divided by the total amount of shareholders' equity is the formula for financial leverage. There is a better chance that the firm will have stable finances if shareholder equity exceeds corporate debt. If the company's debt surpasses its shareholder equity, it might not be able to pay off all its debt.
   To calculate financial leverage, use the following financial leverage formula:

   FL= (Total company debt divided by shareholders' equity)

4. **Firm Size:** The magnitude of a firm's activities is referred to as its company size. A variety of measures, such as assets, revenue, output, market capitalization, workforce size, and invested capital, are used to quantify it.

   Firm size = Ln(TA) = Natural log of total assets

Analysis and Findings

Descriptive Analysis

Descriptive statistical technique employed for each variable in the study that covers from 2013–14 to 2022–23. In addition, we have consideredthe mean values, standard deviation along with minimum and maximum for better understanding of different profitability parameters and their fluctuations over the study period.

Table 1: Descriptive Statistics of Variables of the Indian Insurance Companies over the Study Period 2013–14 to 2022–23

	Minimum	*Maximum*	*Mean*	*Std. Deviation*
ROE	–.48	4.32	.2664	.77531
ER	.04	5.34	.7709	1.10769
FL	.03	191.45	10.1384	27.97022
LnTA	4.08	6.66	5.4999	.59764

Source: Authors' calculation

For descriptive statistics we have selected Return on Equity (ROE), Expenses Ratio (ER), Financial Leverage (FL) and Size of the company (LnTA) in this study. From the results, it may be observed that the value of ROE is 0.2664 whereas minimum amounts to –0.48 and maximum 4.32 during the study period. It suggests that the equity return is higher than the cost of capital. It demonstrates the insurance industry's comfortable equity profit margin.

The ratio of management expenses to gross premium ranges from 0.04 to 5.34, with an average of 0.7709. This indicates that an important proportion of the gross premium has been allocated to management expenses. When the overall debt to equity ratio's standard deviation is more than the mean value, it indicates that the insurance sector is not performing better when looking at leverage. The company's size has been distributed very well.

Correlation Analysis

Below table represent the Pearson's Correlation Matrix of study variable. Result shows the degree of association among the variables used in the study. Correlation between financial leverage and size of the company is positive with profitability. Whereas, correlation between management expenses ratio and profitability is negative, which shows management expenses decreases profitability also decreases in the same direction.

Table 2: Pearson Correlation Coefficient of Different Variables

Variables	*ROE*	*ER*	*FL*	*LnTA*
ROE	1			
ER	–0.122	1		
FL	.904**	–0.172*	1	
LnTA	.327**	–0.592**	0.315**	1

Source: Author's calculation; **correlation is significant at the 0.01 level (2-tailed), *correlation is significant at the 0.05 level (2-tailed)

Furthermore, the correlation matrix shows that the correlation between all the variables is extremely low—less than 0.30. There is no proof that the variables under investigation are multicollinear. Therefore, from the perspective of correlation, the variables selected are adequate. The outcome provides the go-ahead for regression analysis.

Regression Analysis

Below table represents the ordinary least square regression results of predictors. Based on 150 observation the analysis shows the relationship between the external factors and profitability of insurance companies in India. Accordingly, the model explains R-Squared for the regression is 0.821 that is 82.1 percent of the total variability in the performance of insurance companies, while 17.9 percent is influenced by other variables in this study.

From the regression results, the past financial performance (ROE) has depicted positive with the current financial performance. The beta coefficient has been positive throughout the study period. There is a positive effect of ER on ROE, which indicate a significant result between profitability and firm's management ratio.

Table 3: Regression Results for Independent Variables (ER, FL and LnTA) on Profitability (ROE)

Model		*Unstandardized Coefficients*		*Standardized Coefficients*	*t*	*Sig.*
		B	*Std. Error*	*Beta*		
1	(Constant)	–.753	.331		–2.276	.024
	ER	.064	.030	.091	2.117	.036
	FL	.025	.001	.888	24.339	.000
	LnTA	.131	.058	.101	2.264	.025

R-Square: 0.825, Adj. R-Square: 0.821, F-Value: 229.448, F(Sig): .000, Observations: 150

Source: Authors' calculation

Financial leverage has a positive and strong beta coefficient in relation to profitability. The outcome clearly shows that they are heading in the same direction and that profitability is determined by financial leverage. In general, technical reserves make up the majority of the debt held by debt insurance companies, which is mostly composed of debt attached to insurance policies. The degree of financial leverage used by insurance firms is a good indicator of how well they can control their exposure to unforeseen losses. This ratio might influence capital and result in a reserve surplus because of financial claims. A positive and strong correlation has been seen between size and profitability, indicating that when insurance companies grow in size, their profits also tend to rise and vice versa.

Conclusions and Suggestions

India's insurance business has expanded quickly in recent years. Simultaneously, while a large body of research has been done on the variables and elements influencing the financial performance of businesses engaged in the global insurance markets, less research has been done on the variables influencing the performance of Indian life insurers. The study looked at the variables influencing Indian insurance companies' profitability. For ten years, from 2013–14 to 2022–23, the data were gathered from the annual reports of the corresponding 15 insurance firms. The ordinary least square (OLS) regression model was used to evaluate the data. Profitability (ROE) is considered the dependent variable, whereas expenses ratio, leverage, and size are considered the independent factors. According to the correlation analysis performed in course of the study ROE has positive relationship with the size of the company. The regression's findings showed that size and leverage had a substantial impact on profitability. The findings of this study can be used by scientists and insurance professionals for additional research in India and abroad, including industry-based studies aimed at defining factors and creating guidelines and policies for the insurance sector of a particular nation or business. Governmental authorities may utilize the study's findings in conjunction with further research to develop insurance laws and regulations.

References

[1] Bawa, S.K. and Bhagat, N. (2015). Determining the Factors Affecting Profitability of Life Insurance Companies. *Asia-Pacific Finance and Accounting Review.* 3(1). 141–157.

[2] Bhattarai, B.P. (2020). Factors Influencing Profitability of Insurance Companies in Nepal. *International Journal of Management.* 11(9). 8–14.

[3] Bodla, M.S., Tandon, D. and Bodla, S.B. (2017). Profitability Performance of Life Insurance Companies—A Study in Indian Context. *International Journal of Computing and Business Research*, 7(3).

[4] Boyjoo, T. and Ramesh, D.V. (2017). A study on factors influencing performance of General Insurance Companies in Mauritius—An empirical evidence. *International Journal of Conceptions on Management and Social Sciences,* 5(1). 23–29.

[5] Buyinza, F., Francois, J. and Landesmann, M. (2010). Determinants of Profitability of Commercial Banks in Sub Saharan Africa Countries, *Department of Economics Johanssen Keppler University, Linz Austria.*

[6] Daare, W. J. (2016). Factors Affecting General Insurance Companies Profitability: Empirical Study in India. *International Journal of Marketing, Financial Services & Management Research*, 5(12). 1–8.

[7] Lee, C. (2014). The Effects of Firm Specific Factors and Macroeconomics on Profitability of Property-Liability Insurance Industry in Taiwan, *Asian Economic and Financial Review*. 4(5), 681–691.

[8] Nazishishtiaq and Siddiqui, D.A. (2019). Factors Affecting Financial Performance of Life Insurance Sector in Pakistan, *SSRN Electronic Journal*, DOI: 10.2139/ssrn.3400728

[9] Ramji, G. and Das, A. (2021). An Empirical Study on Microeconomic Factors Affecting Stock Price: A Study on Insurance Companies Listed in Dhaka Stock Exchange. *Khulna University Business Review*, 16(1), 25–47.

[10] Rashid, A. and Kemal, M.U. (2018). *Impact of Internal (Micro) and External (Macro) Factors on Profitability of Insurance Companies*, 5(1). 35–57.

[11] Sah, L.K. and Magar, M.R. (2021). Factors affecting the profitability of Nepalese insurance companies. *Nepalese Journal of Insurance and Social Security*, 4(1). 87–99.

[12] Tesfaye, T.T. (2016). Analysis of Factors Affecting Financial Performance Evidence from Selected Ethiopian Insurance Companies. *International Journal of Science and Research*, 7(12), 834–852.

[13] Thirupathi, D.T. and Subhashini, S. (2022). An Empirical Analysis of Key Determinants Affecting the Financial Performance of HDFC Life Insurance Company. *Journal of Positive School Psychology*, 6(6), 2928–2935.

[14] Tsvetkova, L. (2021). Factors Affecting the Performance of Insurance Companies in Russian Federation. *Montenegrin Journal of Economics*, 17(1), 209–218.

[15] Wali, U., G.M., Faisal, M.N. and Zuhra, S.T. (2016). Factors Determining Profitability of the Insurance Industry of Bangladesh. *International Finance and Banking*, 3(2), 138–147.

Annexure

List of Sample Companies

Sl. No.	*Name of the Company*	*Nature*
1.	Life Insurance Corporation of India	Govt.
2.	HDFC Life Insurance Company Limited	Private
3.	ICICI Prudential Life Insurance Company Limited	Private
4.	Kotak Mahindra Life Insurance Company Limited	Private
5.	TATA AIA Life Insurance Company Limited	Private
6.	SBI Life Insurance Company Limited	Private
7.	Bajaj Allianz Life Insurance Company Limited	Private
8.	Reliance Nippon Life Insurance Company Limited	Private
9.	Sahara India Life Insurance Company Limited	Private
10.	Future Generali India Life Insurance Company Limited	Private
11.	Ageas Federal Life Insurance Company Limited	Private
12.	Canara HSBC Life Insurance Company Limited	Govt.
13.	Aegon Life Insurance Company Limited	Private
14.	Star Union Dai-Ichi Life Insurance Company Limited	Private
15.	IndiaFirst Life Insurance Company Limited	Govt.

Study on Trends in Banking Frauds in India

Dipankar Jana[1]

ABSTRACT: The banking sector has been a dynamic one with changes taking place at a rapid pace. The emphasis of the Indian government towards cashless economy and the offer of digital services by the banks have increased customer experience in terms of varied and customized services. The country gas seen the rapid jump in the use of non-cash transactions and the use of plastic money for different form of transactions. However, at the same time, the occurrence of frauds have increased at a very fast pace. The paper aims to look at the trends in banking frauds at the national level that will give an idea about where we are leading to and will create the scope to lay emphasis on increasing customer awareness towards such frauds and how such frauds can be prevented. The secondary data is considered for the period from 2018 to 2023.

Keywords: Banking Frauds, Banking System, Trend of Banking Frauds.

Introduction

The banking sector plays a vital role in the growth and expansion of any country, without a sound effective banking system, no country can have a healthy economy. It affects the country's economy by providing credit, infrastructure and investment. Banking sector went through major revolutionary reforms which enclose a range of measures such as liberalization, deregulation, privatization and technological advancements. These Banking reforms aim to enhance transparency, efficient, stability of banking sector, promote financial inclusion and ensure the availability of adequate credit for economic growth. After economic liberalization, the Indian banking sector has experienced significant growth and changes. Entry of new private sector bank, capital adequacy norms, Basel norms and introduction of information technology has significantly enhanced efficiency and productivity of banking sector. Despite of numerous Government policies, regulation and norms banking sector faced some challenges when it comes to ethical practices, financial distress and corporate governance. In recent year, banking sector in India has been struggling with fraud. Fraud is a deliberately deceptive action designed to supply the

[1] Research Scholar, Department of Commerce, Vidyasagar University, India.
E-mail: iamdipankar94@gmail.com

committer with an unlawful gain or to deny a right to a victim. Fraud involves the false depiction of facts, whether by purposefully hiding important information or providing incorrect statement to another party for the specific purpose of gaining something that may not have been provided without the dishonesty. As per section 17 of Indian Contract Act 1872, fraud is considered to be an act committed by a party to a contract or with his connivance or by his agent with intent to deceive another party thereof or his agent or to induce him to enter into the contract. RBI, as per the guidelines, considers it as a deliberate act of omission or commission by any person carried out in the course of a banking transaction or in the books of accounts maintained manually or under computer system in banks, resulting into wrongful gain to any person for a temporary period or otherwise with or without any monetary loss to the bank. The term fraud can be of various types which includes misappropriation and criminal breach of trust, Fraudulent encashment through forged instruments, manipulation of books of account or through fictitious accounts and conversion of property, unauthorized credit facilities extended for reward or for illegal gratification, cash shortages, cheating and forgery, fraudulent transactions involving foreign exchange and any other type of fraud not coming under the specific heads as above.

Literature Review

Thangam & Bhavin (2019) the main aim of this study is to analyze the nature of frauds in the banking industry, and the role of frauds in public sector banks. It is found that public sector banks are more affected by fraudulent practices in the financial industry than the private sector banks which are less exposed to these types of frauds. Most of the fraudulent practices are committed in the nature of loanisbasement, breach of trust by bank officials, and the use of forged documents. Gupta *et al.* (2023) the studies assess the fraud detection techniques and to suggest remedial measures to prevent E-Banking fraud in India. The findings revealed that online banking fraud, mobile banking fraud, and ATM fraud are the current E-banking fraud risks relevant to Indian banks. It has been found that integrating biometric security and a system that reveals individuals' anonymity with E-Banking systems would aid in mitigating and combating E-Banking fraud. Singh *et al.* (2016) this study detailed analysis the issue such as banking frauds and mounting credit card debt in Indian Perspective. This investigation fully based on secondary data from 2010 to 2013. Researchers observed that public sector banking fraud is more than the private sectors bank in term of both in number of frauds and amount involved in frauds. Singh & Kaur (2023) this study analyzes the trend on banking fraud reported in India and NPA. The authors conclude that despise of several law and regulation banking fraud increase rapidly. Industry is suffering significant losses as a result of unethical behavior by individuals when public funds are involved. Customer funds are misappropriated by taking advantage of various weaknesses and gaps in our financial system. The numerous banking fraud cases and related issues that contributes to the accumulation of non-performing assets. Verma (2021) study contribute basic concept about fraud and include definition of fraud which provide by Indian contract act 1972 and Indian company act 2013. It also shows that trend of banking fraud happened in India in terms of number from 2009 to 2021. This study reported some primary causes of fraud like lack of adequate supervision of top management, faulty incentive mechanism in place for employees; collusion between the staff, corporate borrowers and third party agencies; weak regulatory system; lack of appropriate tools and technologies in place to detect early warning signals of a fraud; lack of awareness of bank employees and customers; and lack of coordination among different banks across India and abroad and mention some preventive measure of fraud.

Hani (2020) study makes an attempt to review and analyze the trend of frauds plaguing the banking sector and its role in the continuous rise of Non-Performing Assets in the India. The study concludes that the number of frauds plaguing the Indian banking sector is on a constant rise in recent years leading to a rise in NPAs and severely impacting profitability of the banking sector in India and finding new means of fraud prevention and reduction is the only way forward for safeguarding the credibility of Indian banks and giving a facelift to the banking sector of the count. Jain and Swadia (2021) aims to study banking fraud trends in Indian banking sector along with measures taken by RBI to combat them. The study is based on secondary data from RBI annual reports. This analysis reveals that increase in frauds, also results in to increase in amount involved in frauds in the same pace and suggests RBI for advanced frame work for detection and prevention of frauds in banking sector. Srinivas (2023) mainly focuses on finding the number of frauds and the amount involvement in the frauds by the banking sector and identifies the frauds in banking operations. This study based on secondary source through annual reports of RB from 2018 to 2022. Study clearly observed that the total number of cases has been increasing from 2018 to 2022 study period and the amount involved in this fraud cases also increasing for the study period and give a suggestion RBI should take more initiatives to overcome of frauds to benefit the customers.

Objectives of the Study

(a) To evaluate the trends of Banking Frauds.
(b) To analyze the number of Fraud cases and amount involved in fraud cases of different type of banks in Banking Sector.
(c) To analyze the Growth of number of fraud cases and amount involved in fraud cases of different type of banks in banking sectors.
(d) To analyze the amount involved in per fraud case of different types of bank in banking sectors.

Research Methodology

The study is based on analytical and descriptive method related to financial fraud in the banking sector. Since the study is based on secondary data, data are collected from the Reserve Bank of India annual report for the period 2017 to 2023.

Findings and Analysis

According to RBI during the course of the last 6 financial years, from 2017–18 to 2022–23 it can be seen that the number of banking scams has climbed dramatically. The number of fraud cases increases year on year. In the year of 2017–18 around 5,916 cases are reported amount involved Rs. 41167 crore and in year 2019–20 cases reached at 8,703 and amount involved Rs. 1,85,468 crore. In year 2022–23 cases reached at around 13,530 amounts involved Rs. 30,252 crore. The highest cases in the year 2022–23 of frauds are reported and highest amount involved in the 2019–20. The lowest cases fraud reported in the year 2017–18 and lowest amount involved in year 2022–23 of fraud are reported. The amount of money involved in fraud on these shows an upward tendency from 2017–18 to 2019–20, then a downward trend in 2020–21 to 2022– 23.

Chart 1: Number and Amount Involved in Banking Frauds

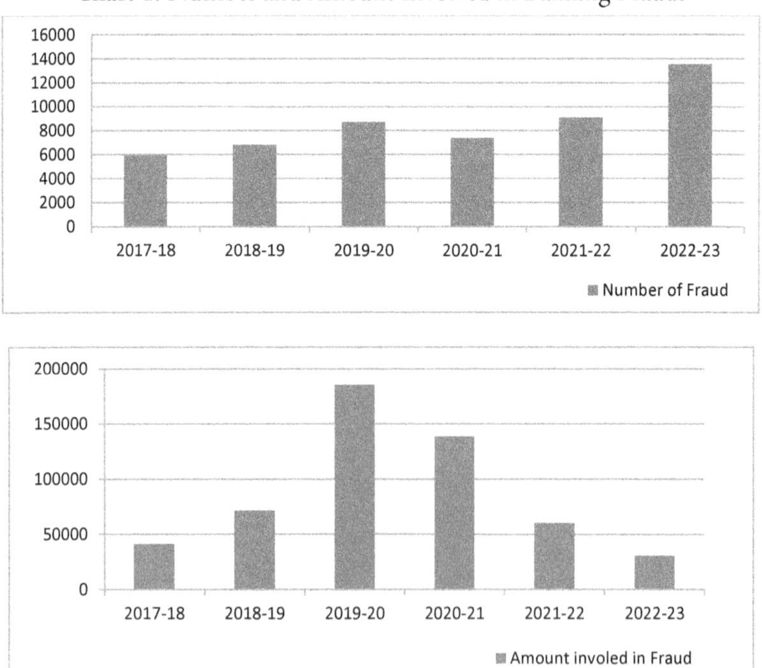

Source: RBI

Table 1: Number of Banking Frauds: Share of Different Banks

Year	*Public Sector Banks*	*Private Sector Banks*	*Foreign Banks*	*Financial Institution*	*Small Finance Banks*	*Payment Banks*
2018	48.78	33.40	16.47	0.20	1.10	0.05
2019	54.49	31.62	11.21	0.41	1.69	0.57
2020	50.68	35.23	11.79	0.17	1.69	0.44
2021	39.44	50.40	7.08	0.34	1.55	1.20
2022	33.82	58.61	5.43	0.11	1.70	0.33
2023	25.17	66.02	5.94	0.07	2.31	0.50
Total	**252.38**	**275.28**	**57.92**	**1.30**	**10.04**	**3.09**

Source: RBI.

From the table 1, represents the analysis of Share of different banks in number of banking Fraud in banking sector. The number of frauds is calculated through percentage from the year 2018 to 2023 in different banking sector. From the calculations it is observed that highest 275.28 percentage fraud share by private sector banks in all the years where 252.28 percent and 57.92 percent share by public and foreign sector banks respectively. Followed by small finance bank, payment banks and financial institution 10.04%, 3.09% and 1.30% respectively. Overall it also observed that all types of banking sector share of banking fraud decrease during last 6 years except private sector share of banking fraud increased rapidly.

Table 2: Growth Rate of Fraud in Different Banking Group

Year	*Public Sector Banks*	*Private Sector Banks*	*Foreign Banks*	*Financial Institution*	*Small Finance Banks*	*Payment Banks*
2018–19	28.39	8.81	–21.77	133.33	76.92	1200.00
2019–20	19.06	42.62	34.65	–46.43	27.83	–2.56
2020–21	–34.17	21.04	–49.22	66.67	–22.45	131.58
2021–22	6.03	43.77	–5.18	–60.00	35.96	–65.91
2022–23	10.62	67.45	62.75	–10.00	101.29	126.67
Average Growth Rate	5.99	36.74	4.25	16.71	43.91	277.95

Source: Computed by researcher

Table 2 shows the Growth rate of fraud of different banking group in banking sector. From the financial year 2018–19 to 2022–23 average growth rate of frauds of public sector bank, private sector bank, foreign bank, financial institution, small finance bank and payment bank is 5.99, 36.74, 4.25, 6.71, 43.91 and 277.95 respectively. It also observed that payment banks have highest average growth of fraud in terms of number of fraud followed by small finance banks. In case of public sector banks average growth rate of fraud is second lowest but there is no trend of growth rate of fraud in different financial year. Interestingly, it has been seen that private sector banks fraud growth rate increased year by year.

Table 3: Share of Different Banks in Amount of Banking Fraud

Year	*Public Sector Banks*	*Private Sector Banks*	*Foreign Banks*	*Financial Institution*	*Small Finance Banks*	*Payment Banks*
2018	92.81	6.01	0.62	0.40	0.15	0.00
2019	89.76	8.12	1.34	0.77	0.01	0.00
2020	79.92	18.45	0.52	1.10	0.01	0.00
2021	59.17	33.47	2.39	4.94	0.02	0.00
2022	66.68	29.11	2.00	2.16	0.05	0.00
2023	69.83	28.85	0.97	0.23	0.10	0.02
Total	**458.17**	**124.01**	**7.84**	**9.6**	**0.34**	**0.02**

Source: Computed by researcher

Table 4: Growth Rate of Fraud Amount of Different Banking Group

Year	*Public Sector Banks*	*Private Sector Banks*	*Foreign Banks*	*Financial Institution*	*Small Finance Banks*	*Payment Banks*
2018–19	67.81	134.42	273.05	235.15	–87.10	122.22
2019–20	130.85	488.93	1.78	270.34	37.50	0.00
2020–21	–44.75	35.44	241.05	233.94	172.73	0.00
2021–22	–50.82	–62.04	–63.62	–80.92	0.00	–50.00
2022–23	–47.56	–50.38	–75.79	–94.64	3.33	600.00
Average Growth Rate	11.11	109.27	75.29	112.78	25.29	134.44

Source: Computed by researcher

Table 3 shows the analysis of amount involved in bank frauds in various banking sectors. The amount involved in fraud cases are calculated through percentage from the year 2018 to 2022 in banking sector wise. Its observed that highest percentage of amount involved in bank frauds by Public sector banks 458.17% and followed by private sector banks 124.01%, Financial institution 9.6%, Foreign Banks 7.84%, Payments Banks 0.02%.

Table 4 shows the analysis of growth rate of fraud amount involved in various banking sectors from financial year 2018–19 to 2022–23. Similar to average growth rate of number of fraud, payment bank has highest average growth rate amount involved in fraud. In case of public sector bank, private sector banks, financial institution and foreign bank growth rate of fraud amount has been showed a decline trend. In compared to other banking sector fraud, average growth rate of public sector bank is minimal. It has also been found that growth rate of small finance banks from 2019 to 2021 increasing trend then it declines to zero in 2022.

Table 5: Amount per Fraud (in Crore)-Bank Group Wise

Year	*Public Sector Banks*	*Private Sector Banks*	*Foreign Banks*	*Financial Institution*	*Small Finance Banks*	*Payment Banks*
2018	13.26	1.25	0.26	13.75	0.95	0.30
2019	17.33	2.70	1.25	19.75	0.07	0.05
2020	33.61	11.16	0.95	136.53	0.07	0.05
2021	28.21	12.49	6.36	273.56	0.26	0.02
2022	13.09	3.30	2.44	130.50	0.19	0.03
2023	6.20	0.98	0.36	7.78	0.10	0.10

Source: Computed by researcher

Table 5 shows that amount per Fraud (in Crore)-Bank Group Wise from 2018 to 2023. It has been found that public sector bank, private sector bank and Financial Institution amount per fraud upward trend from 2018 to 2021 and last two years decline. In case of payment bank fraud per amount decrease year by year. It also observed that amount per fraud of financial institution highest than the other sector in all the year. Compared two giant sector banks, amount per fraud of public sector more than the private sector in all the year.

Conclusions

It is undeniable that the post-liberalization era has given the Indian banking industry new colours of growth, but it has also introduced new challenges.

Banking frauds affect the fashionable quality of life and imposes a detrimental effect on the national growth. The study revealed that from the year 2017–18 the number of fraud cases has been increasing year by year and in the year 2020–21 the fraud cases were registered less compared to 2019–20. Later, in the year 2021–22 the fraud cases again started increasing where amount involved in fraud also increasing year by year for a first 3 years, later from the year 2020–21 started decreasing. From the year 2018 to 2023 private sector banks contribute maximum share of number of fraud case in comparison with others sector bank where public sector banks contribute highest share of amount involved in fraud. The basic reason behind is big amount of loans has been sanctioned by public sector banks but weak monitoring of post loan period. It has also been found that average growth rate of both number and amount involved in fraud of private sector bank is more than the public sector bank. In case of amount involved per fraud of public sector and financial institution is higher than the others sector in the study period. And interestingly, it can be seen that in 2020–21 pandemic period amount per fraud higher than the others period. The frauds may be primarily due to Poor financial governance, technological laggards, poor monitoring, immoral behavior, and political meddling are important factors that contribute to banking fraud. Measures such as strengthening of regulatory and supervisory framework of banks and financial institutions in line with global best practices and updated technology for efficient customer services and effective fraud detection can help in reduction of frauds in banking sector.

References

[1] Gupta, C. and Sharma, A. (2021). Banking Frauds in India: Trends and Legal Challenges. *International Journal of Education, Modern Management, Applied Science & Social Science*, 03, (01), 276–280.

[2] Gupta, R., Gupta, S. and Ajekwe, C. (2023). Electronic Banking Frauds: The Case of India. DOI: 10.4018/979-8-3693-1190-5.ch009.

[3] Hani, P. (2020). Impact of Frauds on the Indian Banking Sector. *International Journal of Creative Research Thoughts*, 8(4).

[4] Jain, M. and Swadia, B. (2021). Study on Banking Frauds Scenario in India. *Journal of the Maharaja Sayajirao University of Baroda*, 55 (1).

[5] Kaur, A. (2020). Banking Fraud: A Conceptual Framework of Dredging up Various Banking Scams, Causes and Preventive Role of Law Enforcement Agencies. *PJAEE*, 17 (6).

[6] Srinivas, B. (2023). A Study on Frauds in Indian Banking Sector. *Central European Management Journal*, 31(2).

[7] Singh, C., Pattanayak, D., Dixit, S., Antony, K., Agarwala, M., Kant, R., Mukunda, S., Nayak, S., Makked, M., Singh, T. and Mathur, V. (2016). *Frauds in the Indian Banking Industry*. IIMB-WP N0. 505.

[8] Singh, G. and Kaur, S. (2023). Bank Frauds Reported In India: A Case Study. *Journal of Pharmaceutical Negative Results*, 14(2). DOI: 10.47750/pnr.2023.14.S02.38.

[9] Thangam, M. and Bhavin, P. (2019). Banking Frauds in India; A case Analysis. *Journal of Emerging Technologies and Innovative Research*, 6, (1).

[10] Vyas, A. and Shah, N. (2023). The Trend Analysis of Bank Frauds in India. *Journal of Multidisciplinary Studies,* 32).

[11] Verma, A. (2021). Banking Fraud—Its Detection, Prevention and Reporting. *Student Company Secretary002E*

Potentiality of Social Media Platforms in Digital Marketing: A New Plethora of Opportunities in India—A Study

Sumedha Majumder[1] and Dilip Barik

ABSTRACT: Digital marketing, specifically social media marketing, has revolutionised the way businesses connect with and attract potential customers. This study delves into the effectiveness of these strategies, exploring how they can be utilised to create a seamless and captivating customer journey. The study also identifies challenges associated with social media marketing, such as maintaining consistency, managing negative feedback, and staying ahead of evolving algorithms. However, it also highlights opportunities for businesses to leverage emerging technologies like AI-powered content creation and influencer marketing to further refine their strategies. Assess the effectiveness of digital marketing, particularly social media marketing, in attracting potential customers. This includes analysing the impact of social media on brand awareness, customer engagement, and lead generation. Identify key strategies and best practices for utilising social media to attract potential customers.

***Aim of the study:** This involves examining different content formats, engagement tactics, and targeting strategies. Explore the challenges and opportunities associated with social media marketing for customer acquisition. This includes investigating issues such as algorithm changes, managing negative feedback, and staying competitive. Analyse the cost-effectiveness of digital marketing compared to traditional marketing methods for attracting potential customers. This will involve comparing the cost per lead and customer acquisition costs for various marketing channels. Evaluate the role of social media in building communities around brands and fostering customer loyalty. This includes exploring the impact of social media on brand advocacy and organic customer acquisition. Investigate the potential of emerging technologies like AI and influencer marketing to enhance social media marketing efforts for customer attraction. This will involve analysing how these technologies can be used to personalise content, optimise targeting, and increase brand reach.*

***Main outcome:** Develop a comprehensive framework for utilising digital marketing, especially social media, as a smooth and effective path for attracting potential*

[1] Assistant Professor, Department of Commerce, Kabi Sukanta Mahavidyalaya College, India. E-mail: sumedhamajumder1987@gmail.com

[2] Associate Professor, Department of Commerce, Lalbaba College, India. E-mail: dilipbarik541@gmail.com

customers. This framework will provide actionable recommendations for businesses to optimise their customer acquisition strategies in the digital age.

By achieving these objectives, this study seeks to contribute valuable insights and practical knowledge to the field of digital marketing, specifically regarding its role in attracting potential customers. The findings will be beneficial for businesses of all sizes, helping them leverage the power of digital and social media to reach their target audience, generate leads, and drive conversion.

Future scope of the study: *The study is based on the secondary data. In future after incorporating primary data, the study can able to frame a future ray towards all level marketers. The study also will be able to guide the new businesses to retain their customer base.*

Keywords: Customer acquisition, Digital Marketing, Potential Customers, Social Media Marketing.

Introduction

In today's digital age, the way businesses connect with and attract potential customers is undergoing a significant transformation. Traditional marketing methods, while still relevant in certain contexts, are increasingly being supplemented by the dynamic and interactive world of digital marketing. In particular, social media marketing has emerged as a powerful tool for businesses to engage with their target audience, build brand awareness, and drive customer acquisition.

This study aims to delve into the effectiveness of digital marketing, with a particular focus on social media marketing, as a smooth and successful path for attracting potential customers. Through a comprehensive analysis of key strategies, best practices, and emerging technologies, the study seeks to provide valuable insights and practical recommendations for businesses to optimise their customer acquisition efforts in the digital era.

By investigating these objectives and examining the intricate landscape of digital marketing, this study seeks to shed light on how businesses can leverage the power of social media and other digital tools to attract potential customers and achieve their strategic goals. The findings have the potential to benefit businesses of all sizes, enabling them to navigate the ever-evolving digital landscape and develop effective customer acquisition strategies for long-term success.

The digital landscape has transformed the way businesses interact with and attract potential customers. Digital marketing, particularly social media marketing, has emerged as a powerful tool for reaching a wider audience, building brand awareness, and ultimately driving conversions. This analysis explores the effectiveness of these strategies, drawing upon data and insights from various sources.

Literature Review

Ranjan (2023) commented that a large number of people are still living in Indian rural villages, though all service providers are not ready to serve in rural areas because of a lack of digital literacy among villagers, language-related issues, economic poverty, and so on. The research work also inferred that digital marketing has immense potential in rural India in the future. Hida *et al.* (2021) concluded that digital marketing media is replacing the traditional marketing medium as most of the online entrepreneurs realised that online platforms easily attract potential customers about their offered products and services. Bhuva *et al.* (2020) concluded that online media will gain importance in marketing products and services in rural markets through a digital model. New, more diversified, innovative technologies will also play a major role in reaching rural markets smoothly and conveniently. Mishra *et al.* (2020) revealed that big brands selected Indian markets for their brand promotion. So, it is high time to recognise the importance of digital marketing in rural India. Accordingly, the research paper highlighted the need to explore the e-rural marketing model to serve all people smoothly. Ravinder (2020) revealed that rural consumption and job opportunities for rural youth will be influenced by digital India in the future, and these will help in the positive growth of the nation.

Research Objectives

The research work has the following objectives:

1. To look into the potentiality of social media platforms in the Indian digital marketing scenario,
2. To make a comparison between digital marketing and social media marketing in India.

Research Methodology

The whole study is explanatory in nature which is based on secondary data. The study based on quantitative as well as qualitative data considers published data collected from several e-contents. The data for 2022 and 2023 are considered which uses data based on few reports.

Analysis and Findings

To discuss the potentialities of social media in the era of real-time connectivity by considering the several reports on social media use as a vital strategy for digital marketing in India.

Table 1: Varied Social Media Users in 2023 in India

Number of Indians watching videos on YouTube	225 million
Active Indian posted on Instagram	50 million
Number of social media users to influence purchase decisions of potential buyers	574 million
Number of social media users want to discover a brand's personality through social media	1160 million

Source: AXIS My India, social beat, December 10, 2023)

The report by AXIS My India revealed that India is the second-largest internet users' country across the globe. The said report also interestingly revealed that a huge number of Indian customers are influenced by social media platforms in their purchasing decisions. Not only that, but also approx. 1160 million Indian social media users want to discover a brand's personality through social media. In short, we can observe that social media has a great influence on consumer behaviour that is truly different from traditional marketing patterns.

Table 2: Active Social Media Users in 2023 in India

Social media used percentage out of total internet users	*Instagram used by 74.70% of Indian internet users*	*71.20 % internet users have their face book profile in India*	*Twitter handled by 42.90% of Indian internet users*	*35.7% internet users active in LinkedIn*	*Moj operated by 29.50% internet users of India*	*29% internet users used Pinterest*	*Moj Lite Plus operated by 26.20% internet users of our nation*
Active users	516.92 million	492.70 million	296.87 million	247.04 million	204.14 million	200.68 million	181.30 million

Source: https://www.forbes.com/advisor/in/business/social-media-statistics

Several reports have highlighted that in India, WhatsApp is the most used platform to connect with each other. But several perceptions mentioned that WhatsApp is a community-based group. So, in the above table, we are not considering the same. However, the collected data revealed that Instagram users on the Internet have the highest stake in other social media platforms.

Table 3: Top 10 Most Used and Liked Social Media Platforms in India, 2022

Top 10 Most Used Platforms	*Top 10 Most Liked Platforms*
Whatsapp	Instagram
Instagram	Discord
Telegram	Whatsapp
FB Messenger	Facebook
Twitter	Telegram
Snapchat	Pinterest
Linkedin	Snapchat
Pinterest	FB Messenger
Mx Takatak	Twitter
Moj	Linkedin

Source: https://oosga.com/social-media/ind

From the above table, we can observe that in India, mostly people use community-based groups to connect with each other as compared to other social media platforms. But the report revealed that preference on Instagram was increasing day by day. We observed that most people prefer real-time communication ways to share their views without considering geographical boundaries.

Table 4: Comparative Impact of Social Media as Compare to Digital Marketing

Digital Marketing	*Social Media Marketing*
Promoting or attracting customers through digitally either internet based or others.	Attracting, informing, viewing through social media platforms regarding any products, incidents, situations, cooking etc.
Definitely a very wider reach of this platform.	Limited to only social media platform users.
Real time interaction with potential customers is missing.	Very prompt communication with potential customers is there.
Action of buying impacted slowly.	Quick buying decision can be taken.
24*7 connectivity is missing	Social media users always trying to connected with their viewers/followers.

Source: Author's own interpretation

To assess a comparison between digital marketing and social media marketing in India to influence customers effectively.

Table 5: Choosing Social Media Platform in Digital Marketing

Aspect of Analysis	*Description*
Platform Selection	Identify the primary social media platforms used for marketing.
Target Audience	Define the demographics, behaviors, and interests of the target customer base.
Content Strategy	Assess the types of content (videos, images, blogs, etc.) and their effectiveness in engaging the audience.
Engagement Metrics	Analyze key engagement metrics (likes, shares, comments, etc.) and their correlation with customer acquisition.
Influencer Partnerships	Evaluate the impact of collaborating with influencers or industry leaders on attracting potential customers.
Paid Advertising	Explore the effectiveness of paid campaigns on social media platforms in reaching and converting customers.
Conversion Tracking	Discuss methods used to track and analyze conversions from social media efforts.
Customer Feedback	Consider the role of customer feedback and reviews in optimizing social media strategies.
Trends & Innovations	Highlight emerging trends and innovative approaches in social media marketing for customer acquisition.

Source: https://business.adobe.com

Potentialities of social media use in the digital marketing era

- **Increased Brand Awareness:** Social media platforms offer a powerful platform to reach a wider audience, amplify brand messaging, and establish a strong brand presence.
- **Enhanced Customer Engagement:** Interactive content formats, personalised interactions, and responsive customer service foster deeper connections with potential customers, building trust and loyalty.
- **Targeted Advertising:** Precise audience targeting capabilities enable businesses to reach the right people at the right time with personalised messages, maximising campaign effectiveness.
- **Cost-Effective Marketing:** Compared to traditional marketing methods, digital marketing offers a more cost-effective way to reach large audiences and track campaign performance.
- **Building Communities:** Social media facilitates the creation of online communities around brands, fostering brand advocacy and organic customer acquisition.

Concluding Remarks

The study concludes that digital marketing, particularly social media marketing, plays a crucial role in attracting potential customers. By implementing effective strategies and adapting to the ever-evolving digital landscape, businesses can create a smooth and compelling customer journey, driving engagement, conversions, and long-term success.

This study has comprehensively explored the effectiveness of digital marketing, especially social media marketing, as a smooth and effective path for attracting potential customers. The analysis reveals a multitude of benefits, including increased brand awareness, enhanced customer engagement, targeted advertising, cost-effectiveness, and community building.

In today's digital age, where consumers spend a significant portion of their time online, social media platforms offer businesses unparalleled access to a vast and engaged audience. Through strategic content creation, personalized interactions, and targeted advertising, businesses can effectively connect with potential customers, build trust, and ultimately drive conversions.

References

[1] Bhuva, K.K. and Vyas, V.H. (2020). "A study on use of digital marketing platforms as a tool for rural marketing in India". *The International journal of analytical and experimental modal analysis*, XII(1).

[2] https://www.researchgate.net/publication/347907488_A_Research_Paper_On_A_Study_On_Use_Of_Digital_Marketing_Platforms_As_A_Tool_For_Rural_Marketing_In_India

[3] Nur, H.A.R. and Respati, D.Y. (2021). "Marketing strategies through Instagram to increase sales". Advances in economics, business and management research, volume 193, proceedings of the BISTIC Business innovation sustainability and technology international conference (BISTIC 2021).

[4] Mishra, R. and Shahid, A. (2020). "Advanced strategies for development of digital marketing in rural area". *International Journal of Management*, 11(5), 1797–1810.

[5] https://www.researchgate.net/publication/365126239_Advanced_Strategies_For_Development_Of_Digital_Marketing_In_Rural_Area

[6] Ravi, R.K. (2023). "Digital marketing's impact on Indian Rural Marketing: A Study". *Shodh Samagam*, 117–120.

[7] https://www.researchgate.net/publication/368364527_Digital_Marketing%27s_Impact_on_Indian_Rural_Marketing_A_Study

[8] Ravinder, D (2020). "Impact of digital marketing on Indian rural marketing- a study". *Journal of Management Research and Analysis*, 1(4).

[9] https://www.researchgate.net/publication/361810969_Impact_of_Digital_Marketing_on_Indian_Rural_Marketing_-A_Study

[10] http://creativecommons.org/licenses/by-nc/4.0

[11] https://www.statista.com/statistics/278407/number-of-social-network-users-in-india
[12] https://business.adobe.com/blog/basics/smm-benefits
[13] https://oosga.com/social-media/ind
[14] https://www.theglobalstatistics.com/india-social-media-statistics
[15] https://www.socialbeat.in/social-media-marketing

Performance of Selected Mutual Funds in India: A Study on Large, Mid and Small Cap Funds

Chhattu Kamila[1], Debasish Bera[2] and Saoni Pal[3]

ABSTRACT: A mutual fund is a managed fund where investors' money is pooled and invested in stocks, bonds, debentures, and other asset classes, both domestically and internationally. This study aims to analyze the performance of selected large-cap, mid-cap, and small-cap mutual funds in India and compare them with the Nifty Fifty, Nifty Midcap, and Nifty Smallcap indexes. The study considered 10 mutual fund companies in each category, rated 4 to 5 by CRISIL. Secondary data from Moneycontrol and Groww app were used. The study analyzed the three-year (30th Nov 2021 to 30th Nov 2023) returns, standard deviations, beta, Sharpe and alpha ratios to interpret the results. Results showed that ICICI, MOTILAL, and HDFC large-cap mutual funds, SBI, MOTILAL, and TATA mid-cap mutual funds, and TATA, NIPPON, and ICICI small-cap mutual funds demonstrated good risk-adjusted returns. Additionally, the three-year returns of the Nifty Fifty, Nifty Midcap, and Nifty Smallcap indexes were tested and found to be lower than the three-year average returns of the 10 large-cap, 10 mid-cap, and 10 small-cap mutual funds respectively. This indicates that mutual funds are a good investment option for investors, although it is important to note that they are also linked to market risks and volatility.

Keywords: Mutual Fund, NAV, NIFTY FIFTY, Sharpe Ratio, Alpha & Beta.

Introduction

It is crucial for a developed economy to have a strong financial market with broad participation (Suvarna, 2022). India's first mutual fund, Unit Trust of India (UTI), was established in 1963 (SAMADDAR, 2018). A mutual fund is a financial product that offers a modern and effective way to invest capital in both money and capital markets (Sharma, 2023). Mutual funds are managed by asset

[1] Research Scholar, Department of Commerce, Vidyasagar University, India.
E-mail: talk2chhattu@gmail.com

[2] Research Scholar, Department of Commerce, Vidyasagar University, India.
E-mail: mcomdb2014@gmail.com

[3] M.Com Student, Department of Commerce, Vidyasagar University, India.
E-mail: pal.saoni26@gmail.com

management companies, which collect funds from investors seeking to maximize returns on their capital but investors may lacking idea about investing in the markets (Bhagyasree & Kishori, 2016). The collected funds are then invested in various financial instruments such as stocks, bonds, debentures, and gold, which can impact the fund's return and risk (Gandhi & Perumal, 2016). Certified fund managers invest these funds in the markets under the supervision of the asset management company, aiming to provide maximum returns to the fund's subscribers (Suvarna, 2022).

The Net Asset Value (NAV) is a crucial metric in the context of a mutual fund, calculated by subtracting the fund's liabilities from its assets and then dividing by the number of shares outstanding. NAV determines the price of a mutual fund scheme and is adjusted after the market closes (Murthy *et al.*, 2022). This value fluctuates based on the market index due to the direct investment of the fund's portfolio in the stock market (Maheswari, 2022). Market conditions, such as bull or bear market periods, can indirectly affect the NAV of a mutual fund scheme. Effective management and a diversified portfolio are essential in such conditions.

There are two types of mutual funds: open-ended and closed-ended funds. Open-ended funds allow investors to invest and withdraw capital at any time, while closed-ended funds provide new units for a limited time. Investors can invest in mutual funds through systematic investment plans, allowing for regular interval investments, or lump sum investments, enabling investors to invest their capital at once. Both methods offer flexibility for modification and withdrawal at any time.

Literature Review

A mutual fund is an investment instrument that allows small investors to invest in the stock market on a SIP or lump sum plan basis, with limited knowledge of the stock market. Jayesh Somaiya conveyed a paper on ELSS mutual fund schemes using Standard Deviation, Beta, Sharpe's Ratio, Jensen's Alpha, and Treynor Ratio. He found that all the ELSS funds had significant recovery and provided high returns after the initial impact of the Corona pandemic. The mutual fund is managed professionally, making it the safest investment mechanism for small investors. The value of mutual fund investments is directly affected by the Net Asset Value (NAV) of the scheme, which is calculated by dividing the market value of the scheme's assets by the total number of units issued to investors. Murthy *et al.*, and Vimla Virparia (2022) examined the performance of large, mid and small-scale mutual funds in India. They revealed that the returns of most sample schemes were not significantly different from their market returns during the study period. Similarly, Shivam Tripathi (2023) conducted on the performance and risk measurement of selected large, mid and small-scale mutual funds, and also used Standard Deviation, Beta, Sharpe, Jensen's Alpha, and

Treynor's Ratio to interpret the results. The result showed that large-cap mutual funds make consistent and decent returns over different periods. Today, the world is witnessing growth in the financial services and technology sectors, and according to this perspective, Shuhita Singh (2023) conducted a study on the performance of Environmental, Social, and Governance (ESG) mutual fund schemes in India. He suggests that while there is an increase in ESG fund investment in India, the growth is still slower compared to other major economies, possibly due to Indian investors not fully embracing the idea of discounting ESG factors when constructing a portfolio. S. Das (2022) examined the performance of open-ended multi-cap mutual funds against the benchmark index of SENSEX and S&P 500, using standard deviation, beta, alpha, Sharpe ratio, and Jensen ratio to interpret the results. He concluded that more than 65% of the fund beat both short and long-term CAGR, risk-adjusted return in terms of its performance against the benchmark. A study on the performance of the selected mutual fund in India (Subha & Bharathi, 2007) used 54 open-ended mutual funds from 2004 to 2005, with S.D, Sharpe, Jensen alpha, and S&P benchmark index. The study concluded that the majority of the funds generated good returns compared to the benchmark index in this period and Jensen's measure, alpha is positive for 98% of the funds, indicating that the funds are generating good returns.

Research Gap

For our study, we reviewed fifteen literature on the risk and return of mutual funds in India. Most researchers focused on various types of mutual fund schemes, including large, mid, and small-cap mutual funds. We also found that there were limited studies on performance of mutual funds against the Nifty fifty, nifty mid cap and nifty small cap indices. Hence, it is important to note that the study tries to compare different types of mutual fund returns and risks to the returns of the Nifty indexes.

Significance of the Study

As we all know, proper investment mechanisms help to build a nation's economic growth, while also facilitating investors in creating sustainable financial assets. In this study, we will discuss what a mutual fund is, its types, different risk parameters, and returns. Additionally, we will cover the historical returns of the Nifty and gold. This study will be helpful to research agencies, academicians, mutual fund investos, business school students, and mutual fund companies while choosing the best investment that maximizes return and minimizes risk.

Objectives of the Study

1. To study the performance of selected mutual funds in India.
2. To compare the performance among different mutual fund schemes and others stock market indexes.

Research Methodology

The study is based on secondary data related to the 3 years annualized return of each mutual fund scheme, as well as the yearly return of both the gold and NIFTY index. Data from 2021 to 2023, for every 30th October of NAV, NIFTY index prices were taken into consideration. All data were collected online from the Groww brokerage site and Money Control. Ten different large, mid, and small-cap mutual funds rated between 4 to 5 by the CRISIL rating agency were chosen for the study. The market size of the fund, risk, and returns varied between each mutual fund. Standard Deviation, Beta, Sharpe, and Jensen's Alpha were used to interpret the results. Each mutual fund's performance, NAV return, volatility, and risk-reward return were calculated, ranked, and given point-wise scores to interpret the position of each mutual fund scheme.

Tools for Analysis

Standard Deviation: Standard Deviation is a statistical tool that measures the variability of returns from the expected value, or volatility. It is denoted by the symbol sigma (σ). The standard deviation of a fund measures the degree to which the fund fluctuates about its mean return; the average return of a fund over some time. For example, if Fund A and Fund B have both given 9% returns in the last 3 years, but Fund A's standard deviation value is lower than Fund B's, it indicates that there is a higher chance that Fund A will continue giving similar returns in the future, whereas Fund B's returns may vary.

Beta: Beta indicates the systematic risk in the fund or any securities, which represents the fluctuations of any fund or securities with their respective benchmark. If the beta is greater than 1, the stock is said to be riskier than the market. If the beta is less than 1, indicates that the stock is less risky in comparison to the market. If beta is zero, then the risk is the same as that of the market. A negative beta is rare.

Sharpe ratio: The Sharpe ratio is a risk-adjusted evaluation method of return on investment. It indicates how well an equity investment is performing compared to a risk-free investment, taking into consideration the additional risk level involved with holding the equity investment. According to the Sharpe ratio, a positive value with a higher ratio is a good indicator for portfolio assessment. If the Sharpe ratio of a mutual fund scheme is greater than that of the market portfolio, it means the fund has outperformed the market. For example, if Fund A and Fund B both have 3-year returns of 15%, and Fund A has a Sharpe ratio of 1.40 while Fund B has a Sharpe ratio of 1.25, we can choose Fund A, as it has given a higher risk-adjusted return.

Jensen Alpha: Alpha is a risk-adjusted return of a mutual fund that measures its performance against a benchmark return. Alpha is also an important indicator of the fund because it shows the capabilities of the fund manager and how they generate returns for the particular fund for their investors. For example, if Fund A benchmarks its returns with Nifty50 returns and has an alpha equal to 1.0, it indicates the fund has beaten the Nifty returns by 1%. So, the higher the alpha, the better.

Data Analysis and Interpretation

Table 1: Large Cap Mutual Fund-Rank Wise Performance

Fund Name	*Market Cap (Cr)*	*3yrs Annual Return (%)*	*Rank*	*S.D*	*Rank*	*Beta*	*Rank*	*Sharpe Ratio*	*Rank*	*Alpha*	*Rank*
ICICI	41264	21.24	4	13.60	1	0.91	1	1.12	4	4.81	3
SBI	38597	18.53	8	14.28	6	0.95	6	0.96	6	1.67	7
NIPPON	16637	25.65	2	15.03	10	0.99	10	1.33	1	7.38	1
TATA	1518	19.31	5	14.21	4	0.98	9	1.11	5	1.48	8
MOTILAL	2390	27.81	1	14.86	9	0.92	2	1.24	2	2.82	4
MAHINDRA	267	18.76	6	14.47	7	0.97	7	0.93	7	2.43	5
EDELWEISS	557	18.74	7	13.94	2	0.94	3	0.91	8	2.02	6
MIRAE	34376	16.17	10	13.97	3	0.94	3	0.72	10	0.62	9
HDFC	25772	22.76	3	14.61	8	0.97	7	1.17	3	6.10	2
INVESCO	785	18.37	9	14.24	5	0.94	3	0.75	9	0.11	10

Source: Computed by researchers

Table 2: Large Cap Mutual Fund- Point Wise Performance

Fund	*3 yrs Return p.a (%)*	*SD*	*Beta*	*Sharpe Ratio*	*Alpha*	*Total Points*
ICICI	7	10	10	7	8	42
SBI	3	5	5	5	4	22
NIPPON	9	1	1	10	10	31
TATA	6	7	2	6	7	28
MOTILAL	10	2	9	9	7	37
MAHINDRA	5	4	4	4	6	23
EDELWEISS	4	9	8	3	5	29
MIRAE	1	8	8	1	2	20
HDFC	8	3	4	8	9	32
INVESCO	2	6	8	2	1	19

Source: Computed by researchers

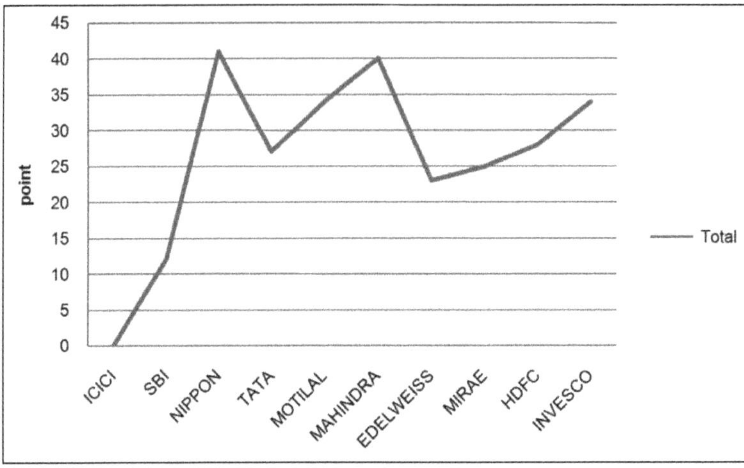

Figure 1: Large Cap Fund

Source: Computed by researchers

Interpretation: In Table 1, ICICI large cap mutual fund S.D and beta have been ranked 1, indicating effective management of volatility and risk. Nippon has shown a good risk-adjusted return against the benchmark return. However, Mirea mutual fund has the lowest return among all mutual funds and lacks in risk-adjusted return. INVESCO has the 9th rank in annualized return, with a Sharpe and alpha ratio of 9 and 10 respectively, making it a worthy scheme for investors. After ranking the performance, the points for each mutual fund were added to estimate the overall performance. Table 2 and figure 1 display the total points for each fund. ICICI funds secured the 1st position with 42 points out of 50. INVESCO, Mirea, SBI, and Mahindra large cap mutual funds obtained 19, 20, 22, and 23 points respectively. This indicates that these funds have not been well-performing or well-managed. On the other hand, the remaining funds have performed and managed on an average level.

Table 3: Mid Cap Mutual Fund Fund-Rank Wise Performance

Fund	*Market Cap (cr)*	*3 Yannual return (%)*	*Rank*	*S.D*	*Rank*	*Beta*	*Rank*	*Sharpe Ratio*	*Rank*	*Alpha*	*Rank*
ICICI	4252	27.25	9	15.43	7	0.95	9	1.35	10	0.18	8
SBI	13202	32.71	5	14.63	3	0.84	1	1.57	3	4.41	2
NIPPON	19081	33.01	3	15.49	8	0.92	7	1.50	6	2.79	4
TATA	2521	27.99	8	14.12	2	0.87	3	1.67	1	0.96	7

Fund	*Market Cap (cr)*	*3 Yannual return (%)*	*Rank*	*S.D*	*Rank*	*Beta*	*Rank*	*Sharpe Ratio*	*Rank*	*Alpha*	*Rank*
MOTILAL	6059	36.58	1	15.84	10	0.84	1	1.62	2	6.92	1
MAHINDRA	1553	33.35	2	15.74	9	0.93	8	1.45	7	2.13	6
EDELWEISS	3792	31.40	6	14.04	1	0.95	9	1.51	5	–0.38	9
MIRAE	11783	29.82	7	14.81	5	0.87	3	1.45	7	2.20	5
HDFC	19081	33.01	3	15.31	6	0.90	5	1.54	4	3.54	3
INVESCO	3418	27.23	10	14.76	4	0.90	5	1.42	9	–0.51	10

Source: Computed by authors

Table 4: Mid-cap Mutual Fund- Point Wise Performance

Fund Name	*3Y Annual Return (%)*	*S.D*	*Beta*	*Sharpe Ratio*	*Alpha*	*Total Points*
ICICI	2	4	2	1	3	12
SBI	6	8	10	8	9	41
NIPPON	8	3	4	5	7	27
TATA	3	9	8	10	4	34
MOTILAL	10	1	10	9	10	40
MAHINDRA	9	2	3	4	5	23
EDELWEISS	5	10	2	6	2	25
MIRAE	4	6	8	4	6	28
HDFC	8	5	6	7	8	34
INVESCO	1	7	6	2	1	17

Source: Computed by researchers

Interpretation: In Table 3, the Motilal mid-cap mutual fund stands out with a top ranking in annualized return, beta, and alpha, indicating a very good risk-adjusted return. On the other hand, SBI has also achieved a good risk-adjusted return compared to the benchmark return. However, INVESCO has shown the lowest return among all mutual funds, and has not demonstrated as a strong risk-adjusted return. Similarly, ICICI's annualized return is ranked 9th, with Beta, Sharpe, and Alpha ratios ranked 9, 10, and 8 respectively, making it a reliable investment option for potential investors. Once the ranking of performance was completed, the points garnered by each mutual fund were tallied to evaluate the overall scheme performance.

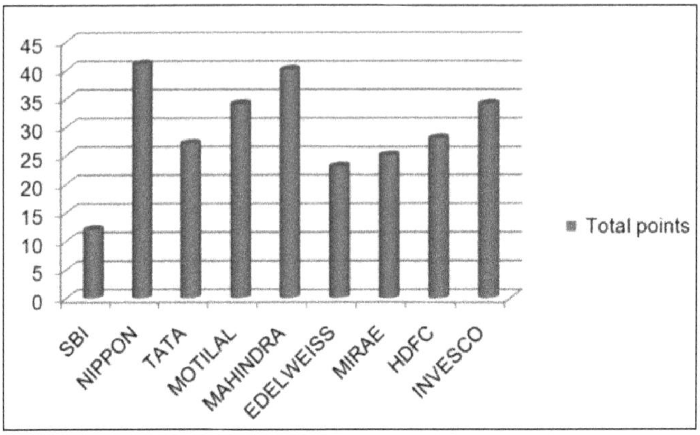

Figure 2: Mid Cap Mutual Fund

Table 4 and Figure 2 illustrate the total points for each fund. SBI and Motilal funds secured the 1st and 2nd positions out of 50 points. In contrast, INVESCO and ICICI midcap mutual funds obtained 17 and 12 points respectively. Based on these points, it can be inferred that these funds have not performed well and are not well managed, making them less desirable for investment. Conversely, the remaining funds have demonstrated average performance and management.

Table 5: Small-Cap Mutual Fund Fund-Rank Wise Performance

Fund	*Market Cap (cr)*	*3 yrs Annual Return (%)*	*Rank*	*S.D*	*Rank*	*Beta*	*Rank*	*Sharpe Ratio*	*Rank*	*Alpha*	*Rank*
ICICI	6,989	37.44	7	14.45	3	0.76	3	1.74	4	6.07	4
SBI	20,911	30.35	10	13.18	1	0.70	2	1.58	7	3.71	9
NIPPON	37,374	43.43	2	16.16	7	0.89	7	1.87	1	7.99	1
TATA	6,014	39.44	4	14.68	4	0.76	3	1.80	3	7.59	2
MOTILAL	452	35.08	8	17.38	9	0.99	9	1.34	9	–1.44	10
QUANT	9520	46.26	1	19.96	10	1.04	10	0.30	10	4.95	5
EDELWEISS	2473	38.03	6	15.13	5	0.81	5	1.64	5	4.49	6
AXIS	16369	32.83	9	13.33	2	0.69	1	1.62	6	4.31	7
HDFC	22560	39.62	3	17.32	8	0.90	8	1.83	2	7.12	3
INVESCO	2869	38.39	5	15.27	6	0.82	6	1.58	7	4.09	8

Source: Computed by researchers

Table 6: Small-Cap Mutual Fund- Point Wise Performance

Fund	*3 yrs Annual Return (%)*	*SD*	*Beta*	*Sharpe Ratio*	*Alpha*	*Total Points*
ICICI	4	8	8	7	7	34
SBI	1	10	9	4	2	26
NIPPON	9	4	4	10	10	37
TATA	7	7	8	8	9	39
MOTILAL	3	2	2	2	1	10
QUANT	10	1	1	1	6	19
EDELWEISS	5	6	6	6	5	28
AXIS	2	9	10	5	4	30
HDFC	8	3	3	9	8	31
INVESCO	6	5	5	4	3	23

Source: Computed by researchers

Interpretation: From table 5, we can observe that the Nippon small-cap mutual fund holds the top rank for the Sharpe and alpha ratios, indicating that it effectively manages risk-adjusted returns compared to the benchmark. In contrast, the Tata fund has delivered average performance across all parameters. Finally, the Motilal mutual fund ranks lowest among all mutual fund returns in the series. To evaluate the overall performance of the schemes, we calculated the total points for each mutual fund based on its rank.

Table 6 displays the total points for each fund. Only the Tata Small Cap fund secured the top position with 39 points out of 50. Similarly, Nippon and ICICI small-cap mutual funds scored 37 and 34 points, respectively. Based on these points, we can conclude that the top three mutual funds in Table 6 have performed and managed relatively well. These would be worthy choices for investment. On the other hand, the remaining funds have performed and managed below average.

Table 7: Other Assets Class Returns

Assets Class Name	*Average 3 Yrs Return*
Nifty Fifty Index	12.95%
Nifty Mid Cap 100 Index	21.23%
Nifty Small Cap 100 Index	19.73%
Selected Large Cap Mutual Fund Return	20.73%
Selected Mid Cap Mutual Fund Return	31.24%
Selected Small Cap Mutual Fund Return	38.08%

Source: Computed by researchers

Interpretation: We made a comparison of performance between direct and indirect investment methods. It was found that the returns from all indirect investment methods surpassed those of direct investment methods. In Table 7, it is shown that the three-year average returns for Nifty Fifty, Nifty Mid-Cap 100, and Nifty Small-Cap 100 are 12.95%, 21.23%, and 19.73%, respectively. In contrast, large-cap, mid-cap, and small-cap mutual fund schemes have delivered average returns of 20.73%, 31.24%, and 38.08%, respectively. Furthermore, the Nifty Small-Cap, Nifty Mid-Cap, and Nifty Fifty indexes ranked 1st, 2nd, and 3rd, respectively, based on their returns. Conversely, small-cap, mid-cap, and large-cap mutual funds have ranked 1st, 2nd, and 3rd, respectively.

Concluding Remarks

A mutual fund is a popular investment option where a fund manager invests a pool of capital in stocks, bonds, and other asset classes to meet the financial objectives of the investors. This study aimed to evaluate the performance of selected mutual fund schemes compared to various indices such as NIFTY FIFTY, NIFTY midcap 100, and NIFTY small-cap 100 indexes. The study used 3 years of returns, standard deviation (S.D), Sharpe ratio, beta, and alpha ratio of the mutual fund schemes to analyze their performance. The empirical evidence from this study suggests that ICICI and Motilal large-cap mutual funds generated good risk-adjusted returns, while the performance of other large-cap mutual funds was average. SBI and Motilal midcap mutual funds exhibited good risk-adjusted returns. On the other hand, TATA, NIPPON, and ICICI small-cap mutual funds showed good risk-adjusted returns based on the S.D, Beta, Sharpe, and Alpha ratios. Nifty fifty, nifty mid-cap, and nifty small-cap indexes performed well, outperforming the return of large-cap, mid-cap, and small-cap mutual funds respectively. Therefore, it can be concluded that mutual funds offer a good option for investors to gain reasonable returns, but the risk associated with these mutual funds cannot be ignored. In summary, this study provides guidance to investors on how to select mutual fund schemes for investment purposes and also highlights the performance of mutual fund companies deemed worthy in this study (Bhagyasree & Kishori, 2016).

References

[1] Somaiya, J. (2022). Effect of corona pandemic in performance evaluation of selected ELSS Mutual Funds In india. *International Journal of Management Public Policy and Research*, 1(4), 1–7. https://doi.org/10.55829/ijmpr.v1i4.73

[2] Gandhi, R.K. and Perumal, R. (2016). Performance of Selected Bank Mutual Fund Schemes Impact in Investors Decision Making. *International Journal of Advanced Research in Management and Social Sciences*, 5(3), 361–370.

[3] Tripathi, S. (2020). Performance Evaluation of Selected Equity Mutual Funds in India. *A Global Journal of Social Sciences*, 3 (1), 65–71.

[4] Bhagyasree, N. and Kishori, B. (2016). A Study on Performance of Mutual Funds in India. *International Journal of Innovative Research in Technology*, 2 (11), 42–48.

[5] Maheswari, Y. (2021). Performance Evaluation Of Select Mutual Funds In India. *Social Science Research Network.* https://doi.org/10.2139/ssrn.3959872

[6] Das, S.K., Das, S. and Seth, S. (2023). Performance of Mutual Funds in India: A Study with Reference to Select Equity Multi-Cap Funds. *Management Journal for Advanced Research*, 3(1), 8–14. https://doi.org/10.54741/mjar.3.1.2

[7] Murthy, J., Anjaneyulu, M.S.R., Bhatt, H. and Kumar, D.S. (2022). Performance Evaluation of Mutual Funds: A Study on Selected Equity Mutual Funds in India. *Journal of Positive School Psychology*, 6 (9), 1124–1132.

[8] Das, S.K. (2022). Examining the performance of selected multi-cap funds in India. *Journal of academic advancement*, 1 (2), 58–68.

[9] Samaddar, K. (2018). A Study on Performance evaluation of Mutual Funds in India. *Journal of Emerging Technologies and Innovative Research*, 5(7), 475–481.

[10] Sharma, A.K. (2023). An Empirical Analysis of Performance and Evaluation of Mutual Funds in India. *Management Journal for Advanced Research*, 3(4), 30–35.

[11] Sharma, K.B. and Tripathi, S. (2023). Performance Analysis and Risk Assessment of Indian Mutual Fund Through SIPs: A Comparative Study Of Small, Mid, And Large Cap Funds. *Vidya A Journal of Gujrat University*, 2(2), 108– 117.

[12] Singh, S., Bahl, S., Sharma, J., & Sharma, A. (2023). Performance Evaluation of ESG Mutual Funds in India. *Journal of Survey in Fisheries Sciences*, 10(3S), 1133–1143.

[13] Suvarna, A. (2022). Timing and Selectivity Performance of Mutual Fund Managers: Application of Conditional Models to Indian Equity Diversified Mutual funds. *Jindal Journal of Business Research*, 11(1), 81–98. https://doi.org/10.1177/22786821221084937

[14] Virparia, V. (2022). Performance Analysis of Mutual Funds in India. *International Journal of Management, Public Policy and Research*, 1(3), 22–34.

www. moneycontrol.com

www. grow.com

www.investing.com

Incorporating Green Bonds in India's Climate Finance: A Resolution to Achieve Net Zero Target

Agnishwar Mukherjee[1]

ABSTRACT: India's dream to achieve Net zero carbon emission by 2070 and to provide a healthy and sustainable ecosystem to the upcoming future generations can be achieved when the Indian financial system will be able to divert the funds towards providing financial supports to the green projects. On 1st Feb. 2022 Ms. Nirmala Sitharaman Union minister MOFCA (Ministry of Finance and Corporate Affairs) announced of launching sovereign green bond to mobilize the funds for building up green infrastructure. Green bonds are the instruments which drive the funds towards setting up projects for environmental protection and also help to set in more projects which are beneficial for sustainable development.

Green bonds are one of the most important financial instruments which is helping the country to achieve its SDG's target as well as in fulfilling the country's commitment to achieve Net zero carbon emission target by 2070 in the United Nations framework convention on climate change (COP26). The paper is been frame to examine extensively the growth of green bond market in India from its point of inception, the projects that are been funded by the top five green bond issuers. It provides insight regarding the future growth prospects and the regulators of the green bond markets.

Keywords: Green Bonds, Green Projects, Sovereign Green Bonds, Sustainable Finance.

Introduction

Green bonds are the financial debt instruments issued by the government, financial institutions for financing the projects that solely dedicated towards investing in renewable energy, water conservation, and sustainable green energy projects. The use of green bonds in the specific green projects differentiates it with the other bonds which prevail in the market.

In the global arena the green bonds are been regulated by the guidelines stated by the ICMA (International capital market association) in its green bond principles. In our domestic territory the green bonds market is been regulated by

[1] Research Scholar, Department of Commerce, Vidyasagar University, India.
E-mail: agni281996@gmail.com

the Securities Exchange Board of India (Issue and listing of non-convertible securities regulation 2021).

India's commitment towards preserving the environment is been embalm in its Article 48-A of the constitution. The Government of India had taken several steps to maintain equilibrium between its economic growth and environmental sustainability. At COP 26, India took a pledged to start a one word movement "LIFE" which stands for "Lifestyle for environment"

This puts a compulsion for the utilization of the resources rationally and generously and puts a bar on wasteful consumption. Our honourable prime minister had further enhanced the ambitious climate control measures in Glasgow 2021 which includes five control measuring steps stated as "Panchamrit" which are as follows:

1. To achieve 500 GW non-fossil energy capacity by 2030.
2. 50 per cent of the energy requirements will be derived from renewable energy by 2030.
3. Reduction of total projected carbon emissions by one billion tonnes from now to 2030.
4. Reduction of the carbon intensity of the economy by 45 per cent by 2030, over 2005 levels.
5. Achieving the target of net zero emissions by 2070.

Review of Literature

The green bonds is opening up a new avenues and its helping in promoting sustainable projects, government should keep on encouraging more use of green bonds which is going to help India in moving towards more greener and sustainable future.[1] Educating, nurturing, spreading awareness among the investors as well as issuers and improving better reporting standards will create strong and vibrant green bond markets.[2] There always remain a risk whether the investment in green bonds is going to help in the sustenance of the green projects from various natural calamities or there will be requirement of more funds to protects such green projects from it, whether the investment is going to give a fruitful and impactful results in the long run.[3] The fund must be channelized to proper green projects so that a need of urgent financing can be fulfilled to stop the loss of biodiversity, human and capital loss and proper mitigation and adaptation strategies must be adopted through channelling government, retail and corporate sector funding towards more green sectors project.[4] Green bonds helps in achieving sustainability targets and also initiate the process of emitting low carbon emissions.[5] Standardisation of issuance process and proper transparency by the regulating bodies will help the green bonds to achieve its long term perspective.[6]

The Trajectory of Green Bonds in India

The green bond was first introduced in the Year 2015 by the Yes bank of INR 1000cr followed by the bonds value of 600 cr by the CLP India. The first certified International green bond issuance was of 500 million USD which was been issued by Axis bank limited. The green bond markets had gradually expanded from its point of inception to several public sector undertakings, state- owned financial institutions, commercial banks and corporate. From January 2015 till the financial year 2021 the green bond market stood over 6 billion US dollars. On 1st February 2022 ministry for finance and corporate affairs had issued sovereign green bonds to mobilize the funds to contribute towards setting up green infrastructure, on 25th January 2023 the first tranche of INR 80 billion of green bond was been issued and on the same year in the month of February another tranche was been issued of the same valuation.

Sovereign Green Bonds: Process of Issuance

The process of issuance of sovereign follows the four core components of ICMA green bond principles which see the use of the i) proceeds of the green bonds, ii) the evaluation of the projects and its selection iii) to manage the proceeds and iv) Evaluation. To maintain further transparency the ICMA also issues an advisory to provide a green bond framework which will be access by the investors and also advises for an external review.

The green projects are been classified on the base of following principles:

1. Encourages energy efficient projects and proper utilisation of resources.
2. Reduction in carbon emission and various green house gases.
3. Promotes adaptability towards the climate change.
4. Improves the state of biodiversity in accordance with SDG principles.

Government of India will use the proceeds raised from the sovereign green bonds in financing and refinancing the eligible green projects, the eligibility of green projects is been determined upon the satisfaction of the following criteria:

Table 1

Green Project Category	*Environmental Objective*	*Eligibility Criteria*
Renewable Energy	Climate Change Mitigation, Net Zero Objectives	• Investments in solar/wind/biomass/ hydropower energy projects that integrate energy generation and storage. • Incentivizing adoption of renewable energy

Green Project Category	*Environmental Objective*	*Eligibility Criteria*
Energy Efficiency	Climate Change Mitigation	• Design and construction of energy-efficient and energy saving systems and installations in government buildings and properties. • Supporting public lighting improvements (e.g. replacement with LEDs). • Supporting construction of new low-carbon buildings as well as energy-efficiency retrofits to existing buildings • Projects to reduce electricity grid losses.
Clean Transportation	Climate Change Mitigation	• Promote public transportation including its electrification and transport safety. • Subsidies to adopt clean fuels like electric vehicles including building charging infrastructure.
Climate Change Adaptation	Climate Change Adaptation	• Projects aimed at making infrastructure more resilient to impacts of climate change, as well as investments in information support systems, such as climate observation and early warning systems.
Sustainable Water and Waste Management	Climate Change Mitigation	• Promoting water efficient irrigation systems. • Installation/upgradation of wastewater infrastructure including transport, treatment and disposal systems. • Water resources conservation. • Flood defence systems.
Pollution Prevention and Control	Climate Change Mitigation, Environment protection	• Projects targeting reduction of air emissions, greenhouse gas control, soil remediation, waste management, waste prevention, waste recycling, waste reduction and energy/emission-efficient waste-to-energy (Feedstock will primarily include: Sewage, manure, wastewater, bagasse, biomass, wood pellets, etc.)
Green Buildings	Climate Change Mitigation	• Projects related to buildings that meet regional, national or internationally recognized standards or certifications for environmental performance.

Green Project Category	*Environmental Objective*	*Eligibility Criteria*
Sustainable Management of Living Natural Resources and Land Use	Natural Resource Conservation	• Environmentally sustainable management of agriculture, animal husbandry, fishery and aquaculture. • Sustainable forestry management including afforestation/reforestation. • Support to certified organic farming. • Research on living resources and biodiversity protection.
Terrestrial and Aquatic Biodiversity Conservation	Biodiversity Conservation	• Projects relating to coastal and marine environments. • Projects related to biodiversity preservation, including conservation of endangered species, habitats and ecosystems.

Sources: Framework of sovereign green bonds GOI

All the proceeds gets allocated within 24 months following the issuance, any funding that is been done by any other government agency will be excluded to avoid double counting the proceeds will be released in tranche depending upon the achievements of the target mention in the approved project document.

Steps to Fund the Green Expenditures

1. The various Ministries which includes Ministries of Environment, Forest and climate Change, Ministries of Housing and Urban Affairs, Ministries of Agriculture and Farmers welfare, Ministries of New and Renewable Energy and Other Ministries will be identifying the Projects and will handing it over to Green Finance working Committee for Internal Evaluation.
2. The Initial List of the Projects got selected will be Prepared.
3. The Project Evaluation will be done by the Green finance working committee which comprises of the Following members such as:
   (i) Chief Economic Advisor who would be chairing the selection committee.
   (ii) Additional Secretary, Infrastructure Finance secretariat (member Secretary).
   (iii) Ministries of Environment, Forest and climate Change.
   (iv) Ministries of New and Renewable Energy.
   (v) The experts and Specialist in the field of Climate Change from the NITI Aayog.
   (vi) Public Debt Management Cell, Budget Division and the Ministry of Finance.
   (vii) Any other Ministries those are been Consulted from time to time.

4. The Eligible Green Projects Final list will be Summarized and finalized.
5. The Public Debt Management Cell will be Issuing Bonds, Allocate funds Proceeds to the Eligible green Projects. The process of is been done yearly Basis.

Table 2: Green Bonds Issuance in Two Tranches

	1st Issuance		*Reopening*	
Issue Date	Jan. 25, 2023		Feb, 9, 2023	
Amount	INR 40 billion ($490 million)	INR 40 billion ($490 million)	INR 40 billion ($484 million)	INR 40 billion ($484 million)
Tenure	5 years	10 years	5 years	10 years
Coupon/Yield	7.10%/7.10%	7.29%/7.29%	7.10%/7.23%	7.29%/7.30%
Oversubscription	2.4x	3.8x	1.7x	2x

Sources: Case study India's green bond World Bank report

The following table depicts the issuance of green bonds in two tranche that to 80 billion INR been divided into two tenor one is of 5years and the other is of 10 years, coupon rate of first issuance and the reopening varies as 7.10% & 7.29% of the first issuance and 7.10%/7.23%, 7.29%/7.30% of the latter. Both the issuance were been oversubscribed as follows first issuance 2.4x (40 billion for 5 yrs) and the other half was 3.8x (40 billion for 10yrs) time

The reopening were been also oversubscribed 40 billion 1.7x times for 5years and the other half of 40 billion were been oversubscribed 2x times which was having a tenor of 10 years.

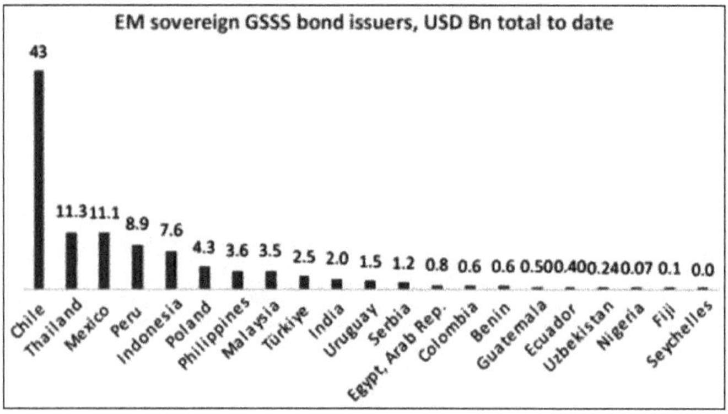

Figure 1: Issuance of Emerging Market GSSS Bonds

Source: Quarterly news letter World Bank (September 2023)

As the figure depicts the emerging markets of sovereign green, social, sustainability and sustainability linked bonds Chile been the highest issuer of green bonds stands at 43 billion USD. India stands at 2.0 billion USD of GSSS bonds issued and is been placed 10th among the rest of the nations.

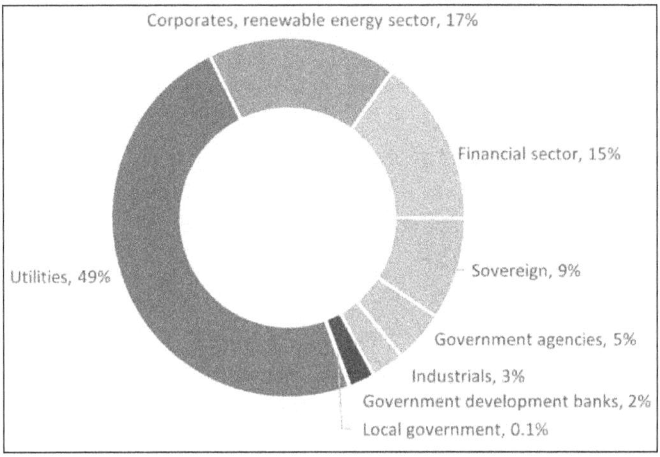

Figure 2: Issuance of Green Bonds by Private Players and Local Government Bodies

Source: Green bond amounts issued in India by type of issuer
World Bank with data from Bloomberg

The financial institutions and government agencies were been using green bonds instrument since 2015. The Private sectors were playing the major role in the issuances of the bond which stands around 84% of the total issue; Greenko group the largest green bond issuer in India is funding the major green projects which include the major renewable power sources for energy generation. The major noticeable area regarding the issuance of green bonds is that two local government bodies Ghaziabad Nagar Nigam and Indore Municipal Corporation had issued 20 million USD in 2021 and 87 million USD in 2023 respectively.

Recommendations

(a) A lucrative scheme must be launched so that the green bonds could become more attractive from the investors point of view.

(b) Tax benefit/tax exemption should be introduced for the bondholders for the interest that they are receiving.

(c) A more dedicated structure of bond issuance must be made so that the proper assessment could be done whether the funds that are been drive in towards the green projects are been utilised generously or not.

(d) A proper credit rating agency must be developed for the rating of the bonds on the basis of the viability of the projects on which such bond issuance are been invested. Moody's had launched such green bond credit rating mechanism in the year 2016; such kind of agency is required for assessing the green bonds domestically.

(e) Conscious and awareness must be there among the investors regarding the betterment and upliftment of their environment than only it's possible to issue green bonds and we can drive such funds towards green projects.

(f) The Participation of Corporate must be there so that they must incorporate green bonds in their CSR investment activities that too with environmental sustainability goals.

(g) The encouragement and Involvement should be there for the public private partnership entities in building up renewable energy infrastructure with the green bond funding as the key funding source.

Conclusion

The green bond market is utterly a very new concept in India and it will take a time to build up its own image. The consciousness of the investors, their rational decision making power is going to help the green bond market to grow at its fullest potential it will help the government to fulfil its nationally determined contribution. The net zero target by the Indian railways by 2030 will alone help in the reduction of carbon emissions by 60 million tonnes annually but this could only be possible if the power generation is been done through certain green projects or infrastructure. The mobilization of the funds towards the funding of sustainable projects will help India in achieving its net zero targets, the introduction of sovereign green bonds and the entry of the GOI into the green bond markets is going to bring in an optimistic wave in the investment of various green projects which is going to help the country in achieving its international commitments and will help in to bring a sustainable and inclusive growth of the economy.

References

[1] Verma, A. and Agarwal, R. (2020, April). A study of green bond market in India: A critical review. In *IOP Conference Series: Materials Science and Engineering*, 804(1), 012052). IOP Publishing.

[2] Faske, B. (2018). Turning billions into (green) trillions: Tracking the growth and development of the green bond market in China, France, India, and the United States. *Tulane Environmental Law Journal, 31*(2), 293–325.

[3] Franco, B.M.O. (2022). *Does the Issuance of Green Bonds provide a cheaper source of capital to firms?* (Master's thesis, ISCTE-Instituto Universitario de Lisboa (Portugal)).

[4] Azhgaliyeva, D., Kapoor, A. and Liu, Y. (2020). Green bonds for financing renewable energy and energy efficiency in South-East Asia: a review of policies. *Journal of Sustainable Finance & Investment, 10*(2), 113–140.